To Andrew
Thanks for
all your
on my late
Journey
Coach Fre

NO LIMITS

ONE COACH'S REMARKABLE JOURNEY OF ATHLETIC, SOCIAL, AND CULTURAL SUCCESS ON AND BEYOND THE COURT

MARK AMATUCCI

WITH TODD KARPOVICH AND JOE BAKER

CATHEDRAL
FOUNDATION PRESS

PUBLISHED BY

CATHEDRAL
FOUNDATION PRESS

Printed and bound in the United States of America
First Edition 1 2 3 4 5
Library of Congress Cataloging-in-Publication data is available upon request.
ISBN 978-1885938572

PUBLISHED BY: Cathedral Foundation Press
PUBLISHER: Christopher Gunty
COVER AND BOOK DESIGN: Sara Travlos
COVER PHOTO: Kevin J. Parks
PHOTOS: All photos courtesy Mark Amatucci.
PRINTED IN THE USA

This books is dedicated to my two families -

My wife Pat
My children Stephanie, Jacquelyn, and Michael
Dad, Mom and Kitty

All the players, coaches, mentors and friends
of the Calvert Hall Basketball family.

In Memory of:

Brian G. Kirby
Paul A. Kinney
Craig H. Cromwell
Daryl M. Augustus II

*Special thanks to Joe Baker, Todd Karpovich
and B & A Productions*

CONTENTS

FORWARD

When Mark Amatucci was named the head basketball coach at Calvert Hall College a little more than 40 years ago it wasn't long before he helped change the landscape of high school sports in the Baltimore area forever.

Tucked away in a small corner of the Towson section of Baltimore County, the Calvert Hall basketball program often took a backseat to the school's more storied football, baseball, lacrosse and swimming teams.

That changed when the 24-year-old Amatucci took over as head coach for Tom Ackerman in 1977 and immediately began assembling what would become one of the greatest teams in Baltimore history and one of the country's best high school basketball programs.

He did it by bridging social and cultural barriers and providing a life lesson in dedication and commitment.

He went into the city's basketball-rich recreation centers and brought out a handful of key players – all young African American teenagers – to Calvert Hall's predominately white, Baltimore County campus. Together, they not only helped The Hall win a national championship but also helped elevate Baltimore to what it is today – a basketball gold mine – while forever changing the face of the famed Baltimore Catholic League.

David Blackwell was the first player he recruited to attend The Hall.

He was followed soon after by Paul Kinney, Darryle and Paul Edwards, James "Pop" Tubman, Marc Wilson, and Duane Ferrell, who started on the varsity as a freshman and went on to have a long career in the NBA. Throughout his career his teams would feature a host of Baltimore's marquee hoopsters.

The result? An undefeated season and national championship in 1982 and a group of young men who remain incredibly close today.

I first met Mark Amatucci when he was putting his first teams together and it wasn't long before a wonderful friendship was born. A friendship that still exists today. I saw a fiery and passionate coach who loved the game, his school and his players and who built his championship culture through discipline, accountability, responsibility, trust and camaraderie.

Mark Amatucci remains a guidance counselor at Calvert Hall today and now, along with local sports writer Todd Karpovich, has written a superb story. A story not just about the rise of Calvert Hall to national basketball prominence, but also about the countless players the coach, who they call 'Tooch', helped turn into young men.

Guys like Ferrell, Juan Dixon and Gary Neal, who all played in the NBA, and the Edwards brothers, who helped Mt. St. Mary's College of Maryland reach the NCAA Division II national championship game and whose own kids have now gone on to outstanding high school and collegiate careers of their own.

Together they document Calvert Hall's classic triple-overtime win over Baltimore's Dunbar High School, the memorable championship-clinching win over coach Morgan Wooten's iconic DeMatha, Tooch's journey to Division I and back, life-long relationships that became the Calvert Hall basketball family, and a legacy of excellence that still exists today.

It's a fascinating look back that takes us onto the practice floor, inside locker rooms, and on road trips to gain an inside perspective on Amatucci, his coaches, and players. Amatucci's story leaves us with a clear understanding of what can be accomplished by going beyond the limits of what is expected.

– Keith Mills

Keith Mills has been a journalist on the Baltimore sports scene for over 40 years. Today, as a member of the WBAL-TV news team he is one of the area's most respected sports anchors. Keith is a graduate of Brooklyn Park High School in Anne Arundel County and Towson University. He is a part of the Ravens Broadcast Team and hosts Ravens programming on WBAL-TV 11 and WBAL Plus. He also hosts radio shows on WBAL 1090 AM and 98 Rock.

TOOCH - THE FORMATIVE YEARS

Mark Amatucci with his parents, Phil and Marie.

"You don't walk out on Calvert Hall. Unless it's halftime, you stay in your seats because once we hit our spurt, that's it."

- PAUL EDWARDS, III

As 5,028 raucous fans at the Towson Center began to exit, Calvert Hall coach Mark Amatucci called a timeout with his team trailing 80-71 with 1:24 remaining in the final quarter against Dunbar, a perennial Baltimore powerhouse. Amatucci recalled, "There was no panic in the huddle. It was business as usual. Everyone was focused — no chaos."

The Cardinals had been in this situation before. There was never a doubt.

Preparing for the next 84 seconds and what was to follow started sixteen years earlier when Amatucci applied for ninth grade at Calvert Hall. He had been born with a competitive spirit, the type that can't be taught. Amatucci's father, Phil, was an excellent athlete and businessman. He would nurture his son's competitiveness and lead by example.

When Amatucci was 12 years old playing behind the plate in a rec baseball game, he was hit in the head with a foul ball. Catchers wore face masks, but not helmets at the time. Amatucci finished the inning and returned to the bench when the coach noticed blood coming from a gash in his head. Amatucci's father drove him to a medical center on York Road in Timonium, Maryland, where he received a Novocain injection and five stitches.

Leaving the medical center, they realized there was still time to return to Ridgeley Junior High School to finish the game. Phil Amatucci asked his son if he wanted to resume his duties behind the plate. Mark enthusiastically said "yes," but his coach prudently declined the offer.

"That experience illustrates the way I look at life," Amatucci said. "When you're expected to do something, you have to go out and get it done. Sometimes, you have to block things out of your mind."

In eighth grade, Amatucci continued to be a standout baseball player, especially on the mound. Sprouting to 5-feet-10 before his teens, he was also turning into a potentially solid basketball player. The added height enabled him to be effective clearing the boards at both ends of the court. Amatucci set his sights on Calvert Hall because of the academics, athletics, and the fact that many of his friends were planning to attend the school, including best pal and future assistant coach Phil Popovec.

However, Amatucci had always struggled in math and science, a problem later attributed to attention-deficit/hyperactivity disorder. As a result, the school's entrance exam proved to be a challenge. Fortunately, Amatucci had a strong ally in his eighth-grade teacher, Kitty McNeal (nee Walker), at St. Joseph Texas in Cockeysville. Amatucci regards her as a "second mother," and she played a pivotal role in his life.

Amatucci remembered his first impressions of McNeal. "She was young and enthusiastic," he said. "She was dedicated to making sure I could move onto Calvert Hall. Very early on, I gained a lot of respect for her and knew she was there to help me be successful in high school."

Amatucci earned Bs and Cs but had trouble processing many of the elements of math and science — no matter how long or hard he studied. McNeal tutored Amatucci in math and provided practice tests to prepare him for the entrance exam at Calvert Hall.

Meanwhile, Amatucci's mother aspired for him to attend Loyola Blakefield because of a family legacy. Amatucci had a different plan. He was determined to attend Calvert Hall with the rest of his friends from St. Joseph's.

Amatucci did not get into Loyola. The scenario initially worked in his favor because it opened the door for Calvert Hall, provided he could pass the test. Unfortunately, just a few days later, another rejection letter arrived from Calvert Hall. Amatucci was heartbroken.

Not accepting Amatucci's rejection, McNeal intervened by meeting with Monsignor Stanley J. Scarff, a Calvert Hall alum, to plead her student's cause. He suggested McNeal meet with Brother John Moore, who was Calvert Hall's vice-principal of academics. McNeal presented her case three times; each time Moore declined to accept Amatucci. McNeal was relentless and returned to Monsignor Scarff, who then suggested she return one more time and vouch for her pupil.

McNeal recalled how Amatucci was the catalyst for organizing football, basketball, and baseball teams at St. Joe's, despite the lack of funds. The football team wore shirts with numbers drawn with markers. The school hosted bake sales every Sunday after mass that helped pay for suitable baseball uniforms. McNeal knew how much Calvert Hall meant to Amatucci, and she was determined to help him every step of the way to get into the school.

"He wanted so badly to go to Calvert Hall," McNeal said. "I knew he would have a hard time with the entrance exam. Mark and I would work regularly after school to prepare for the test. He was a boy who had a goal in mind, and that's all he wanted. I told Brother John, there has to be a way. He really had to go to Calvert Hall. As It turns out, he has spent most of his life connected to The Hall."

Finally, Moore said Amatucci could attend summer school at The Baltimore Institute located in downtown Baltimore. If he secured at least a B in math, English, and reading classes, he would be admitted. Attending summer school required Amatucci to catch two public buses from his home in Cockeysville every morning.

"It was my whole summer — 9 to 2 daily from June to late August," Amatucci said. "The last day of class we got our report cards, and I had earned three Bs. I remember taking the bus home being overjoyed with my grades. I used to get dropped off on Bosley Road by Dulaney Valley Road, which was still a good distance from my house. That final day, I just skipped along knowing I would start classes at Calvert Hall in two weeks."

Without Kitty McNeal's relentless persistence, Amatucci's journey would likely have a different ending.

McNeal and Amatucci have remained close over the years. McNeal's son, Dan McNeal, was killed in the Sept. 11, 2001, terrorist attacks in New York City. The McNeal family established a scholarship award at Loyola Blakefield in Dan McNeal's name that annually goes to an outstanding senior. The scholarship was another example of Kitty's relentless drive and passion to establish a proper legacy to honor his memory.

Despite the discipline and academic rigors, Amatucci quickly acclimated to life at Calvert Hall. There were some eye-opening moments, like the time a Brother smacked a pen from the mouth of a student, aptly known as "Fish," because it looked like a cigarette.

"It taught you a lot about discipline," Amatucci said. "It made you consider consequences of your behavior. If you didn't learn to accept rules and authority, you were going to be in trouble."

Amatucci made the freshman basketball team, and this is where he crossed paths with his future mentor, Joe "Snooky" Binder, who was a hard-nosed teacher and coach. He was well-respected by the student-body. He would also leave a life-long impression on Amatucci.

"Snook was the epitome of the type of person I wanted to play for," Amatucci said. "He was demanding, aggressive, in your face. No excuses. If you don't want to play hard, you can leave. I liked this guy."

During a game against Baltimore Catholic League foe Cardinal Gibbons, a player threw an elbow that landed on Amatucci's head. Amatucci retaliated with a punch of his own before the opposing player spit at him. Amatucci then went after him again, and a brawl ensued. While Amatucci was tied up in the scrum, the player he was supposed to be guarding ran down the court and scored an easy basket.

After the game, Binder summoned Amatucci into his office. A life lesson was awaiting.

"He jumped right in my face," Amatucci remembered. "I thought he was going to pat me on the back. Instead, he lashed out saying, 'You didn't get back on defense. Don't ever let a distraction interfere with getting your job done.' That became an absolute."

The following year, Amatucci got into another "misunderstanding" with the same player from Cardinal Gibbons. This time, the player was pushing around Amatucci's teammates. At halftime, Calvert Hall JV coach Joseph Carlozo asked for a volunteer to retaliate against the Gibbons player and send a message. Amatucci eagerly raised his hand. Soon after the second-half tip, Amatucci proceeded to throw an elbow at the player. Another brawl ensued. Amatucci was ejected, much to the disappointment of his father, as he was escorted out of the gym by Calvert Hall Athletic Director Brother Andrew DiNoto and Brother Gregory Cavalier for his own protection.

That type of feistiness would carry over to Amatucci's playing and coaching career. This also meant giving 100 percent in practice. Amatucci always took exception to teammates and players who didn't play hard. This meant altercations that sometimes ended with a handshake … or not.

While Amatucci made varsity basketball in his junior year, he made his mark earlier as a pitcher on the baseball team. By his sophomore year, his fastball was clocked at 87 miles per hour. The following two years, Amatucci was consistently throwing in the low 90s. He was named team captain and earned All-Metro honors.

As a senior, in a critical match up with archrival Cardinal Gibbons, Amatucci pushed himself to the max for his team. He pitched 12 innings in a tight loss, allowing six hits with 12 strikeouts and two walks. "I never came out of the game," Amatucci said. The winning pitcher for the Crusaders that day was Lou Eckerl, who later became one of Amatucci's closest friends and the athletic director and baseball coach at Calvert Hall. Amatucci received a few looks from major league scouts before he headed off to Juniata College in Huntingdon, Pennsylvania, where he became a starting pitcher his freshman year. He managed a stellar career for the Eagles, even though an arm injury decreased his pitching velocity from the 90s to the mid-80s. Nearing graduation, he earned a tryout with the Philadelphia Phillies and interest from the Los Angeles Dodgers.

"Tooch", far right, with Juniata seniors and Lou Eckerl, far left.

At Juniata, Amatucci was also a creative writer with an interest in psychology and sociology. Social and cultural issues intrigued him. In the spring of 1974, as graduation neared, his heart was set on professional baseball. When an offer from the majors never came, he decided he wanted to coach and teach. Athletics were in his blood, and he felt most comfortable around a baseball diamond or on a basketball court.

His father, Phil, was not thrilled with his career decision. He envisioned a life in the business world for his son. While Amatucci deviated from his father's advice with his career choice, the values that were instilled by him at a young age lasted a lifetime.

Be humble.

Work hard.

Don't let your ego get the best of you.

Phil Amatucci had excelled at baseball, football, and boxing. Sports just seemed to come naturally to him. He was a successful businessman and a top salesman at C.R. Daniels Inc., a textile and manufacturing firm. He worked his way to vice president and was a member of the Board of Trustees.

"In terms of my personality, I have a lot of my father in me," Amatucci said. "The only difference between me and my dad is my dad never raised his voice and was much less animated. But early on, I learned when my dad said something, you better be listening. He was not only a great father, but an outstanding athlete. I honed my baseball and football skills from his instruction." He added, "My dad always made time for me."

One Saturday morning during his senior year at The Hall, Amatucci was reading an article highlighting his performance as his father walked into the room. He grabbed the newspaper and said, "People who walk around talking about how good they are probably aren't." He continued, "Always make sure you congratulate the people who support you, because they're the ones most important to your success." Phil Amatucci expected his son to be passionate and go beyond what is expected in school, athletics or in his choice of profession.

In his first year after graduating from Juniata, Amatucci learned valuable lessons working with young adults at Sheppard Pratt Health System. He gained appreciation for critical people skills: patience, compassion and care. Afterward, Amatucci began working for a friend at a gas station and was eventually given an opportunity to run his own business. However, Binder contacted Amatucci about a couple of open coaching positions at Calvert Hall, namely junior-varsity baseball and freshmen basketball. Binder added that there was also a teaching position available in the social studies department.

This opened the door for a new career.

Brother Timothy Dean, Calvert Hall's principal, hired Amatucci for the teaching position, along with the freshmen basketball and JV basketball coaching jobs. "Brother Timothy gave me the opportunity of a lifetime," Amatucci remembered. During that summer, he furthered his studies at Towson University to develop his teaching skills.

Amatucci is first and foremost a teacher, and that translates well to the basketball court. The court is his classroom. His style is sometimes viewed as brash and demonstrative, but the goal is always to make his students and players perform at a higher level.

Amatucci adapted his philosophy from Binder. Amatucci's first freshman hoops team was successful. The following year as the JV coach his team was Baltimore Catholic league champs.

Only in his second year, Amatucci's coaching philosophy was reaping benefits. He recalled, "The guys bought into the words hard work and total commitment. The long hours of practice and attention to detail was expected and never challenged."

On the varsity level, Calvert Hall's program was unraveling. There was little identity and poor results. There was a need for new direction.

The pieces were beginning to fall in place for what was to follow.

2

PIECES OF THE PUZZLE

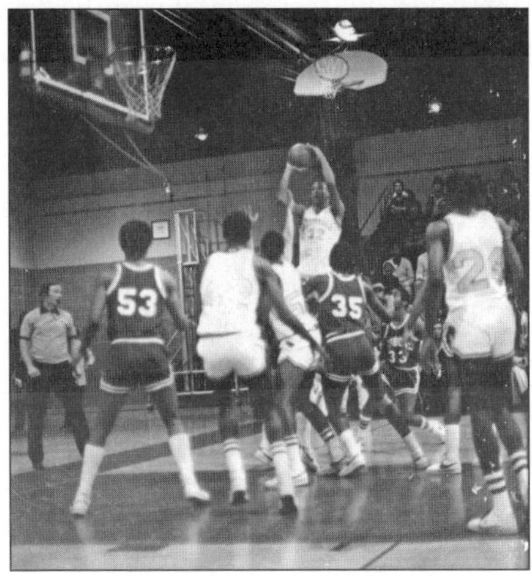

"Gettin' after Cardinal Gibbons."

"Every time I turned around, I see this guy with the London Fog trench, sunglasses, and the Calvert Hall hoodie, and I know it's Tooch."

- JAMES "POP" TUBMAN

Tom Ackerman stepped down as the Calvert Hall varsity basketball coach following the 1976-77 season. The program had admittedly lost some of its direction. Athletic Director Brother D. John Smith asked Amatucci if he was interested in applying for the job on the success of guiding the junior varsity program to the Catholic League title.

Amatucci was enthusiastic about the opportunity and agreed to meet about the opening. About a week later, Brother D. John asked Amatucci to explain his philosophy on coaching, recruiting, and where he wanted to take the program. The interview was not just about basketball. Brother D. John believed academics played an important role with athletics. This fit right in with Amatucci's philosophy. If a coach could not depend on a player to make the effort in the classroom, then he certainly could not be trusted to perform in the last two minutes of a tight game — no discussion. Back to hoops, Amatucci made Brother D. John his own offer that was difficult to refuse.

"If I can't get the job done in four years, you can fire me," Amatucci proclaimed.

Shortly thereafter, Brother D. John summoned Amatucci to his office and offered him the position. Although just 24, Amatucci had a budding confidence about building a successful program. Amatucci recalled, "I had an aggressive plan from the start. I got the job and headed to the Dome at Madison Rec." Amatucci knew the program needed more talent, and he was willing to go into Baltimore City to find the right players.

The Catholic War Veterans league had been a hotbed for recruits for Baltimore Catholic League teams for years. St. Mary's Govans featured one of the top 8th graders in the city — Darryle Edwards, a tall, lanky, versatile sharpshooter. Amatucci set his sights on Edwards after seeing him play only one game. He saw him as a complete player who could be a star. Edwards was considering arch-rival, Loyola Blakefield. St. Mary's had a tradition of sending top players to Loyola. As a part of the recruiting process, Amatucci made it a practice to visit the homes of prospective student-athletes, something his rival coaches did not do.

"The home visits gave me an edge that I used to my full advantage," Amatucci said. In the home, he told Edwards, "You are going to be the rock of the program. We are building the program around you."

During his visit, Amatucci highlighted Calvert Hall's academics as

Darryle Edwards getting up against Archbishop Curley.

a key part of his presentation. Edwards' mother and father greatly appreciated his focus on being successful in the classroom. It also helped that Amatucci was a faculty member who would be able to closely monitor Darryle's academic progress. Mom and dad were sold. Dad, well known as "Big Paul," broke out a bottle of scotch to celebrate his son joining the Cardinals.

Edwards' enrollment at Calvert Hall in the fall of 1977 would change both the direction and overall culture of the program. In September, Amatucci made the tough decision to have Edwards play his freshman year on the JV to best prepare him to be the impact player he envisioned by his sophomore year.

A year earlier as JV coach, Amatucci targeted David Blackwell from Madison Square in East Baltimore. Blackwell had played for the Madison Buccaneers. He enrolled at Calvert Hall in the fall of 1976 and had no trouble adjusting to Calvert Hall's challenging curriculum. He was a seamless fit into the school community. Blackwell —outstanding in the classroom and on the court — set the bar for the future players that Amatucci wanted to help build a championship team.

Blackwell started for Amatucci's championship JV team in his first year and then became a key member of the varsity squad for the next two seasons. "He was athletic, he was lightening quick, and I just put him at the two-guard and let him go," Amatucci said. "From day one my game plan was baseline to baseline defense and transition offense. David had the same mentality." Sensing what Blackwell would bring to the table, Amatucci made up his mind that the Madison Buccaneers would be a constant focus of his recruiting efforts.

The next order of business during the summer was to meet individually with the returning players. He wanted to make sure they all gained an early appreciation for his no-nonsense coaching style. Not everyone got the message. When Amatucci's inaugural season began, only three players would return from the previous year, including a talented 6-foot-6 junior named Tony Morris. Morris would prove to be one of Amatucci's first challenges as a head coach. The remainder of the squad was made up of members of Amatucci's JV championship squad.

Entering the season, Blackwell shared the backcourt with point guard Brian Kirby, a standout soccer player who was quick and could handle the ball. Marty Blair, a three-sport athlete and outstanding student who eventually went to The Citadel, was a major contributor. In the years to come, there would be more Kirbys and Blairs, multi-sport athletes who bring their winning mentality to Amatucci's program.

With the exception of Morris, the frontcourt did not bring a lot of height to the floor, but the players had heart. "We played our butts off without a whole lot of size," Amatucci said. Their blue-collar work ethic made life difficult for opponents inside the paint. Frank Fulco, who later played linebacker at the University of Wisconsin, was a force and added to the team's toughness. John "Joe" Walsh, and John Evans were juniors who were relentless in practice, pushing their frontcourt teammates to be better.

The Cardinals took their lumps over Amatucci's first season as he exposed them to tough competition. The team travelled to Philadelphia three times to take on some of that city's top programs. This became a staple of the Cardinals' schedule, one Amatucci maintained throughout his career. He never shied away from playing the best. Amatucci's Cardinals would play anybody, anywhere with one goal in mind — win. Amatucci says, "We never went into any game against anybody expecting not to win; that is how we prepared"

The Cardinals opened the 1977-78 season against West Catholic in

Philadelphia. Amatucci admitted he had "no idea what we were walking into. They were loaded." The gym at West Catholic was tight with two pillars at each end of the court that crossed over the sidelines, a distinct home court advantage. Calvert Hall never found its footing and lost, 86-65.

Amatucci then picked up his first win as a varsity coach by beating Boys' Latin, 65-51, the following game. The Cardinals then topped Northeast for a second straight victory before heading back to Philadelphia for a game against North Catholic. This time, the Calvert Hall players were better prepared for the hostile environment and came away with a 69-57 victory.

The next weekend, the Cardinals loaded the van for a third trip to Philadelphia and a game against Monsignor Bonner. The Friars have produced several top players over the years, including Rodney Blake, who later played at St. Joseph's University. Another Bonner player, Tom Gormley, played collegiately for Amatucci at Loyola College of Maryland. Calvert Hall hung tough most of the way before losing 70-67. While Amatucci wanted to win, the results were not nearly as important as the experience of playing those big games, especially at such an early stage of the program. Amatucci related, "Playing the best and learning how to win on the road are critical experiences that serve as a foundation for building a culture of success."

Talking about the Philly trips Amatucci reflected, "There were not many African-American team members on Bonner or North Catholic. But West Catholic did have several African-American players on the roster. This was an opportunity for our guys to mingle with players of color. That was something I thought was extremely important."

After a preseason of mixed results, the Cards headed into their Baltimore Catholic League season. At that time, BCL Hall of Fame coach Jerry Savage had built Loyola Blakefield into a powerhouse program. The Dons were led by Tony Guy, who scored 1,499 points over his high school career, played collegiately at Kansas, and was drafted by the Boston Celtics. Loyola dominated the Cardinals in both of their matchups during that 1977-78 season, winning 99-64 and 69-41. Calvert Hall also dropped games to strong Towson Catholic, Mount St. Joseph, and an outstanding Cardinal Gibbons squad led by All-American Quintin Dailey, finishing the year 9-14.

The losing record was not as disappointing as some of the players' attitudes over the final stretch of the season.

"After we lost to Loyola a second time, my seniors packed it in," Amatucci said. "It had started as a very encouraging year playing with heart and determination against really good teams. By the end, we were not ready to go to the highlight reel yet. Some guys hit the wall."

Amatucci was angry some of the players appeared to quit and did not put forth the necessary effort to win late in the season. He went to his mentor Binder, who agreed with the assessment. Binder was known as a no-nonsense coach and disciplinarian. A losing attitude among the players never sat well with him. He had no patience for players who didn't work hard. Binder had stepped down from coaching basketball in 1976 to focus on baseball. His Calvert Hall baseball program was eventually regarded as one of the best in the entire nation.

"You have to get kids to believe what you're doing," Binder said. "Then, you have to motivate them and talk about how everyone is going to go about it the same way. When kids believe in that and are all pulling for one another, now you have it going. I always said to the kids, 'Don't be happy sitting the bench. Show me you want to play by working hard.' Sometimes, that's not always the best player. Mark came from that. He worked his tail off. When you get guys going, you're going to win more than you're going to lose."

Amatucci knew the program still needed a significant change in the mindset and culture of his players. The first player Amatucci addressed after the season was Morris, who had been benched late in the year. The coach laid out a plan for workouts during the summer. Amatucci gave Morris an ultimatum.

"If you're not on board with the summer workouts, you are not going to be around in October," Amatucci remembered telling him. "You have a losing mentality and you do not play to your potential. You're selfish and all you do is worry about Tony Morris scoring points."

It was a wakeup call that Morris would not take lightly.

Following Easter break, Amatucci had the players work out three days per week. There was no summer holiday. From the third week of June until late July, Amatucci led rigorous workouts. The players bought in, and Amatucci was encouraged by the effort. Morris was a key presence in these workouts and set an example for his teammates.

Still, finding the rest of the pieces to build a successful program meant hitting the recruiting trail even harder and finding new, innovative ways to land difference makers.

Amatucci went back to East Baltimore and set his sights on two top players, Paul Edwards III and Paul Kinney. Edwards, known as LP, was Darryle's younger brother. Kinney also had a connection to Calvert Hall. His older brother, Vince, attended the school and was a top-tier athlete. Vince graduated from The Hall 1974 and went on to play football at the University of Maryland and for the Denver Broncos.

Amatucci had gotten a lead on Kinney from Darryle Edward's dad, "Big Paul," who was good friends with Kinney's dad, Luther. Kinney, already 6-foot-5 and a stellar athlete, came from a solid family in the Old Northwood neighborhood of Baltimore City. Amatucci had concerns about Kinney's transcript, and stressed the priority of academics over hoops to the family. To drive home his point about the importance of education, Amatucci talked about the study hall he held between the end of school and beginning of daily practice.

Amatucci let the Kinneys know that Paul Edwards III had already agreed to attend Calvert Hall. The trio of the Edwards brothers and Kinney could be the best in the Catholic League. The Kinney family agreed. Paul would wear Cardinal and Gold.

Luther opened a bottle of his favorite scotch to celebrate a new era for his son at Calvert Hall. The celebration moved to The Haven, a well-known jazz club in the Northwood Shopping Center. When Amatucci walked in, quite noticeable as the only white person in the club, the crowd became noticeably quiet. Luther Kinney eased any suspicions by pointing at Amatucci and yelling, "Calvert Hall! He's okay." The celebration continued.

Both Paul and LP arrived at Calvert Hall for the 1978 school year. Kinney entered as a sophomore and played varsity. Edwards arrived as a freshman and spent one year on the junior varsity before playing his final three seasons for Amatucci.

"When I came in as a freshman, Darryle was a sophomore, so any issue I ran into, he would be my buffer," Paul Edwards remembered. "He kind of told me what teachers to look out for. The only disappointing thing for me was that I didn't play varsity as a freshman. That upset me a little bit. It didn't go over well."

Paul Edwards used his time on JV as a learning experience that would prepare him to become a major impact player on the varsity. At that time, neither he nor the rest of the players saw the big picture. They were just focused on playing basketball and getting a good education.

"I don't think we realized we would have a great team if everybody came together," Edwards said. "Everyone brought their own talents, and it just gelled. Nobody was talking about championships."

Tooch staring down legendary Cardinal Gibbons coach Ray Mullis.

Amatucci remembered, "Edwards was being highly recruited by Cardinal Gibbons coach Ray Mullis, who doggedly pursued him. He went so far as to corner Edwards at Calvert Hall during a grade school tournament. I saw Mullis talking to Paul and I was incensed. I got in Mullis' face and made it clear he needed to leave the Calvert Hall gymnasium."

Mullis put his head down and exited the premises.

Their enrollment not only helped the basketball program, it opened the door for more minority students to enroll at Calvert Hall. The families of the Edwards, Paul Kinney, and Blackwell put the responsibility on Amatucci to watch over their sons at the predominantly white school, especially if any racial issues arose. Amatucci fully embraced this role. Surprisingly, the guys never experienced any problems and easily incorporated themselves into the school environment.

"I hit the jackpot with those kids because of their personalities," Amatucci said, "They were not here just to play basketball — they really loved the place."

Assistant coach, Joe Baker added: "The students loved them and bonded with them. Teachers liked them. They were solid students. They were humorous and engaging. One of the key things for us is we always had guys with good parents. Then we started winning, and it went to another level."

A different Calvert Hall team took the court for the 1978-79 season. The Cardinals had swagger and played hard. Amatucci did an effective job adjusting to his opponents. After being swept by Loyola the prior season, the Cardinals returned the favor by beating the Dons twice, 65-63 and 61-59.

"This will be constant against Loyola. We are just going to pressure the hell out of them for 32 minutes," Amatucci said. "We're going to play transition and make them run up and down the court. I am not taking any prisoners in practice. My mantra is with two minutes left in the game when the other team is gassed, that becomes our time; we are going to rev it up. We're trapping and running. We're really good."

Morris was making a major impact at both ends of the court and won over his coach with his effort. After the second win over Loyola, Amatucci spotted Morris in the parking lot celebrating with his girlfriend.

"I looked at him, he looked at me and I pointed at him and said, 'Have a good night.' It was cool," Amatucci said. "It was a defining moment for me because here was a kid that I had threatened to get rid of. I made demands on him and he came back and played for me. We were good friends from then on."

While Calvert Hall was successful against Loyola, the Cardinals still struggled against Cardinal Gibbons and its star Quintin Dailey, who is still regarded as one of the best players to come out of Baltimore. Dailey played collegiately at the University of San Francisco and spent almost a decade in the NBA with the Chicago Bulls, Los Angeles Clippers, and Seattle Supersonics. His Cardinal Gibbons team swept the Cardinals, 83-65 and 87-78.

The Cardinals split games with Archbishop Curley, which was coached by BCL Hall of Fame coach Dan Popera. The Friars played a different style from Calvert Hall, but were just as motivated. The fierce rivalry with Curley still resonates with Amatucci.

"Popera had those tough, eastside white guys," Amatucci said. "He was in my head every time we played them because his teams played a very different style. They didn't run, played a motion style half-court offense, and a match-up zone. They did that as well as we played transition, trapped, and pressed. It was always a challenge playing over there."

As the season ended, Amatucci was much happier with the state of the program, compared to the same time a year earlier. Players were buying into his system. The hard work was evident in practice and paying off in games. The Cards finished an encouraging 17-7, but even greater moments are on the horizon.

"We got after it," Darryle Edwards said, "We were not the cream of the crop yet, but we competed with everybody."

3

NATIONAL RECOGNITION AND BREAKING BARRIERS

1980 Baltimore Catholic League Champions

"The Cardinals may not fly,
but they sure as heck get there in a hurry."

- CLARK JUDGE,
The Baltimore Evening Sun

In the early spring, Amatucci was cautiously optimistic looking forward to the upcoming 1979-1980 season. With the Edwards brothers and Kinney on board, he was confident the Cardinals had the best front court in the entire Baltimore Catholic League. They were the types of players who could run up and down the floor and create matchup problems for most opponents. Now, he needed a solid backcourt to complete the puzzle to capture a title.

"I was always point-guard oriented," Amatucci said. "If we didn't have a point guard who I could trust and who had the confidence of the other players, we weren't going to get to the next level."

Amatucci believed he had found key pieces to the puzzle. He spent most of the summer of 1979 in East Baltimore aggressively recruiting players. Amatucci had established a solid rapport with Madison Square Recreation Center coaches Andrew Boston and Henry "Sarge" Powell because they saw their players as people with great potential and not just basketball players.

"They were providing the education, structure, and teaching the responsibility that young men need at that time," Amatucci said. "They're East Baltimore guys, they supported Dunbar. They supported Lake Clifton. Two intelligent guys. Great basketball minds, great teachers. We shared the same ideas about putting kids in position to succeed on and off the court. You're not going to see many AAU guys with that kind of mentality."

James "Pop" Tubman and Marc Wilson were playing for the Buccaneers and both were a perfect fit for Calvert Hall. Amatucci soon realized again he was in a fierce recruiting battle for Tubman and Wilson with Cardinal Gibbons coach Ray Mullis, who was highly respected and tightly connected to coaches and players throughout the city. In his favor, Amatucci had established a foothold in the community and strongly believed his visits to the players' homes would go a long way toward convincing Tubman's and Wilson's moms that Calvert Hall clearly was the best choice.

Both Tubman and Wilson were reared by single mothers, Barbara Wilson and Doris Williams (Tubman). Wilson lived in a housing project in the shadows of Little Italy, while Tubman lived nearby on Chase Street in a row home. From his first interactions with the moms, it was obvious to Amatucci that they were committed to instilling their sons with strong values. Living in a neighborhood full of challenges and dangers, Amatucci was extremely impressed with the strength and character of these two women. The efforts of the moms were clearly evident in the respectful and mature way in which the boys carried themselves. Their efforts were also clear in small details. Amatucci says, "On the road, Marc and Pop were well-known for packing an iron to press their shirts and slacks."

In choosing a high school, Tubman and Wilson faced a tough decision. Mullis continued his relentless recruiting for Gibbons, while Dunbar and the local community were applying the same pressure for them to stay in East Baltimore. Both players were equipped to handle pressure from all sides.

"Marc and Pop were independent, confident, and street smart—each with his own unique personality," Amatucci said. Marc was socially shy and uncomfortable speaking in groups. Pop was the advocate, enjoyed the spotlight. He was brash and fearless."

Together, they were a powerful team. On the court, Tubman set the stage, Wilson was the closer. His nickname was "Money." Amatucci said, "They were inseparable and displayed a certain energy when they walked into a room."

Amatucci continued to sell the program to their mothers. He preached the advantages and opportunities that would come from the structure and discipline integral to the Calvert Hall curriculum. Moreover, Amatucci had to deal with the elephant in the room: How were two black students from the inner city going to thrive in a predominantly white school?

Amatucci was determined to become a trailblazer for minority students at Calvert Hall. In 1970, when Amatucci graduated from The Hall, there were only nine African-American students at the school. Eight years later, the number had only grown to thirteen. By 1982, the progress was evident with 45 African-American students attending the school. That number grew to 54 the following year. Today, minorities make up 29 percent of Calvert Hall's 1,200-student body. Amatucci's philosophy had a huge impact on these strides.

Amatucci was honest with Barbara and Doris. He truly believed the school offered a great opportunity for the boys culturally and academically. He also realized and shared the concerns that there was risk involved. Because of the lack of racial diversity in the school, they would be under a microscope. Amatucci felt strongly that Tubman and Wilson had the maturity and street sense to handle the increased scrutiny that could be expected. In addition, he knew the dynamic presence they displayed individually and together would help open horizons for the Calvert Hall community.

Both mothers of Tubman and Wilson eventually acquiesced because they wanted their sons out of East Baltimore and away from the potential dangers lurking around every corner. The trust they had in Amatucci sealed the deal.

"My mother took care of two kids by herself in East Baltimore," Tubman said, "and growing up I seriously thought we were rich. That's how well she took care of my sister and I. We never wanted for anything. Never. My story is not one of government cheese and things of that nature. My mother was never on welfare or public assistance. She started working at the age of sixteen when she was pregnant with my sister. She refused to have her children live like she lived as a child."

Amatucci knew both Tubman and Wilson could make an immediate impact. They were already battle-tested by playing in Baltimore City. The players embraced the opportunity to crack the starting lineup their first year at Calvert Hall.

"Pop was the point guard that I knew was necessary to climb the ladder. I put the ball in his hands and gave him the keys to the bus," Amatucci said. "Marc Wilson was the epitome of the two guard. He was left-handed and could get to the basket. In transition, one-on-one he was money in the bank. He never shot a jumper that he did not think was all net."

Both players entered Calvert Hall as sophomores. Coach Mullis did not know they had decided to attend Calvert Hall. He was convinced both Tubman and Wilson were heading to Gibbons. He was surprised when neither student arrived at Cardinal Gibbons on the first day of school.

"I don't think Mullis took us as seriously as he should have," Amatucci said. "I remember after a game at Madison's Dome that Pop winked at me and I winked back. I knew then that I had him — and where Pop went, Marc would follow."

Tubman was somehow also registered at Dunbar. He remembers his friends asking why he was missing school because the teacher was calling out his name in homeroom. He was never there.

"We had known Darryle and Paul from summer league," Tubman recalls, "Marc and I played at Madison and they played for Lafayette Courts. Marc and I had played together all of our lives. Once we got on the court it just worked."

While both Tubman and Wilson had the pedigree to play immediately, they still had to earn their minutes in practice. Amatucci treated his players equally, and the ones that worked the hardest reaped the benefits.

"I never promise playing time." Amatucci said. "I made it clear that if you went out, worked hard and were committed, both to my standards, then you had the opportunity to start. Starting is grossly overrated. It's the guys on the floor in crunch time that really matter. The thing that we made paramount was that to earn time you had to beat somebody's ass in practice, every day. No debate. Pop outworked everybody."

Calvert Hall opened the season with five African-American players in the starting lineup: Paul and Darryle Edwards, Kinney, Tubman, and Wilson. Amatucci never looked at the color of a player's skin. His focus was putting the best five players on the court. Nonetheless, a few eyebrows were raised when an all-black lineup took the court on December 9, 1980, in the home opener.

Afterward, Charlie Rogers, a close friend of Amatucci, long-time maintenance director at the school, and an African-American, walked up to Amatucci and said, "Tooch, what are you doing? You're starting five black kids. Nobody at Calvert Hall has ever seen anything like that."

Amatucci replied sarcastically, "Mr. Charlie, it never crossed my mind."

Amatucci later admitted: "I was shaking the cage a little bit. Did I worry about it? No. I had the support of the principal, Brother Rene Sterner."

Calvert Hall is operated by the de La Salle Christian Brothers, founded in the 17th century for the sole purpose of providing education for those without resources. Since 1845, Calvert Hall had carried on that tradition providing a strong education to generations of Baltimore's young men from diverse areas of the city. Until this time that commitment to welcoming diversity did not extend fully to the African-American community. The Brothers played a key role in Amatucci's life and helped him attain a Calvert Hall education. Now, he wanted to give back. It was an unprecedented moment having five minority students start for Calvert Hall.

"We just didn't talk about Lasallian values, we lived them," Amatucci said. "I was a believer in the teachings of LaSalle. I wanted to better the understanding of the diversity we had at the school."

Interest in the color of the players who started was a short-lived discussion. Amatucci and his team were focused on basketball. A vital new addition to the team was sophomore Mark Kauffman. He would be a game changer for three years.

Kauffman, who later played football at Towson University, was a standout playmaker and brought "in your face" toughness to the court. Defensively, he made life hell for opposing players. Like Tubman and Wilson, Kauffman came from a single-parent home and displayed the qualities of the type of kid who embraced all of Calvert Hall's values. Also, Jeff Yost, a junior transfer from Towson High School, made an immediate impact, adding to the Hall's blue-collar image with his ability to knock down jumpers. His presence added more depth to the total package.

Most importantly, the team quickly developed a special bond, in which race and socioeconomic backgrounds were not factors. This bond would further develop and extend to include Amatucci. "I truly felt we were building more than a team, we were building a Calvert Hall family," the coach said.

Coming off the previous season, the Cards were certainly expected to play at a higher level. Still, Cardinal Gibbons was the favorite to win the Catholic League. Loyola Blakefield was a force, and Curley played as competitively as any team in the conference. A traditionally strong Mount St. Joseph team was also in the mix.

The Cardinals beat a good Bishop Walsh squad, 74-40, in the regular-season opener on the road and then overwhelmed Loch Raven, 96-56, in the second game. Loch Raven's coach was angry because he thought Amatucci ran up the score. The Cardinals, however, were just deep.

"I only had 11 guys and I played everybody," Amatucci told him. "And, I stopped pressing. It's only my third year. You didn't mind playing me when we weren't this good."

Calvert Hall then reeled off six consecutive wins, including a huge confidence builder with its first victory over Philadelphia's West Catholic. The first setback occurred in Philadelphia against Cardinal O'Hara, which had a gym that was a "bandbox," similar to West Catholic. O'Hara kept the Cardinals off-balance by playing a variety of zone defenses and occasionally switching to man-to-man. The Lions methodically walked the ball up the floor, successfully ran their set offense, and escaped with a 60-58 victory.

In response to that loss, Amatucci picked up the intensity at practice. Invoking an often-used quote of his mentor Joe Binder, Amatucci told the players, "If you're going to make me miserable, I am going to make you miserable." Amatucci taught his players valuable lessons during these intense practices, most notably, "You play like you practice."

The Cardinals were returning from a road victory at St. Mary's High School in Annapolis when Kauffman and Tubman decided to "moon" the car behind the team bus. The driver of the vehicle began honking his horn and Brother James Nash, who was driving the bus, pulled over to the side of the road. The driver then begins yelling at Amatucci because of the players' behavior. Amatucci eventually calmed the man down, and everyone went on their way.

When the team returned to campus, Amatucci told Kauffman and Tubman to get changed into their practice gear for a "no-ball,"40-minute workout. Amatucci was determined to teach the players a lesson about holding themselves accountable for their behavior. About 35 minutes into the session one of the players vomited, and Amatucci's point was made.

"I explained to them that despite the great things that we are building, it only takes one stupid incident like that to have the whole thing crumble," Amatucci said.

There were no further incidents aboard the team bus.

Paul Edwards remembered how Amatucci ran a hard practice, especially if the team did not play well. He was still trying to figure out his coach, who was just 26 at the time. The players, though, always respected his methods. The positive results were further reinforcement.

"Animated is a good adjective, but there are a lot of other ones you could use as well," Paul Edwards said about Amatucci's coaching style. "He had a passion for the game and wanted to win at his alma mater. At that time, we thought Tooch was old. I think he was like twelve years ahead of us, but we thought he was old and crazy. What we did not realize at the time was that he acted the way he did because Tooch was on a mission from day one. There was a method to his madness."

Calvert Hall kept the 1979-1980 season rolling by blowing out Patapsco, Pikesville, and the JV team from Johns Hopkins University. This set up a Friday night showdown with Cardinal Gibbons in the Catholic League opener at a sold-out Calvert Hall gymnasium. The Cardinals started strong and eventually wore down the Crusaders with their constant pressure and transition game in the 69-56 overtime victory. Calvert Hall beat both Cardinal Gibbons and Loyola twice that season and won the regular season title with a league record of 9-1. The balance of power in the league was shifting.

Calvert Hall finished the regular season 24-2 and went on to win its first Catholic League tournament championship. In the title game against Mount St. Joseph, Paul Edwards scored 15 points and made a crucial layup with 10 seconds remaining to seal the 65-62 victory at UMBC. Darryle Edwards had 18 points and Marc Wilson finished with 15. Amatucci's long-term plan was coming to fruition.

Amatucci said, "We were playing with ice in our veins. The tremendous poise of the team when the game was on the line was eye opening. This composure gave a special identity to the team and the program."

"What was significant was the support we were starting to get at home," Amatucci said. "We had sellouts every Friday night and Sunday afternoon. The following year, we sold season tickets and had a section roped off for season-ticket holders. Every home game was like playing in the ACC."

By winning the BCL, the Cardinals were invited to the prestigious Alhambra Catholic Invitational for the first time since Joe Binder's 1973 Catholic League championship team. The tournament was held at Frostburg State University, 154 miles away in the western part of Maryland.

"It was an exciting moment for us — players and coaches," Amatucci said. "It provided an opportunity to not only establish ourselves locally but across the state and maybe nationally."

In the tournament opener, Calvert Hall was matched up with powerful St. John's from Washington, D.C., coached by the venerable Joe Gallagher. The Cardinals came out tight and nervous. Calvert Hall lacked their usual defensive intensity. "If we can't get stops, we can't run," Amatucci said. "If we can't score, we can't press." St. John's was a big team that emphasized getting the ball into the low post. The Cadets put together a 13-point lead at halftime, a seemingly overwhelming deficit against such a good program.

In the locker room, the Cardinal players uncharacteristically had their heads down. Tubman, who was upbeat in the toughest situations, even appeared despondent, which forced Amatucci to pause. Amatucci remembered asking himself if he should go on a tirade about the lackadaisical play or stay calm and convince them everything is going to be okay. He chose the latter and it proved to be a wise decision.

"Hey! Look at me right now," Amatucci told the players. "We can't do anything about the first half. Now, we have to stop them defensively. We can't allow penetration, and we can't allow second and third shots. We have to create turnovers. If we get stops and control the boards, then we can run. We can play Calvert Hall basketball. It's all about doing the little things. But most importantly, you have to forget about the score, be positive and play together."

The Cardinals responded to the speech and outscored St. John's 22-6 in the third quarter to take a 52-49 lead. Wilson scored 14 of his 20 points over that decisive stretch. Calvert Hall remained in control the rest of the way and picked up a signature 62-61 victory. Kinney finished with 20 points.

"The one thing about our team is that we believed we were never out of a game," Tubman remembered. "We always played for one another. It was my responsibility to take the opposing point guard out of his game. Marc had to out-play the two guard and so on down the line. Even in our darkest moments we were always able to channel the necessary strength and energy from one another to come from behind."

Calvert Hall then lost to Gonzaga in the second round but bounced back the following night and beat Father Judge from Philadelphia. The Cardinals finished the tournament in fifth place. "It was another milestone," Amatucci said. "Now, we are going to get some national attention. Indeed, Calvert Hall finished the year 28-3 and was ranked No. 13 in the country.

Despite the success, Amatucci best remembers that season for how his players showed class, restraint, and dignity when facing an ugly situation. The Cardinals were playing a league rival when the opposing students started shouting racial epithets directed at Darryle Edwards. These comments were made directly in front of several of the opposing school's faculty.

"They were brutal on Darryle, but we had to be careful," Amatucci recalled. "I couldn't have my players lose their composure and go after people. Instead, our kids showed great maturity, which spoke highly of their parents and their values."

The Cardinals were down at halftime, and Amatucci made sure to address the issue with Edwards and the rest of the team. He had to defuse a potentially volatile situation. The key was to stay focused on playing basketball. Amatucci did not want his players stooping to the level of the opposing team's fans.

"Darryle, there are two ways we can handle this," Amatucci remembered telling him. "We can let them get in our heads, break our concentration and be a distraction. Or, we can block it out and play the way we're capable. We're not doing that right now. They are making YOU focus on them. It's taking you out of your game."

Edwards single-handedly took over the game in the second half, scoring 20 points. It was a demonstration of his star power. Calvert Hall held on for a close victory. Edwards never uttered a word in retaliation. He let his play do all the talking. Amatucci voiced his displeasure to one of the school's administrators after the game. He also did not lose his composure, setting an example for his players.

The Cardinals quickly put the ugly incident behind them. There were more important goals to achieve and the team was well on its way to unprecedented success.

CROSSROADS - MEETING LIFE HEAD ON

Paul Kinney slamming it home.

PAUL ALLAN KINNEY
1962-1980

"The virtuous man, though he dies before his time,
will find rest ... Coming to perfection in so short a while,
he achieved long life; his soul being pleasing to the Lord,
he has taken him quickly ..."

Wisdom 4:7, 13-14

"Those who had the pleasure of knowing Paul Kinney will remember him not only for his outstanding athletic ability but also for the way his personality touched those he met. He was a special young man, sensitive to others, who took time to make people smile and laugh.

Paul loved his family, and certainly he loved basketball and his teammates, but what Paul loved more than anything was life. No one ever got more out of life than Paul Kinney.

His loss will deeply trouble us, but we may rest assured that Paul has achieved what every man strives for, eternal peace and happiness. Our only consolation is that he did indeed pass our way and touch our hearts."

- MARK AMATUCCI

Amatucci was astounded when other high schools were not heavily recruiting Paul Kinney. He had all the physical tools to make an immediate impact to any program. Kinney could run like a gazelle. Defenders had little chance of taking away his jumper because of the way he could rise above the court. He worked hard in the classroom and always seemed to have a smile on his face.

"He was 6-foot-5, but played like he was 6-8," Amatucci said. "He was always up over the rim. Paul was very versatile. He was the kind of inside player that also had the ability to shoot the 12 to 15 footer."

Kinney perfectly complemented the other Calvert Hall starters — Pop Tubman, Paul and Darryle Edwards and Marc Wilson — because they all ran the floor so well. Calvert Hall could push the ball up and down the court for thirty-two minutes, easily wearing down most opponents. More importantly, the Cards outworked other teams. "We were a very dangerous team at that point," Amatucci remembered.

In the classroom, Kinney had processing issues that made the tough Calvert Hall curriculum a difficult challenge. But he worked diligently to meet the high standards. He took advantage of the school's academic resource centers and regularly met with his teachers for extra help. Kinney never got discouraged. He took everything in stride and wanted to become a better student and athlete.

"You work so hard to get ready for a test or write a paper well, and when you get the work back, it's only a C," said Amatucci, who could identify with his player's processing issues. "The grade not reflecting the time and effort involved is a real disappointment. That can be very discouraging to most kids at that age. I am not saying that he didn't get disheartened about his schoolwork, but he could always regroup. Paul didn't let anything negative linger too long, whether it was athletic or academic. That was the type of attitude that defined us."

Kinney never had problems making the adjustment to the overall environment at Calvert Hall, despite being one of the few African-American students. He was popular among all of his peers and never focused on race. There was some familiarity with the school because his brother Vince graduated from Calvert Hall in 1974, but Paul was determined to forge his own path. He had an engaging sense of humor that resonated with teachers and athletes on the football and soccer teams. He was establishing himself as a force on the basketball court, creating an even bigger upside. As a sophomore, Kinney averaged 18 points with 10 rebounds.

"He was only going to get better, bigger and stronger," Amatucci said. "When he got off the floor with his hands up, he was an incredibly difficult matchup."

As a sophomore, Kinney entered Calvert Hall and immediately cracked the starting lineup. Amatucci led rigorous training sessions, convinced the challenge made his players better each day. The Cardinals were expected to stretch on their own before practice. Once practice started, the pace and intensity shifted right into high gear. Practice sessions were broken down into six parts: 15 minutes of skill work, 20 minutes of defensive fundamentals, 20 minutes of transition offense, 20 minutes of split squad offensive and defensive work at both ends of the court, 20 minutes of situational game instruction with free-throw shooting, followed by 20 minutes of half-court offense.

Paul Kinney receiving his Alhambra Invitational All Tournament Trophy, 1980.

Finally, the day ended with an inter-squad scrimmage, including competitive conditioning. The average practice time was two-and-a-half hours. It was demanding. The players were able to use the lessons they learned in practice in the regular season games.

Darryle Edwards remembered the intensity of those practices over his stellar career. He still carries some of the battle scars. "We just got up and down the court," said Edwards, who had been named captain with Kinney prior to the 1980-81 season. "Part of that was because of what we did in practice. We got after it. Sometimes our practices were harder than the games. Because of the amount of conditioning we did in practice and how we got after each other, when we got into games everything was second nature, and we just clicked. We did not waste time in practice. If you did not want to work, you could go."

Amatucci liked the look of his team heading into that 1980-81 season. In addition to a solid cast of returning lettermen, the Cardinals had a highly recruited freshman, Duane Ferrell. It would not be long before Ferrell would be turning heads in practice. He was poised to be a huge force in Amatucci's arsenal.

The team started strong and ran Fallston High School off the court in the opening scrimmage on the Wednesday before Thanksgiving. Kinney played well with no indication of what was looming ahead. In fact, his only concern was improving on his breakout season the year before. He had already caught the eye of more than forty college basketball coaches.

"The basketball environment we created made Paul better," Amatucci said. "He could shoot, post up, and run the floor. He didn't miss a step. As we got better, he got better, and vice versa. Some guys go to the locker room and bitch and moan about not getting the ball. It's just natural. But he never complained."

On Friday, Amatucci ran a normal practice and the players were upbeat and enthusiastic. Calvert Hall traveled to Parkville High School the following day for an early-morning scrimmage. The Cardinals started strong, establishing their up-tempo pressure game from the tip-off. The Knights were quickly overwhelmed. Amatucci anticipated the opportunity to get an extended look at some of his players who would be fighting for minutes in the regular season.

After Parkville called a timeout early in the first quarter, Kinney said he was winded, and Amatucci subbed him out to get a rest. Kinney casually took a seat next to assistant coach Joe Baker, who lauded his efforts at that point in the game.

The following moments would change the course of everyone's life in the gym that day.

As Amatucci crouched in front of the bench, he heard a loud bang behind him. He quickly turned around and realized that Kinney had fallen backward and violently hit his head against the bleachers. Kinney then fell forward into Amatucci's arms. His eyes had rolled back into his head. Immediately, Amatucci and his coaches knew that something had gone horribly wrong.

At first, the coaches thought he had a seizure, but then it became apparent he had suffered a massive heart attack. The players also knew Kinney was in peril. Paul Edwards ran close to his brother Darryle and pointed out that Kinney was lying on the floor. There was shock and disbelief over what was happening.

The entire Parkville gym fell silent, as there was a mad scramble to aid Kinney. Parkville coach Norm Norris ran over to the Calvert Hall bench and was trying to provide any support that he could. Cardinals lacrosse coach Mike Thomas was in the stands watching the scrimmage, and he went into action delivering CPR to the stricken player. Charles Lyon Sr., the father of a Parkville player, was a physician and also attended to Kinney.

Norris called 9-1-1 and paramedics arrived within minutes because of their proximity to the school. It was clear the situation was dire. Kinney's pulse was revived, but he was not able to regain consciousness. Amatucci rode in the ambulance with his stricken player to St. Joseph's Hospital in Towson. The Cardinals assistant coaches tried to reach Kinney's parents, who were not at the scrimmage, before making their way to the hospital. Kinney was rushed into the intensive care unit, and Amatucci could only sit against the wall of the ER and pray for the best.

From there, players, coaches, and parents arrived at St. Joseph's. Kinney had already been placed on life support. Darryle Edwards remembers seeing Luther Kinney as soon as he arrived in the emergency room.

"DOA, Darryle, DOA," Luther Kinney told him.

At the time, Edwards did not understand what that meant, but he knew it wasn't good.

"No, no, they had him breathing," Edwards remembers saying to Kinney's father, trying to offer some consolation.

The prognosis was grave.

Amatucci's mind had gone blank, and around 8 p.m. Kinney's parents said he should go home and get some rest. There was nothing more he could do. Amatucci reluctantly agreed. He then drove to his nearby, upstairs apartment and just sat in a rocking chair, never bothering to turn on any lights.

The world had come crashing down.

The following morning Amatucci returned to the hospital. However, everyone just had to wait through another day and hope for a miracle. On Monday morning, the decision was made to take Kinney off life support. He died twelve minutes later at the age of eighteen. "He had no history of illness or heart trouble," his mother, Catherine, lamented. Amatucci travelled back to Calvert Hall to relay the tragic news to the shocked and devastated players. The following day a formal announcement was made to a somber student body.

"Paul Kinney was my brother from another mother," Pop Tubman said. "He was one of the greatest guys I ever met in my life. He had one of the biggest hearts I've ever seen a person have. It's unfortunate that his heart was so big that his body couldn't handle it. From that day forward, we would say, '1-2-3, Paul Kinney,' and his spirit would carry us to victory. That's the absolute truth."

The viewing took place at Kinney's home, where a steady stream of visitors paid their respects over two nights. The funeral was held at St. Francis Xavier Catholic Church on East Oliver Street in Baltimore. Coaches from the other schools in the Baltimore Catholic League attended the service. Amatucci and the Calvert Hall players served as pall-bearers. The mood of everyone was summed up by Coach Mullis' sobering comment, "I was sitting crying in my beer over two kids with broken hands and two others who could not practice because of poor grades, then I heard what happened to Paul Kinney and all these problems paled by comparison. Paul's death makes basketball seem pretty insignificant."

After the funeral Mass and burial, the team travelled to Bishop Walsh for the regular season opener that night. Amatucci had initially cancelled the game, but the players wanted to make the trip. Basketball was cathartic. The Cardinals then took their anger out on the Spartans and emerged with a dominant 74-40 victory. Ferrell made the start in Kinney's place and threw down a 360-degree dunk in the first quarter.

Walsh head coach, Joe Carter, a good friend of Amatucci's, approached him after the game and said, "Mark, with no disrespect, I thought with everything you guys have been through this week and missing Paul's presence in the line-up, we would have had an easier time."

The game's result was more than just a blowout win. It was a statement of this team's total commitment to honor Paul Kinney.

After the game, the reality of the situation resurfaced. Calvert Hall was staying overnight in the Cumberland Holiday Inn, and Amatucci thought it was important for both the coaches and players to let off some steam. The coaches were invited by the Walsh staff to check out a local tavern called "My Place" to decompress. Prior to heading out, Amatucci lifted a curfew for the players but warned them not to get into any trouble.

Returning to the hotel around 3 a.m. the five coaches quickly scrambled to grab sleeping space in the single hotel room they shared. Amatucci's request to turn on the air conditioning despite the cold, December chill was vetoed by the other coaches. As a result, he ended up sleeping in the bathtub. A few hours later, Baker, who slept on the floor, was forced to answer the phone at 7 a.m. after none of his roommates bothered to move. He then entered the bathroom to inform Amatucci that the hotel manager needed to have a word with him in the lobby.

The previous night the players were loud and a bit out of control, much to the displeasure of the other guests. However, they did avoid any serious trouble. The manager initially intended to bar the team from future visits to the hotel.

Amatucci relayed the emotional challenges the team had faced the past week, and he promised the team would return in March for the Alhambra Catholic Invitational Tournament. He guaranteed that the players behavior would be totally appropriate. All was forgiven.

However, once the coaches and players returned to Calvert Hall it was still a struggle to get back to normalcy. There was a void left by Kinney's death, and Amatucci even considered stepping down as the coach. "I had some kind of guilt there … maybe I should have seen something, maybe I was being too demanding," Amatucci said.

He was visibly sulking during practice the following Monday. There wasn't the same energy. "I wasn't barking or placing my usual demands on the players," Amatucci said. "I guess I was worried about it happening again."

Darryle Edwards remembers the practices being completely different after Kinney's death. The team wasn't doing any conditioning. Amatucci wasn't imploring his players to quickly push the ball up and down the floor. "He wasn't as emotional as he usually was," Darryle Edwards remembered. "He wasn't getting after us the same way." Finally, the players sat on the bleachers after practice and waited for Amatucci to join them.

"We can get through this," Edwards told Amatucci in front of his teammates. "But we can't get through this if you don't coach us. You have to start coaching us again. You have to get back to the way that you were. We can still do this, but we need you to lead us."

No one in the Calvert Hall gym that day could control their emotions. There were no dry eyes. The players knew and respected that Amatucci was worried about their welfare after the tragedy. However, everyone needed to get back to playing Calvert Hall basketball. It was a way to honor Kinney's memory.

This changed Amatucci's mindset, and he gradually became his old self ... with some significant changes. The team formally dedicated the season to Kinney prior to a game against Mount St. Joseph.

"The kids being that emotional just shows where we were going as a family," Amatucci said. "It was a turning point in my life. I completely changed my approach. If I'm tough on someone, there's a reason for that, and it's not about winning the game. If I am banging on someone it's because I know they need it and it's going to help them grow. It's about building character. There is purpose in my madness. It really was the turning point for everyone."

Amatucci had previously dealt with a tragic death when one of his best friends committed suicide during his freshman year of college. That incident had a lasting impact on him. But after Kinney passed away, Amatucci's entire perspective on death changed.

"Dealing with Paul's death caused me to reflect deeply on my understanding of Christ's mission," Amatucci recalled. "Through my reflections, I came to the awareness that for me, Christ's mission is all about being a witness for his teachings. Unconditionally providing care and comfort for our neighbors, especially during times of pain and suffering, became an absolute. In my world, this faith-based commitment would extraordinarily help when dealing with future death and dying occurrences."

He added, "I used Paul's tragedy as an inspiration to motivate my spiritual mission which included touching the lives of the entire 1981 team. When I think about Paul, I focus on all the remarkable pluses I was privileged to be a part of during his short stay among us. Paul is never out of my thoughts."

Instead of falling apart, the players and coaches rallied around Kinney's memory. The team would play hard every practice and game to honor him. The Cardinals were determined to make his legacy a great one. Many of the players said they could tangibly feel Kinney's spirit that season. They knew he was with them and still a vital part of the team.

"It was a real-life experience that changed a lot of those guys," Baker said. "We were a different team because of losing Paul and what he meant to everybody. They were already a tight-knit group before Kinney passed away. It changed their entire perspective."

"It was surreal how things change over a tragedy in a good way," Amatucci said. "As tragic as Paul's death was, what he was able to pass onto us with his personality was incredible. I can truly say that Paul Kinney's death helped us to become better people, to be caring people, and be more unselfish when it came to helping folks who are in need."

The rallying cry for Kinney elevated Calvert Hall to new heights. The team was destined for something special and they were not going to let opportunity slip from their grasp. The team transcended race, and the entire student body was firmly behind them. It paved the way for a magical season.

5

HERE COMES CALVERT HALL

The Hall – "Sold Out"

"The relentless pressure continued. It came from every which way and finally it all broke loose. The Spartans had run flat out of fingers, had used up all of their toes and everything else at their disposal, and still the rush came."

- DAVE CATER, WILKES-BARRE TIMES
"Calvert Hall Cops WARMland Title"

On New Year's Eve in 1980, Amatucci spent the afternoon with assistants Phil Popovec and Joe Baker watching the movie "Raging Bull" at a local movie theater. Amatucci was still dealing with the aftermath of Paul Kinney's death. As a result, he was not in the mood for any further holiday festivities that evening. Instead, Baker stuck around Amatucci's apartment discussing life, death, and basketball. Baker was expected to pick up his girlfriend and future wife, Cathy, at 8 p.m. The discussion between Amatucci and Baker lasted past 9 p.m. Baker was late for his date, and took one on the chin for his friend.

After the Christmas break, Amatucci still had trouble functioning. One morning, Amatucci decided he needed some time and space to deal with Kinney's death. So he left his office at 10 a.m. and did not return the rest of the day. Baker and another fellow teacher, George Kropp, travelled to Amatucci's apartment in an attempt to help get him back on track. The healing process was underway, but the grieving would not end easily.

"I was still feeling guilty," Amatucci said. "I took it personally. When you look at where we were at that moment, the basketball family was taking a hit. The players were part of my family. I didn't have any children at the time. They were my kids. That's how important the guys were to me. Basketball gave me an opportunity to develop young men's minds and values. Culturally, guys were coming from different environments. I needed them and they needed me."

On the court, Amatucci was slowly bouncing back and his players had no inkling that he was still struggling with Kinney's death. The practices were once again intense and the team was clicking at both ends of the court. The players were channeling their sadness over Kinney onto their overwhelmed opponents. The Cardinals were playing with an energy few teams could match, and they rolled through the early portion of their schedule.

After dominating Bishop Walsh in the opener, Calvert Hall won eight of its next nine games before heading into its Catholic League schedule. Over that successful stretch, the Cardinals beat a tough West Catholic team on the road in Philadelphia, 83-51. The only setback was a controversial 63-62 loss to Dunbar of Washington, D.C., that was plagued by several questionable calls in the final minutes. Anthony Jones, who would later play at both Georgetown and UNLV and spend four years in the NBA, hit a game-winning jumper for the Crimson Tide with ten seconds left. Calvert Hall would have its revenge for that game the following year.

"The train is rolling," Amatucci said. "Before every game and after every practice, it's '1-2-3 Paul Kinney.' I never had to remind them to do that. Until you experience something like Paul's death, you don't realize how it's going to hit you. With our guys, black or white, we were driven by Paul's memory. Some people say that's a cliché, but it's reality. We were taking it out on whoever was on the other bench. That's how we were resolving our anxiety, anger and frustration. For sure, we approached opponents without fear."

The Cardinals further advanced their reputation by winning the noteworthy WARMland Holiday Tournament in Wilkes-Barre, Pennsylvania. Calvert Hall took down La Salle, 73-55, and then beat Wyoming Valley West, 79-57, for the title. Ferrell was named the tournament MVP after scoring 17 points with 13 rebounds in the championship game.

"Winning that tournament helped us gain more national recognition," Amatucci said. "The guys were not only rallying around Paul, but they had a chip on their shoulder. It didn't matter who they were playing. Paul Edwards exemplified the players' level of confidence. He was a quiet intimidator. He'd walk up to someone on the opposing team, pat them on the ass and say, 'Have a nice game tonight.' Or he'd whisper at the foul line to the shooter, 'I hope you make that one-and-one.' But he did it very quietly and always with a smile on his face. He could get in your head. It wasn't arrogance. It was the confidence coming out."

After Christmas, the Card headed to Arlington, Virginia, for the distinguished Bishop O'Connell High School Christmas Invitational Tournament. In the first round, they picked up another signature 65-57 win over Philadelphia's St. Joe Prep. The Cardinals dominated Georgetown Prep, 86-57, in the semi-final. That set up a showdown with Holy Trinity Diocesan of Hicksville, New York, in the championship match-up.

The Titans were led by 6-foot-7 center Ken Bantum, who was later an All-American at Cornell, and 6-foot-6 forward Doug Poetzsch, who starred at Siena. The Cardinals emerged with a 68-62 victory, and Darryle Edwards was named the tournament MVP, winning an award that was the size of the Heisman Trophy. It was becoming a habit for the Cardinals to "walk away with the gold," a phrase that would become part of the team's persona.

"On paper, we were not supposed to win that game," Amatucci remembered about the Holy Trinity matchup. "They were probably the best team we had played so far that season. With our pressure defense, we jumped out to an 18-4 first quarter lead. Poetzsch, with 23 points in the game, kept Trinity within striking distance throughout the second and third quarters. As usual, once we got into the fourth quarter and it got late in the game, that's when we took off. We can run. They had to come out and play our style. Trinity could not keep up with us. We're trapping, pressing, and creating turnovers. That was probably one of the biggest wins for the program at the time."

Off the court, it wasn't all business in Arlington. The coaches shared one room once again, which prompted nighttime activities. Assistant coach Charlie "Doc" Reif would commandeer a bed because he had to drive back to Towson for his junior varsity practice each day. Reif would sleep with his clothes inside out and his beard hanging over the covers for reasons still not known to the other coaches.

"Despite his success, there is no pretension about Mark," Reif said. "He did a great job of building that community with the players and the coaching staff. Everybody felt a part of it, no matter what role they played, whether it be a scorekeeper, an announcer, or team manager. He made everybody feel a part of the success the team was achieving, which was remarkable."

The coaches took advantage of Jack Amatucci's local auto dealership, which was a sponsor of the tournament but had no relation to the Calvert Hall coach. Nonetheless, Reif jokingly began referring to Mark

Amatucci as "Jack Amatucky." The coaches would make late-night calls to a local radio station pretending to be Jack Amatucci requesting to play Calvert Hall's team song, "Love Train" by The O'Jays. "More important than winning the tournament was the strength of the bonding experience had by the players and coaches. "We had a great time and won the tournament," Amatucci recalled. "Life is good again."

Returning to Towson, the program had another sobering moment for the players and coaches. Prior to the Baltimore Catholic League opener against Mount Saint Joseph, the Cardinals had a formal ceremony to honor Paul Kinney.

Kinney's parents were presented with a picture of their son in uniform and a plaque from the Calvert Hall players. The team wore black armbands and No. 42 on the shoulder of their warm-ups to honor their beloved teammate. Calvert Hall retired his number.

"It was hard," Amatucci said. "I was scheduled to speak, and I can remember just walking around outside the school for a half-hour to determine whether I could pull it off or not. We got it done."

On the court, Calvert Hall used a balanced attack to beat the Gaels, 70-65. Darryle Edwards led the Cardinal with 16 points, while brother Paul scored 13. Wilson and Ferrell added 11 points apiece. It was not uncommon for Calvert Hall to spread out the scoring. "If we had four players in double-figures, we were going to win a lot of games," Amatucci said. The Cardinals were creating a buzz in the local basketball community. The Calvert Hall gymnasium became the place to be on Friday night. It was more than just Calvert Hall fans in the stands. Hoop fans

Darryle Edwards scores his 1,000th career point.

across the area wanted to the see the Cardinals' electrifying style of play in person.

Later that season, in a sold-out home game against Loyola, fans climbed onto the roof of the gym and watched the action through the skylights. In a blitzkrieg attack, the Cards dominated the Dons in the first quarter 20-8. Loyola never recovered. Final score: 75-61. Defensively, the Cards shut down the Don's talented offense featuring University of Virginia-bound Kenny Johnson.

"Wilson, Pop and Kauffman worked together and communicated so well defensively that I just let them go," Amatucci said. "It was a full-court, run and jump defense. Once the ball was in-bounded, Pop's job was to force the ball out of the middle of the floor. Wilson and Kauffman would work in tandem, one trapping with Pop and the other rotating up for a steal. The forwards in the back reacted to the trap and kept the pressure on. Everybody knew their job and had the versatility to play different positions in the defense. Teams could not handle it. Defense was how we won games."

Kauffman was another one of Amatucci's prize recruits coming out of Madison Rec. He played on Madison teams with Tubman and Wilson. When they reunited at Calvert Hall, it was a comfortable transition. They were tight on and off the court.

"We had an opportunity to build something special," Kauffman said. "We were all guys who liked to get up and down the court. Tooch's style of play, which was a full-court press on defense, and then pushing the ball on offense, perfectly fit our athletic ability. We liked to play like that."

Despite their success, the Cards did have their share of "trying moments" for the coach. Late in the fourth quarter in a home game against Bishop Walsh, Amatucci decided to hold the ball on offense to preserve a five-point lead. Marc Wilson, who rarely spoke around the team, ran by Amatucci and said, "Play ball, man." After the initial shock of hearing Wilson speak, Amatucci benched his premier guard the rest of game for trying to be the coach. The Cards won, 46-41.

During the BCL regular season, the Cardinals beat rival Cardinal Gibbons twice. The Crusaders tried to intimidate Calvert Hall to no avail. Before the away game at Cardinal Gibbons, the Crusader players performed calisthenics like a football team during warmups. Once the game started, the Crusaders also tried to emulate the Cardinals' trademark style by trapping, running, and pressing. The players for Calvert Hall were completely unmoved by this strategy. They attacked the full-court pressure by throwing the ball over the defense for easy layups. On the other side of the court, the Cardinals effectively created turnovers with their pressure. At the end of the first quarter, the Cards led, 18-3. Game over.

Gibbons' game strategy did not just involve the players. Gibbons Coach Ray Mullis was well-known for his efforts to intimidate officials. He always carried a red towel on his shoulder that he would toss in the air to show his displeasure with referees.

As the Cards took control of the game, Mullis put his towel act into play. Amatucci sensed some calls were beginning to swing toward the Crusaders. Amatucci decided to get into the act himself by throwing a chair, earning a technical foul.

"The next time he throws the towel, I'm throwing the chair again," Amatucci told referee Jack Hubbard. Even with all of the shenanigans, the Cardinals ran away with a huge road win, 75-67. Calvert Hall was not going to be intimidated. As with Loyola, the rivalry with Gibbons was becoming one-sided.

Amatucci and the players embraced the role as the new guard in the stodgy Baltimore Catholic League. Amatucci would wear three-piece suits to games, and his body language rubbed some of the opposing coaches the wrong way. Some of the old guard didn't like Calvert Hall's run-and gun philosophy because they considered it "playground basketball." BCL opponents should have spent less time criticizing the Cards style and more time preparing to play against it. Amatucci said, "We were in their heads, and the results speak for themselves." The Cardinals went 29-1 over a three-year stretch against league opponents.

"St. Joe, Gibbons, and Loyola were really good," Baker said. "Even Towson Catholic wasn't bad. It wasn't like everyone else in the league were weak sisters. Dan Popera at Curley had disciplined, motivated guys who could play. If they set the tempo, you were in trouble. They could beat any team in the league. We were winning those games, but they were not cakewalks."

The regular season concluded in a spirited contest with Towson Catholic. Emotions boiled over late in the Cardinals' 76-58 victory. A loose-ball scrum at half court led to a melee with Paul Edwards at the bottom of the pile. His brother Darryle jumped right in with his loyal teammates. Amatucci, trying to be a peacemaker, ran onto the court and started pulling players off the pile. In the chaos of the moment, he was pushed to the floor tearing an extremely expensive brand-new pair of camel-colored linen pants. Incensed, Amatucci was now ready to become a participant rather than a peacemaker.

Coach Chris Devlin, a large man, stepped in and pulled Amatucci away. Calming down, Amatucci turned his head to the bench area only to see Coach Baker making a bull-run down the sideline to have a discussion with the TC head coach. The melee ended as fast as it started. One particular piece of Calvert Hall lore remains from that day, "Where was Marc Wilson during the brawl?" Having no interest in fisticuffs, Wilson calmly sat on the floor by the team bench to watch the action. Baker joked that Wilson, "didn't want anyone stealing the team's shooter shirts."

The Cardinals surged through the rest of the regular season with 14 straight victories, winning the league championship, followed by a second-round BCL Tourney win over Gibbons. Next up, the BCL tourney title match up versus the Loyola Dons.

Prior to the championship game, Amatucci recalled, "We visited Paul Kinney's grave before the game, and I told the guys — nothing too solemn, nothing morbid — but let's win this one for Paul."

Calvert Hall beat Loyola 81-62 to finish the regular season 26-1. The game was never close with the Cards dominating from start to finish and picking up their third victory of the season versus the Dons. The win set up another trip for the team to the famed Alhambra Tournament.

First, though, Calvert Hall and Dunbar had a score to settle over which team was the best in Baltimore. It was a showdown that would be long remembered as one of the greatest games ever played.

6

THE GAME - A NIGHT FOR THE AGES

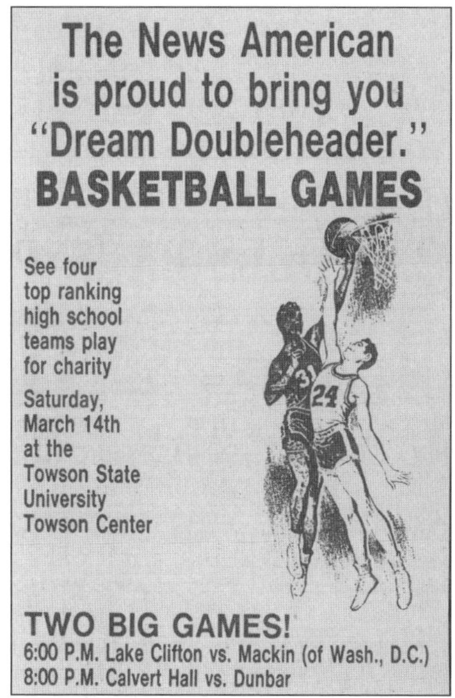
The News American is proud to bring you "Dream Doubleheader." BASKETBALL GAMES

See four top ranking high school teams play for charity

Saturday, March 14th at the Towson State University Towson Center

TWO BIG GAMES!

6:00 P.M. Lake Clifton vs. Mackin (of Wash., D.C.)

8:00 P.M. Calvert Hall vs. Dunbar

"There on the sidelines Amatucci crouched on his haunches. Cool, quiet, he directed his players with hand signals. His words would never have surfaced in that sea of noise."

\- SUSAN REIMER
Baltimore Sun

Amatucci awoke with his usual game-day anxiety on March 15, 1981. This time, he was not preparing for an ordinary matchup. Instead, he was focused on the most highly anticipated game of the basketball season on tap for that evening. No. 1 Calvert Hall would be playing No. 2 Dunbar for supremacy in the Baltimore Metro area. Proceeds allotted to Calvert Hall were designated to the Paul Kinney Scholarship Fund.

The game was part of a double-header at the Towson Center on the campus of Towson University with Baltimore City power Lake Clifton and Mackin of Washington, D.C., playing the 6 p.m. opener. The games sold out almost immediately with an estimated 2,000 people turned away at the gate. There was a palpable buzz leading up to the opening tip. The *News American*, one of the local newspapers, helped put the game together. Officials with Towson University did not charge for the use of the arena, which increased the funds for charity. Dunbar used its money to support the William "Sugar" Cain Scholarship, named after the legendary Baltimore City basketball coach. Tickets were $2, and the *News American* chartered buses to transport fans from Lake Clifton and Dunbar high schools to the Towson Center.

The players were allotted ten tickets each, which were more valuable than a local lottery stub. Mark Kauffman gave all of his tickets to friends, who then proceeded to scalp them outside the arena. "I only had one buddy use the ticket, and he wound up seeing the greatest game in Baltimore basketball history," Kauffman remembered. The other players also gave away their tickets to family and friends who packed the Calvert Hall side of the court. "One thing that I'll never forget is that I gave my father tickets and he didn't show up for the game," Pop Tubman said. "He missed one hell of a game."

Amatucci was on edge most of the week. He even attempted to alter the practice routine by playing music during warm-up drills. Pop and Darryle vetoed this move. They implored him to get back to normalcy. Amatucci had reason to be nervous because Dunbar's roster was loaded with talent. Forward David Wingate later played at Georgetown and was a second-round pick by the Philadelphia 76ers in the 1986 NBA Draft. Reggie Williams also played at Georgetown and was a first-round selection of the Los Angeles Clippers. Gary Graham furthered his playing career as a member of the highly regarded Rebels of UNLV.

The Cards also had their own share of stars and were not the least bit intimidated.

When Calvert Hall arrived at the Towson Center, they were relegated to a small dressing room in the arena as opposed to one of the regular team locker rooms. This did not help Amatucci's mood. However, his jitters began to recede as soon as he started the pre-game speech. "I'm usually a nervous guy until I get into my game-day routine," Amatucci said. "I wasn't happy with the accommodations at the Towson Center. In reality, they were a good distraction which got me amped up."

Lake Clifton topped Mackin, 87-83, in the first contest. The game finished on schedule, which allayed Amatucci's concern that a lengthy ending would impact the Card's pre-game preparations.

The Cards had played in front of large crowds all season, and they knew most of the players on Dunbar. However, they also fully understood the magnitude of the game and its place in local and national basketball landscape.

"It wasn't a game that you would think people would pick sides because of race or color," Paul Edwards said. "Calvert Hall was Calvert Hall and Dunbar was Dunbar. It wasn't a black or white game. If you had friends who went to Calvert Hall, then you rooted for Calvert Hall. If you were from the city then you just rooted for Dunbar. It never got to be racial. It was just a great game because we played with those guys in the summer. It was a lot like a summer league game with Lafayette playing Madison, only we had some of their players and they had some of ours."

The game was intense from the opening tip. Kauffman and Williams almost immediately got into a confrontation when they ran to the same spot on a jump ball. "There was a lot of trash talking going on," Kauffman said. From there, the Cardinals and Poets settled down and got into the rhythm of just playing basketball. The teams traded baskets and Dunbar held an 18-16 edge at the end of the first quarter. The Cardinals were hampered because Darryle Edwards picked up two quick fouls and was forced to the bench. As a rule, Amatucci always pulled players with two fouls in the first half and held them out until the second half.

"Of all the games to get into foul trouble, that was the worst," Darryle Edwards remembered. "One of the reasons we got down was because I was out. It was a big stage. When I came back, we started rolling."

The seesaw battle continued in the second quarter as both teams effectively ran their offenses. The Poets made a few more plays at both ends of the court and held a 38-35 lead at the break. Graham came up huge for Dunbar, scoring 12 of his 19 points in the opening half. In the locker room, Amatucci maintained his confidence because he knew his players had the legs and stamina to aggressively pressure the Poets throughout the final two quarters.

However, it was the Poets who came out of the locker room with increased energy and began to pull away. Wingate and Williams were dominant and they dictated the tempo by making shots from around the perimeter and inside the paint. Dunbar began to get some separation and outscored Calvert Hall 24-17 in the third quarter and led 62-52 heading into the final period.

"They were doing exactly what we didn't want them to do," Amatucci said. "Wingate and Williams were getting off. Kevin Woods' offensive spurt added to their fire power. We were getting beat in transition, allowing penetration and not effectively defending the low post. But, we had been down before. I also knew to never discount Paul Kinney's influence on these players."

With Darryle Edwards back on the court, Calvert Hall regrouped in the fourth quarter. The Cardinals were aggressive and began to get stops and force turnovers with their pressure defense. They slowly chipped away at the margin. The Poets, though, managed a run of their own late in the quarter and amassed a seemingly insurmountable 80-71 lead with just 1:24 left in the game, forcing Amatucci to call a timeout.

Fans started to head toward the exits because they believed the game was over, prompting Paul Edwards to say, "You don't walk out on Calvert Hall. Unless it's halftime, you stay in your seats because once we hit our spurt, that's it." Those proved to be prophetic words.

In the huddle, Amatucci knew it was the critical moment for this team to make a decisive run at the Poets. Amatucci looked into the eyes of his players and didn't see any panic. "I said, 'Look, we're going to have to hurry.'" Coming out of the timeout, the Cards ran an inbounds play against the Poets zone defense.

"We scored on the inbounds play out of the timeout," Amatucci recalled. "And then we jumped right into our full-court pressure creating a couple of turnovers. Before you knew it, we were right back in the game."

With thirty-eight seconds remaining in regulation the Cardinals had cut the margin to 80-79.

With the arena already at a fever pitch, another uncanny turn of events unfolded.

After Calvert Hall seemingly took an 81-80 lead on a jumper by Darryle Edwards, a chair near Dunbar's bench was flung onto the court. The most likely culprit was esteemed Poets coach Bob Wade, who vehemently denied doing a Bob Knight imitation. A technical foul was initially called for the infraction. Calvert Hall now had an opportunity for a pair of free throws and possession of the ball when the game continued. It appeared that The Hall was in position to take over control of the game.

Gerry Jackson, a long-time editor at the Annapolis Capital and The Baltimore Sun, was working at the scorer's table that night as a student intern for the Sports Information Department and stats crew at Towson University. He recalls seeing Wade throw the chair. "We had the full stat crew on hand for that game," Jackson said. "It was like a college game. To this day, and I've seen hundreds of basketball games, from college to high school to pro, and that was the most intense game I ever remember watching. You were just on pins and needles the entire game."

Bill Glauber, who was covering the game for The Baltimore Sun, could not confirm Wade threw the chair amid the chaos. "It was just bedlam," said Glauber, who now writes for the Milwaukee Journal Sentinel.

A bit of pandemonium broke out as the Poets sideline extensively protested the ruling. The officials gathered at half court and decided to take away both Edwards' basket and the technical foul because seemingly no one could accurately identify who actually threw the chair and there was an issue with the clock. It was an astonishing turn of events. Nonetheless, the Cardinals remain unfazed and focused on closing out the game.

"We had come all the way back and were down one point," Darryle Edwards said. "I scored the go-ahead bucket that put us up by one. The chair comes out on the floor and they don't count my basket. The crowd was going crazy."

Amatucci added, "We weren't panicking. We believed we could create another turnover and score quickly. It was a very mature, very business-like mentality."

At the time, Dunbar had not played many close games. On the other side of the court, the Calvert Hall players had been in several hard-fought contests against teams from Philadelphia and the tough Baltimore Catholic League. The Cardinals were battle-tested and that turned out to be the biggest difference that night.

"They had never been in a situation with someone putting constant pressure on them as we did," Amatucci said. "Dunbar felt the game was already won."

The Cardinals appeared to take the lead again when Paul Edwards converted a put-back off a Wilson shot. However, the basket was disallowed because Edwards was called for a foul for jumping over the back of a Dunbar player. The Poets then went up 81-79 on a free throw by Woods. In situations like this, down one or two, late in the game, the Cards were trained to run their fast break and look for the first open shot. On Woods' made free-throw, the Cards quickly outlet the ball and pushed it to Tubman running the outside lane. From the corner, Pop's shot fell short, but Darryle Edwards, filling his spot on the break was there for a put-back to tie the score, 81-81. Edwards still can't believe the sequence of events.

"Of all the people on our team, why the hell do we want Pop to shoot the ball?" Darryle Edwards said with a laugh. "You got me, Paul Edwards, Marc Wilson and Duane Ferrell, and Pop is going to shoot the ball. When the shot went up, I was in perfect position for the rebound. I grabbed the ball and put it back in."

The Poets had one more chance to win the game as the ball found its way to Woods on the inbound. The Cardinals, however, got a little help from some divine intervention at the buzzer.

"They beat the press and threw the ball to Kevin Woods, who could jump out of the gym," Darryle said. "He catches the ball and nine out of ten times, he makes a dunk. Instead of dunking it, he tried to lay it in and the ball bounced off the back of the rim. Time expired. We said, 'That was Paul Kinney who saved us right there.' If someone asks me one hundred times, I will repeat that story the same way. Woods made that play all of the time."

Neither team scored in the first extra period and the crowd noise was virtually deafening at the sold-out arena. In the second overtime, Dunbar took a late lead on a pair of free throws by Russ Williams. However, freshman Duane Ferrell responded for the Cardinals with a layup and the game was tied, 83-83, with twenty-three seconds remaining, setting up a third and final extra period. After the game, Ferrell commented to reporters, "People talked all week about how I was so young, but I think I proved to everyone that I could play at that level."

"I think I tried to coach too much in the first two overtimes," Amatucci said. "Instead of continuing to be aggressive as we had been in the fourth quarter, we came out at a slower pace, trying to manage the clock and run set offensive plays. That was really not our style of play. By the third overtime, it was just, 'Okay, let's just go out and get them again.'

"And we did!"

Calvert Hall finally took control by scoring the opening six points in the third overtime period to take an 89-83 lead. The teams traded field goals before Tubman's free throws in the final seconds earned a 94-91 victory for the Cards. Wilson led Calvert Hall with 27 points, while Paul Edwards scored 25. Dunbar was paced by 24 points from Williams, while Wingate and Woods scored 19 apiece.

Wade was not happy with the officiating, telling reporters: "There were a lot of questions in that game. I don't normally gripe about officiating. But you know, you saw it. My kids were afraid to do anything. They were afraid because the guys were calling anything. Some of those fouls were out-and-out blatant. I'm just a little ticked off. Calvert Hall won and they are a good team. But there are a lot of questions still." The Cardinals were called for 27 fouls, compared to 25 for Dunbar.

Pandemonium broke out after the final buzzer as players and students stormed the court in celebration. Charlie Rogers, the long-time maintenance director at Calvert Hall, did a dance atop the scorers' table. "It was like winning the ACC Tournament or getting into the Final Four," Amatucci said. "It was bedlam, it was electrifying ... just unbelievable after the game." The team later chanted Kinney's name in the locker room. It was an emotionally draining night on several fronts. The Cards showed the heart of a champion. The effort was a source of pride for the entire school community.

Amatucci remembered just sitting down on the bench amid the celebration and soaking in the atmosphere. After finally leaving the Towson Center, the Calvert Hall coaches and their friends went to a local restaurant for dinner and drinks, but the celebration was subdued. There was a tremendous sense of accomplishment, but total exhaustion had set in because of the emotions of the game, the week, and the season. "Okay, we got it done," Amatucci said. "There was no celebration. Everyone was in a fog."

There was not much time to celebrate the victory over Dunbar because the Cards had just a few days to get ready for the Alhambra Catholic Invitational Tournament. Players and coaches were still emotionally and physically drained from the weekend. Amatucci implored his players to re-energize in preparation for the legendary tourney.

While checking-in to the Holiday Inn in Cumberland, the team quickly recognized the anticipation of their arrival. Tourney regulars and media were abuzz with an anticipated Calvert Hall versus DeMatha showdown in the championship game.

"It really was a big-time atmosphere the entire week," Amatucci said about Alhambra.

The Cardinals had a shoot-around at a local YMCA hours before playing Father Judge in the opener. It was a tough matchup, and Calvert Hall started that game sluggish with some uncharacteristic defensive breakdowns. Father Judge played typical Philadelphia Catholic League basketball with an effective zone defense and half-court sets on offense. Nonetheless, Calvert Hall rode the hot hand of Wilson, who scored 27 points and paved the way for a 79-73 victory.

"They stayed in the game," Amatucci said about Father Judge. "We didn't pull away. We didn't play well defensively and gave up too many points. You could see the Dunbar game took a lot out of us." The players admitted they were not at their best. "We weren't psyched for the game," said Darryle Edwards, who scored nine points. "We've been sluggish all day."

Nonetheless, the victory set up a second-round game with Archbishop Carroll of Washington, D.C. This time, fatigue caught up with the Cardinals against a hot-shooting team coached by Jack Bruen. Calvert Hall struggled to get its transition game going against Carroll's tough man-to-man defense. The Cardinals had a cold night from the field shooting just 23 of 68. Meanwhile, Carroll made 50 percent of its shots and won 73-63, snapping Calvert Hall's 23-game winning streak.

"We got beat at both ends of the floor," Amatucci said. "We never got any rhythm going offensively, and they put up 73 points. They were well-coached. It was a poor effort from our team."

After the game, Amatucci tore into his players, reminding them about the significance of the Alhambra. He stressed there was no excuse for coming out flat two games in a row, especially after having such a successful season. The Cardinals had a showdown with Philadelphia's Roman Catholic on the final day for fifth place. He emphasized to the players that they needed to be ready to play the next day. His final message was that they better make sure everyone is in their rooms at curfew. Any violators would be sent home. The message was clear.

Amatucci and the rest of the coaches let out their frustrations following the Archbishop Carroll game with a trip back to "My Place." After returning to the hotel, Doc Reif and Baker went to the hospitality room in search of refreshments, but everything was shut down. Instead of food and drinks, they returned with a borrowed fez hat from a local Shriners organization. Adding to the hijinks of the evening/early morning, the Calvert Hall players congregated outside the door of Roman Catholic coach William "Speedy" Morris and chanted his name. The hat did make it back to its original resting place before anyone noticed.

The Cardinals did not show any ill effects from the previous night during the morning shoot-around. Calvert Hall was focused and determined to finish the season strong. "We talked a long time about who we are and how we are expected to perform," Amatucci said. "I told them we haven't done that the last two nights. Like my dad said, 'You can't go around talking about how great you are when you don't back it up.' We were not backing it up. How much did this game mean right then? It was our championship game. Forget Dunbar, this was the biggest game of the year."

Roman Catholic had a solid team led by Randy Monroe, who later became the head coach at the University of Maryland Baltimore County, and Tommy Lee, who would play for Amatucci at Loyola College. "They got after it defensively and were disciplined on offense. We were going to have our hands full," Amatucci said. The Cardinals were down at halftime, prompting Amatucci to throw an errant luggage bag at his players to get their attention. The Cards responded by pulling away for a 64-57 victory. Darryle Edwards made first team all-tournament, and Wilson was named to the second team.

Calvert Hall finished the season 29-2 and was ranked third in the nation.

"From outside looking in, to win two out of three after going through what we experienced the week before, I don't think anyone would be upset with that," Amatucci said. "We beat some really good teams and ended on a high note. It was something special. Truthfully though, we were not satisfied with how the season ended."

Now, the pieces were in place for another historic run the following season.

The Cardinals had been in this situation before. There was never a doubt.

WIRE-TO-WIRE UNRIVALED PERFECTION

Tooch and Pop – a dynamic duo.

"That team was at its best during the most critical moments of the game, refusing to buckle under pressure when confronted with a formidable opponent or the inevitable adversity that can cause others to capitulate."

- BERNIE MIKLASZ
St. Louis Post-Dispatch

The hype surrounding the 1981-82 Calvert Hall basketball team began in the summer when most schools were typically preparing for football, soccer, and other fall sports. National media publications, including USA Today and Basketball Weekly, were quick to declare the Cardinals as the No. 1 team in the United States. Calvert Hall had four returning starters from the previous season—Pop Tubman, Marc Wilson, Paul Edwards and Duane Ferrell. The bench went eight deep, and Amatucci had confidence in the entire roster.

"I truly believed we embraced the idea of being ranked the No. 1 team in the country, and we were excited for the challenge," Wilson said. "It meant a lot to us because we worked so hard individually and as a team to prove we were excellent basketball players and people. The team had faced many challenges and came through with flying colors. We felt we were the best."

Darryle Edwards had graduated and was playing at Mount St. Mary's (MD). Pat Sass, a sharp-shooting, 6-foot-3 guard, transferred to Calvert Hall from St. John's in Washington, D.C., and replaced Darryle in the starting lineup. "He was just a pure jump shooter," Amatucci said. "He fit right in. He developed an immediate chemistry with the veterans." Sass showed his commitment to playing for The Hall by making a daily forty-mile drive from Crofton to school every day. He often arrived home late at night because Tubman, Wilson, Kauffman, and Paul Edwards piled into his family station wagon for a ride home after practice.

The top preseason ranking did not fluster the Cardinals' players or coaches. The hard work in practice and the number of wins on the court the past two seasons culminated in their earning national respect. The players had a swagger. They were prepared to take on any team, anywhere. "There was not a lot of locker room chatter about the ranking," Amatucci recalled. "They were not impressed by it, they believed it." The Cardinals were prepared to take care of unfinished business on the court.

"We were not intimidated by it," Mark Kauffman said about the preseason ranking. "Was there pressure? I didn't feel any. We just pushed the ball up the floor and tried to run people out of the gym."

Amatucci put together one of the toughest schedules in the entire nation, playing teams from around the United States in tournaments in Las Vegas, Philadelphia, and of course, the Alhambra. No one with any basketball common sense was able to make an argument about the Cards playing soft opponents to pad their ranking.

"We didn't need to go around and draw attention to ourselves and remind everyone that we were No. 1 in the country," Amatucci said. "What we had accomplished over the last two years spoke for itself. We were going to play anybody, anywhere, at any time, and always believed we would chalk up a win. We knew who we were and we knew what we were capable of doing. It was going to be fun.

Although he knew the outstanding talent of his team, Amatucci had no intention of becoming complacent. From day one the players could tell by his body language that he was all-business. Tooch took his ever-present intensity and amped it to a new level. He knew this group was capable of doing something special. The players responded with a determined work ethic and had great spirit. Practices were competitive. Amatucci rarely had to interrupt the sessions to address any lack of effort. All of the players were expected to go 100 percent all of the time, anything less was completely unacceptable.

"I don't care who you are, once you cross that line onto the court, your ass better be prepared to practice," he said. "I didn't play favorites. If anything, I was harder on the guys who had more talent."

Amatucci boosted the scrimmage schedule to get his team bat-

The Cardinals' 1980-82 coaching staff.

tle-tested for the regular season. The Cardinals played an experienced and physical Annapolis team on the road and a confident Essex Community College squad that was ranked in the top five in the national JUCO polls. Calvert Hall won both games by running away in the fourth quarter. "Scrimmaging ranked teams helped us jumpstart our preparation for the first game against Washington power, Spingarn," Amatucci said. "Those scrimmage wins were a huge confidence-builder."

The national media were impressed with the schedule. Hall-of-Fame basketball journalist Dave Krider, who wrote for USA Today, Street & Smith's, Basketball Weekly, Basketball Times, and Sports Illustrated in his illustrious career, thought the Cardinals might have overdone it with the level of competition they were facing.

"The killer schedule is the biggest stumbling block between Calvert Hall and the national high school basketball championship," Krider wrote Nov. 27, 1981. "Basketball Weekly likes the Towson, Md., school as the No. 1 team in the preseason, but it will have to earn it the hard way."

Despite the early accolades, a controversy was building before the season even tipped off.

From the start of the preseason, the local media was clamoring for a Calvert Hall/Dunbar rematch. "It came up right away; do we want to play again?" Amatucci said. The Poets had a deep team with David Wingate, Gary Graham and Reggie Williams returning. Muggsy Bogues, a transfer from Southern, and Tim Dawson, who transferred from Towson Catholic, added to Dunbar's star power. Dunbar wanted to stake its claim to the #1 ranking.

"They were already arguing their case and the season had not even started yet," Amatucci remembered.

Amatucci was asked throughout the entire summer about a potential rematch, but there were obvious challenges with Calvert Hall's schedule. He already had a full tilt of games and the only alternative would be to play Dunbar after the Alhambra Tournament. "We were focused on two goals: win the Baltimore Catholic League again and take the Alhambra Tournament crown," Amatucci told the media. "We have unfinished business at the Alhambra. I would be more than happy to schedule a game with Dunbar, but at an appropriate time."

The outcry for the game created area wide debate with local residents writing letters to newspapers about the potential rematch. There was also growing division between the two programs. The Calvert Hall players from Baltimore City were falsely accused of taking payouts for attending the school and bypassing Baltimore City. "When other kids decided to go to other schools, it was their decision. But when we go to Calvert Hall, people were saying they bought us cars or something," Tubman told The Baltimore Sun. "I've been told to use my basketball as a tool and not let it use me. I could break a leg, but people can never take your knowledge away."

Dunbar coach Bob Wade even defended Calvert Hall's recruiting and said the school was being unfairly victimized for recruiting black players. "Everyone is knocking Calvert Hall because they're winning," Wade told The Baltimore Sun. "When they were 9-15, no one was paying attention to them. Now they're villains, so to speak." Amatucci added, "Bob and I have always had a good relationship. I respected him as a person and a coach. He always put his players first."

Still, the perception only added more intrigue to the potential game. Some reporters in the local media were convinced the Cardinals and Poets had to play to decide who was the true No. 1 team.

"Not only Basketball Weekly, but Street & Smith have rated the Cardinals as the No. 1 in the nation, but it's not clear whether Calvert Hall is No. 1 in Baltimore, let alone the entire country," Susan Reimer wrote in The Baltimore Sun. Woody Williams, of Lake Clifton, added "I think the wrong team is rated No. 1 in the country."

Amatucci played down the outside detractors. He knew the Cardinals would have to earn that No. 1 ranking by winning out, and they still weren't quite as strong as the end of the prior season.

The hype surrounding a Calvert Hall/Dunbar rematch eventually died down before erupting again midseason. Amatucci and the players weren't about the controversy—loftier goals were directly in front of them beginning with the regular-season opener at Spingarn in Washington, D.C.

When the Cardinals arrived at the northeast Washington school, the front doors were bolted shut. It was a daunting environment. Spingarn was a tough team led by Michael Graham, who later played at Georgetown and was a fourth-round pick by the Seattle SuperSonics. Calvert Hall started slowly and trailed by seven at the break. However, Wilson and Paul Edwards picked up their games in the second half and the Cards were effective forcing turnovers with their trapping pressure D. The Cardinals wore Spingarn down in the fourth quarter and pulled away for a 63-51 victory.

"We were able to take Graham out of his game because of the defensive pressure," Amatucci said. "The most critical difference was we took better care of the ball in the second half, which we didn't do in the first two quarters. After the game, I told the team that tonight's game had a clear message for them. Everybody was going to have to look in the mirror and question himself, because we were going to be on the road a lot against nationally ranked, quality teams. We had to be ready to play. Spingarn was the first challenge we had, and we came out flat."

Calvert Hall once again had a tough matchup the following game against another highly rated Washington school, Mackin, at Catholic University. This time, the challenge was shutting down Johnny Dawkins, who later starred at Duke and was the 10th overall pick in the 1986 NBA draft by San Antonio. Dawkins was supported by Dominic Pressley, who went on to play for Boston College and was drafted by Seattle.

The Cardinals struggled early, trailing by twelve at the half. "They run up and down the court. They play the same style as we do," Amatucci said. "They're a disciplined team, extremely well coached by Paul DeStefano, a close friend of mine. They play quickly, and they'll come at you aggressively on the defensive side of the ball. It wasn't a lack of motivation on our part. Mackin just outplayed us that entire first half."

The second half was a familiar script for Calvert Hall, which jacked up the pressure defensively and precisely moved the ball on offense in their cat-like transition game. Wilson had one of his best defensive efforts against Dawkins. "It was a macho thing: Who was the best guard on the East Coast? Marc Wilson or Johnny Dawkins," Amatucci said. "Dawkins' abilities were far more publicized than Wilson's were, but Marc convincingly won the battle. He proved to me that he was capable of having a better defensive effort than what he had shown in the past. That was a key."

Wilson added, "I tried denying him as much as possible. I knew if he didn't touch the ball, Mackin would struggle. I wasn't a defensive stopper, I was a scorer. But Tooch challenged me all year long to improve my defense to be prepared for the next level. So, I made a concerted effort to do it. I played games with myself. If I stop the good players, get a steal or two, I could score, get dunks and enjoy this 'horrible' thing called defense! Defensively, I take credit in holding JD to what, 25 points?"

Wilson and Dawkins eventually became friends. They connected when Dawkins was an alternate on the 1985 U.S. Olympic team when those players practiced at Minnesota, where Wilson played collegiately and finished his career as the Golden Gophers' top-ten all-time list for scoring, assists and steals. Dawkins also contacted Wilson when his NBA teams, the Pistons and Spurs, passed through Minnesota. "He even helped my son meet and have a picture with Grant Hill," Wilson said. "

At one point late in the fourth quarter, Pressley was preparing for a critical free-throw attempt when Paul Edwards walked behind him, gently patted him on the backside and whispered in his ear, "I hope you make this." Pressley missed the shot and the Cardinals eventually pulled away for an 82-77 victory.

"This team's story is not about being the biggest, the strongest or the most talented team in the country," Amatucci said, "but it is about showing that no one plays better together than we do. That's a fact."

The starters were dominant, but the Cardinals were also getting important contributions from their bench. Sophomore Eddie Oliver helped spark the offense with a textbook jumper and a fearless ability to take the ball to the rack. Oliver, Ferrell's best friend from grade school, also added an enthusiastic spirit and a fierce competitive drive to the makeup of the team. Vernon "Joe" Hill, a 6-foot-4 sophomore who played like he was 6-foot-7, had an uncanny ability to block shots and rebounded aggressively at both ends of the court. A versatile player, he could run the floor as well as any of the Cardinals and take defenders to the hole using his quickness and strength. Hill later played for Amatucci at Loyola College.

"We were living up to our reputation after we beat Mackin," Amatucci said.

After those two tough road games, Calvert Hall returned home to a sell-out crowd for the opener against La Salle of Philadelphia. Coach Baker had put together a season ticket plan because of fan interest. The plan included a section of the gym roped off for all the home games. The Cardinals put on a show and ran past the Explorers, 81-66.

After the Cardinals breezed past Bishop Walsh, 93-23, they were ready for a rematch against Dunbar of Washington, D.C. This time, the game was being played at Calvert Hall, and the night was full of controversy once again. A snowstorm hit the region as Dunbar began its trip to Towson from D.C., which snarled traffic.

Amatucci never considered postponing the game, and despite the weather, the gym was sold out. Because the game was running late, Amatucci and the officials did not give the Crimson Tide the customary twenty-minute warm up. Dunbar coach Joe Dean Davidson was not happy his players only had fifteen minutes to shake off the travel and his disdain carried over to the game.

Dunbar was big and fast, but lacked Mackin's discipline. Still, the Crimson Tide hung with Calvert Hall throughout the first half before wearing down in the third quarter. Davidson was on the referees from the opening tip, complaining about calls he felt went against his team.

Late in the fourth quarter, Davidson confronted Amatucci about the perceived bias and threatened to pull his team off the court. Calvert Hall assistant Chris Devlin eventually had to get between the two coaches as the tensions came to a head.

"I thought this was a Christian school," Davidson said to Devlin. "I didn't think I was going to come up here and be treated like this."

Devlin replied: "I'll show you what good a Christian I am. I am going to grab you and nail you to a cross."

Now, Amatucci had to separate Devlin and Davidson. The fans enjoyed a great show as the Cardinals closed out a 77-65 win over another ranked opponent. Long ride home.

The next day, Amatucci and Baker drove to Philadelphia to attend the press conference for the Pepsi Challenge High School Basketball Tournament, which was being held in January. Camden (N.J.) coach Clarence Turner, whose team was ranked No. 2 nationally behind Calvert Hall, added intrigue to their future matchup by saying, "It doesn't matter who we play. If we have the opportunity to bury you we are going to do it." He stared directly at Amatucci as he made those comments. Amatucci glanced at Baker, and then laughed at Turner. The Cardinals had other business in front of them before having to worry about Camden. That score was going to be settled on the court in the coming weeks.

Calvert Hall was clicking on all cylinders heading into the WARMland Holiday Tournament in Scranton, Pennsylvania, to defend their previous season's tourney championship. The whole area was excited to be hosting the No. 1 team in the nation and hung signs welcoming the Cardinals. An ad in the local paper read, "Guess who's coming to WARMland?"

"It was just incredible," Baker said. "The kids loved it because people were asking for their autographs and we were on the radio. We were pumped. It was like playing at home because everyone was rooting for us." Calvert Hall did not disappoint and blew out Bishop Hannon (Scranton, Pa.) 94-55 and Bishop O' Reilly (Kingston, Pa.), featuring

North Carolina recruit Dave Popson, 84-50.

Amatucci's fast break design was specific: get to the opposing team's basket in four seconds off a turnover and five seconds off a field goal. The primary tenet of the design was keep the ball off the floor. This lightening attack put opponents at a disadvantage. His players executed the break to perfection. For the fans, there was a real beauty in the movement of the players and the ball. The ability to play so quickly was instrumental in the team's quest to hold the No. 1 ranking for the entire season.

After the WARMland tournament, the Cardinals faced their biggest challenge to date at the Nike Prep Holiday Classic in Las Vegas. Prior to the tournament, Amatucci had to come up with $6,000 for the team's airfare. To raise money for the trip, Amatucci and Baker decided to host a bull roast at a local UAW hall on a Saturday afternoon in the fall. Amatucci was able to secure live music through long-time friend, referee, and former University of Baltimore coach Woody Powell. His wife Monica was the lead singer in a local band. The overflow crowd had a great time and did not want the party to end. The coaches cajoled Monica and her band into doing an encore set. The Cardinals successfully raised $6,500 and they were off to Vegas.

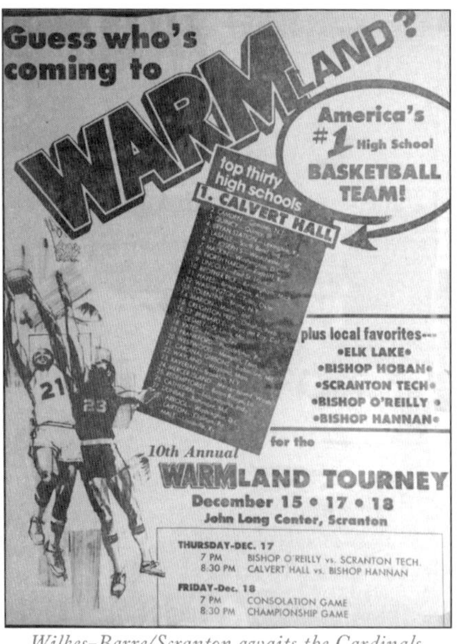

Wilkes-Barre/Scranton awaits the Cardinals.

The team flew to Nevada on December 26. The trip did not get off to a good start because the accommodations at UNLV were just plain dirty. As a result, Amatucci gave an ultimatum to tournament director, Larry McKay: pay for the team to move to better accommodations or they were flying back to Baltimore. "I told him he was in a no win situation. If he didn't pay for upgraded accommodations he would either be explaining why we left because he had us staying in filthy dorms or explaining why the No. 1 team in the nation decided to not play in the tournament," Amatucci said. The Cardinals were provided with an upgrade at a local hotel.

Calvert Hall beat Western of Las Vegas, 103-80, in the opening game led by Ferrell's 36 points. He was substituted out late in the fourth quarter for Charles Sikorsky, who later played at Johns Hopkins, graduated from law school and eventually became a Roman Catholic priest. Sikorsky, affectionately known to this day as "Ski", managed to score six points in his limited action, and for years would remind everyone how he and Ferrell combined for 42 points.

The Cardinals then rolled past Clarke of Las Vegas, 85-54, the following night, but all was not well in the land of the Cards. The forwards were not happy. Following that second game, Ferrell, Hill, Sikorsky and Edwards said they were "going on strike" because the guards were not getting them the ball enough. After several unsuccessful efforts at an amicable resolution to the dispute, Amatucci called a team meeting.

During that gathering, things got so heated that Tubman threw an empty bottle at Edwards. The projectile missed Edwards and whizzed past Amatucci's ear. Fed up with the unproductive discussion, Amatucci suspended team democracy telling the players, unequivocally, either play together or turn in your gear. Smart enough not to debate Amatucci's declaration, the players quickly resolved their issues and team unity was restored. They would need that unity because the matchups in Las Vegas became much more difficult in the later rounds.

"We had great camaraderie to be honest," Wilson said. "Boys will be boys. Like any family you have disagreements, arguments, what have you, but when game time came around we were all on the same page. Everyone knew their roles as well the others' role on the team."

"We did argue about who got touches and who didn't, but none of it carried onto the court. That's one thing I preach now as a coach," Wilson added. "You must let the off-court things go for at least two hours or so.

Go out and do your job. Coach Amatucci always preached togetherness, and we as players were always there for one another. So true today, because I believe we genuinely loved each other."

The Cardinals faced their toughest opponent, St. Bernard of Los Angeles, in the third game. The Bernards were ranked 20th in the nation and were deep with talent. They were led by Corey Gaines, who played at UCLA and Loyola Marymount before becoming a third-round pick by Seattle in the 1988 NBA Draft.

The Cards controlled the early part of the game, but Amatucci was unhappy with some of the officiating. Late in the second quarter, he picked up a second technical foul, which was one shy of being ejected at the time. Calvert Hall led by seven at the half before the Bernards made a run. The game quickly unraveled for the Cardinals who trailed by nine with 1:52 remaining in the final quarter. Once again, there were no sweaty palms among the players because they had been in that situation previously.

The Cardinals chipped away and trailed just 64-63 with seconds remaining. Calvert Hall forced a jump ball on a mad scramble that provided a glimmer of hope. On the ensuing jump ball, Ferrell was not able to win the tip. However, Wilson, with his outstanding games sense, jumped in front of a Bernard player, grabbed the ball and made a layup with three seconds remaining that sealed a 65-64 victory. "Game over. Have a nice day. That's why they call Wilson, 'Money.'," Baker said. "That was the closest we came to losing that entire season."

It was another Paul Kinney moment.

"My only thought was our undefeated season was in jeopardy," Wilson said. "In a jump ball situation at half court, Duane Ferrell tipped it my way and I drove it and scored to preserve the game and our undefeated season at that point. That's when my nickname 'Money' was born."

Wilson finished with 22 points, while Ferrell scored 18 and grabbed 12 rebounds. The Cardinals lived up to their lofty billing and were headed to the championship game against the hometown team, Valley High

School, the two-time defending state champion in Nevada.

In the title game, Calvert Hall came out as if they were sleepwalking and trailed by 12 points at the end of the first quarter. Once again, the Cardinals bounced back utilizing their renowned transition game and smothering defense. They went on a 16-4 run that tied the game 28-28 with 3:50 left in the half. A layup by Ferrell provided a 38-36 margin at the break.

The teams then traded baskets throughout the second half. A layup by Wilson off a pass from Ferrell gave the Cardinals some breathing room, 68-65, with 1:08 remaining in the game. From there, Calvert Hall never trailed. A pair of free throws by Wilson in the final seconds sealed the 70-69 victory. Ferrell, a sophomore, was named MVP of the prestigious tournament. Amatucci recalled, "After this tournament, our coaching staff began referring to Ferrell as 'The Great One.'"

The overall showing in Las Vegas—winning four games over five nights—allowed the Cardinals to put a bigger stamp on the No. 1 ranking. Amatucci was pleased with the overall experience out west, including his luck at the casinos, arriving home $100 richer. There were still big challenges ahead, especially with the opener in the Baltimore Catholic League just a few weeks away. The bullseye on the Cardinals' back as the top-ranked team had gotten bigger. Every opponent was looking to knock down Goliath and earn its way into the national headlines.

Calvert Hall, however, was not going to let the top ranking slip from its grasp.

The Cardinals returned to the East Coast for a game against Eastern of Washington, D.C., at Cole Field House on the campus of the University of Maryland. The game was part of a doubleheader with Maryland matched up against No. 1 North Carolina after the high school game.

"The kids were really pumped up about playing at Cole," Amatucci said. "Ferrell was being recruited by North Carolina as well as Georgia Tech and every other team in the country."

On the court, Calvert Hall dominated from the opening tip and took full control by outscoring Eastern 30-9 in the second quarter. Wilson finished with a game-high 24 points, Paul Edwards scored 14, and the Cardinals ran away with an 89-67 victory.

Despite the win, Amatucci was not happy with the performance. The Cardinals were sloppy near the end of the game. Amatucci was especially disappointed with his reserves, who did not maximize their opportunity to play in the fourth quarter.

"Their effort was disappointing," Amatucci said. "We were committing too many unforced errors and defensively did not make stops. Even though we won by 22 points, it could have been 40. We get back in the locker room and it was not good. I'm usually chewing the starters out for lackluster play with big leads which prevents me from giving the other guys an opportunity to receive substantial minutes. This time it was the reverse. Directing my frustration at the reserves, I said, 'I give you all of that time in the fourth quarter to show you deserve to be on that floor and play for the No. 1 team in the country and you fall flat on your face.' It was unacceptable. It was a good thing we were playing away or we would have gone back out on the court and practiced."

The Cardinals refocused and the following Friday routed Towson Catholic, 82-54, in the Baltimore Catholic League opener. The momentum carried over to the following game as Calvert Hall breezed past Archbishop Curley, 72-42. A non-conference game against East Patterson of New Jersey produced a similar result, with the Cardinals pulling away for an 87-65 victory at Villanova University.

"At this point, I'm happy with what we're doing defensively," Amatucci said.

Following the string of victories, the lackadaisical attitude that appeared against Eastern emerged once more. The players seemed to lose some of their edge in practice heading into a key game against Mount St. Joseph. Amatucci was annoyed with their attitude and was determined to solve the problem immediately.

"It was the first time I sensed their body language saying, 'Hey, we're

Calvert Hall. We're the No. 1 team in the country. We're blowing people out. We got this.' Taking a step back, this was not sitting right with me," Amatucci said. "We needed to re-focus or Mount St. Joe was going to kick our butt. They were a well-coached, solid team."

On the day prior to the game against the Gaels, Amatucci ran a practice without providing any basketballs. The players ran sprints and suicides until they appeared to regain some of their focus. Amatucci was still not satisfied and decided to increase the intensity of the workout. He then had the team play back-to-back scrimmages on one of the shorter cross-courts in the gym. The coaches sat in the bleachers, games were to five, no fouls, and winners ran for the losers. The setup of the scrimmages combined with the tighter confines of the side court led to rising emotions amongst the players. In addition, if Amatucci saw something he did not like in the action, he simply made the players run—over and over again.

"I intentionally wanted them to get pissed off at me to bring them together," Amatucci said, "I was gambling that this psychological ploy would shake up the team."

The players got angrier as the scrimmages continued and began to push and shove one another on every possession. The session ended with Ferrell and Wilson getting into a full-fledged fight. The players separated the combatants while the coaches remained on the sidelines. After the heated exchange, Amatucci addressed the team.

"You put yourselves in this situation today," he told the players. "You cannot come out here and take where we are for granted. The minute you start thinking about how good you are, you are not that good. We are not going to be ready for St. Joe, and it's on you." Lowering his tone, Amatucci strongly suggested "getting together in the locker room and deciding where we're going forward from here."

The Cardinals responded with a hard-fought 72-69 win over the Gaels. Calvert Hall played team ball and shook off the frustration from the previous practice. Amatucci was confident the players were back on track. They would need to be at their best for the next huge obstacle—the inaugural Pepsi Challenge High School Basketball Tournament at The Spectrum in Philadelphia.

The Cardinals were matched up against Long Island Lutheran High School of Brookville, N.Y., in the first round of the tourney. The Crusaders were the defending New York State Class C champions and were coached by Bob McKillop, who took over the program at Davidson College in 1989 and became the school's all-time wins leader. Long Island Lutheran High School had a traditionally strong program that produced several All-Americans, including Steve Rivers (Maryland), Matt Doherty (North Carolina), and Bill Wennington (St. John's).

The Crusaders proved to be a formidable foe for Calvert Hall and led, 28-26, at the half. The Cardinals rebounded in the third quarter, outscoring them 25-10 to take charge of the game. Once again, Wilson was the catalyst with a game-high 19 points in the 68-55 win. Tubman had 13 points, while Ferrell and Edwards scored 11 apiece. Kauffman, who had been named The Baltimore Sun's Player of the Year in football in the fall, came up big defensively and had five assists.

The Cardinals win the 1982 Pepsi Challenge Tournament, The Spectrum, Philadelphia (Pa.)

The victory set up a showdown with Camden of N.J., which was still ranked second behind Calvert Hall in the national polls. The Panthers were led by Billy Thompson, the nation's No. 1 recruit who was averaging just over 30 points per game, Thompson later played at Louisville and was a first-round pick by the Atlanta Hawks in the 1986 NBA Draft. Camden also had a speedy, 6-foot-2 guard named Kevin Walls, who also played at Louisville, where he won a national championship as a freshman. Camden had beaten Frankford of Philadelphia, 85-80, to advance to the title game.

Panthers coach Clarence Turner had already rankled Amatucci with his comments in the pre-tournament press conference. Amatucci had informed his players about Turner's disrespectful remarks directed at the Cardinals, which provided extra motivation. On the day before the game, Turner downplayed the matchup, saying. "It's going to be a big game, but we've played big games before. Every game we play outside our conference is a big game. But they are No. 1, whatever that means." These comments incensed Amatucci. Camden warmed up with tiger-striped warmups the day of the game. The Cardinals were neither impressed nor intimidated.

The Panthers started strong behind Thompson, who was dominant inside the paint. Calvert Hall was just 13 of 32 from the field and trailed, 33-29, at the break. The Cardinals picked up the pressure in the second half and forced several key turnovers. Kauffman once again sparked the defense, while Wilson paced the offense. Still, Calvert trailed, 44-41, heading into the final quarter. The 3,306 fans were on edge throughout the game.

A thundering dunk by Thompson gave Camden a 55-50 lead with just 4:30 remaining in the contest. Taking a time out, Amatucci remembered, "My assistant, Steve Misotti (aka Wolfie) approached me right away and said, 'It's time to make a move or this game is over.'" In response, Calvert Hall went to a half-court, zone trap defense and forced two straight turnovers to cut into the margin.

The Cardinals took a 61-60 lead on a layup by Wilson with 1:40 left. The Panthers had a chance to retake the lead in the final thirty seconds, but Tubman stole the ball from Thompson and Ferrell made a layup for a 63-60 margin. A three-point play by Edwards sealed the 67-62 win for the Cardinals, ranking as one of The Hall's best hoop victories.

"Once again, we proved who was No. 1," Amatucci said. "When we played Dunbar, it was for bragging rights in Baltimore. Against Camden, we proved we were No. 1 in the nation."

Tubman had 15 points, three steals and three assists and was named MVP of the tournament. Edwards also came up huge, finishing with 13 points, eight rebounds and four steals. Ferrell contributed 11 points and 12 rebounds. Thompson had 22 points for Camden, who were not happy with the officiating.

"They're always around the ball, doing something with the ball," Turner told The Baltimore Sun after the game. "They're a fortunate group doing something at the ball and not committing fouls. You can read between the lines if you want to." Cards get a big win; disappointed losers make excuses. Not a new scenario for the talented Cardinals.

On the heels of the results in Las Vegas and Philadelphia and despite Turner's protestations, the rest of the nation regarded Calvert Hall as the No. 1 team. The Cardinals returned to their Baltimore Catholic League schedule and had to move their game against Cardinal Gibbons to the Towson Center because of the demand for tickets. A sell-out crowd of 5,300 spectators braved a snowstorm to watch the highly anticipated matchup.

The Crusaders were 19-1 overall and 3-0 in the Catholic League, but that success was overshadowed by the success of the Cardinals and Dunbar, which were both getting local, regional and national attention. Several Calvert Hall players received prank phone calls the night before the game. "I've been getting obscene calls at night from people, saying 'Gibbons gonna win,' or they don't say anything," Ferrell told The Evening Sun. "Man, that just pumped me up even more."

It was also the so-called "Get Ray Week" for Calvert Hall, alluding to Cardinal Gibbons' BCL Hall of Fame coach coach Ray Mullis, that helped boost the spirited rivalry to another level. The day prior to the game, the snow had started and the students were excused early from classes. As usual, Amatucci still held practice. After practice, Amatucci and Baker requisitioned a school van to get Wilson, Tubman, Kauffman, and Edwards home because of the weather. On the way back toward Calvert Hall, the van got stuck in the snow, forcing Amatucci and Kauffman to push the oversized vehicle up a hill on Cold Spring Lane in Baltimore City.

Returning to school, the night was just beginning for the coaches, who decided to brave the elements and head out for the evening. Assistant Chris Devlin owned a conversion van that included a perpetually tapped keg, and the coaches piled in for the ride downtown. The coaches bar-hopped for several hours, and at one point, were joined by a state legislator who was a big fan of the school. The coaches eventually wore out their welcome because of their spirited antics that included dancing on a table and a toppled chair. On the way back to the van during a snowball battle, Amatucci got blind-sided by a parking meter dislodging the pole from the ground. Regrettably, for the parking meter, Amatucci got the better of the collision. The night ended with Devlin's van doing a NASCAR-like victory lap around a local golf course.

Once they got on the court the following evening, the Calvert Hall players and coaches were totally focused on beating the Crusaders. The Cardinals started fast and led 34-32 at the half. The second half was a familiar script with Calvert Hall powering up the defense and pulling away. Wilson, who finished with 24 points, scored three straight times in the final 1:30 of the third quarter that provided a 56-49 lead.

The Cardinals made nine consecutive shots in the final period that helped seal the 84-74 victory and improved their record to 18-0. Ferrell had 24 points and 12 rebounds, while Edwards scored 14. Tim Coles, who later starred at the University of Connecticut, led Cardinal Gibbons with 26 points and eight rebounds.

Darryle Edwards, who was a freshman playing at Mount St. Mary's (MD), was in the stands at the Towson Center that night. He invited his teammates to make the trip from Emmitsburg to watch the No. 1 Cardinals. He was beaming with pride over his alma mater.

"I talked all kinds of trash," he said. "My high school team was No. 1

in the country. We're going to roll with this thing. My entire team came down to watch Calvert Hall. They were still my boys. It felt good to come down and support them."

After this game, the Cards continued to cruise through their league schedule. In their 80-70 win over Loyola, Marc Wilson reached a milestone, notching his 1500th point and solidifying his standing as the Hall's all-time leading scorer.

The Cardinals second matchup against Cardinal Gibbons was held at the University of Maryland Baltimore County because of the demand for tickets. Uncharacteristically, Tubman and Wilson were late to the game so Amatucci banished them to the bench for the first quarter. The duo made up for their mistake as Wilson had 17 of his 25 points in the second half and Tubman scored seven in the 74-67 victory before 3,500 spectators.

The victory set up the regular season finale against archrival Loyola, which was subsequently dismantled, 86-63. The Cardinals extended their winning streak to 29 games and entered the Baltimore Catholic League Tournament as the top seed. A packed crowd filled Loyola's gym to see the Cards and their arch-rivals. Adding to the excitement, a photographer from Sports Illustrated was taking pictures for a Sports Illustrated article featuring the Cards being written by Franz Lidz. Baker remembered, "We knew the photographer was coming, we didn't realize he was hanging hi-powered flashes in the Loyola gym. With each photo he took, the whole crowd could see a flash." The final article included a memorable photo of Amatucci and Tubman strategizing on the sideline.

"The talent that we had and just going out and winning games, my senior year when we wound up being the No. 1 team in the country, was amazing," Paul Edwards said. "But it wasn't anything that anybody strived to do. All we ever tried to do was win the game we were playing. When you add it all up at the end, then you're 28-3, 29-2, or 34-0."

After enjoying a bye in the first round, Calvert Hall took down Loyola again, 75-57, in the BCL semifinals. The Dons had pulled within two points with less than two minutes left in the third quarter. The Cardinals responded by scoring 12 of the next 14 points and pulling away. Wilson made eight of nine shots from the field and finished with 18 points. In the other semifinal, Mount St. Joseph upset Cardinal Gibbons, 62-48, and earned an opportunity to avenge a pair of losses at the hands of the Cardinals in the regular season.

The championship game was held at UMBC. More than 2,500 people filled the arena to see if Calvert Hall could win its third straight title and head to the Alhambra Tournament undefeated. The upstart Gaels stayed with the Cardinals throughout the game. Mount St. Joseph chipped away at a 10-point deficit and pulled to within 58-57 with 6:13 left in the third quarter.

The Cardinals responded with a short jumper by Ferrell and a layup by Hill over an eleven-second span to get some breathing room. Calvert Hall maintained the lead the rest of the way. Wilson scored nine of his 18 points in the final quarter, and the Cardinals came away with an 85-81 victory and improved to 31-0 on the season. The Gaels were paced by Rob Nieberlein, a George Mason recruit who made eleven of thirteen shots from the field and finished with a game-high 31 points. After the game, the Mount St. Joseph players gave the Cardinals a standing ovation.

"It was just something we wanted to do," Gaels coach Pat Maggio told the News American. "We respect them a lot and enjoy playing against them. You can't ask much more for a situation where you can coach and face a team like that in your own league. That's what the game is all about."

Amatucci left UMBC and drove back to Calvert Hall to watch the Paul Kinney Tournament, which featured local grade-school teams. Calvert Hall principal, Brother Rene Sterner, approached Amatucci in the stands to congratulate him on another BCL championship before the conversation shifted to the future.

"You're not going anywhere, are you?" Sterner whispered in Amatucci's ear, inquiring whether the coach was interested in taking over a college program.

"I'm not going anywhere," Amatucci responded. "This is where I belong and this is where I am going to stay." A statement he might soon rethink.

Calvert Hall had ten days to get ready for Alhambra, looking to become the first team from Baltimore to win the tournament since 1962. The Cardinals players were not taking the high stakes lightly and returned to practice fully focused on closing out the magical season. "We had business to take care of," Amatucci said. "Everyone was charged up. There was no need to crack the whip."

Amatucci placed a special emphasis on half-court zone pressure in the practices leading up to the tournament, Much of his practice plans were directed towards preparing for DeMatha, the Washington powerhouse and defending Alhambra champion. Amatucci remembers, "It was a strong tournament field, but we really felt that DeMatha was the team in the path of our quest for the perfect season."

Turning to the offensive side of the floor, Amatucci focused on Wilson's scoring. Amatucci said, "We knew 'Money' was more effective scoring the ball from the right side of the court. We practiced sets and screens to free him up with the option to take a short jumper or drive to the basket from that side of the court. He just seemed more comfortable coming from the right side.

However, the trip to Alhambra did not get off to a great start. Amatucci and his players were forced to pile into one van for the three-hour journey. "This is the No 1 team in the nation and we have one friggin' van," an exasperated Amatucci said. "Luckily we only carried ten players. We all had to cram into that thing." Amatucci sat in the door well because of the lack of space. On the bright side, LP (Paul Edwards) recovered a four-leaf clover in a box of Cracker Jacks. It also happened to be St. Patrick's Day. He took that as a positive sign.

"Coach Tooch, Coach Tooch, we're going to win this tournament because I just found a four-leaf clover," LP said, grasping the lucky charm.

"I wasn't going to tell you until after we won the game." Amatucci reflected, "I guess LP got caught up in the excitement and let the cat out of the bag a little early."

Once the team arrived in Western Maryland, the Cardinals were ready to put the rough ride behind them and focus on winning basketball games. Calvert Hall was matched up with a tough Monsignor Bonner High (PA) team in the first round. The Cardinals jumped out to an early 10-2 lead before Bonner began to change the tempo of the game. Calvert Hall led, 33-29, at the break. A huge concern for Amatucci was that Wilson, Edwards, and Tubman were forced to the bench with two fouls in the second quarter.

The Friars stayed within striking distance and pulled to within 51-49 late in the third quarter. Calvert Hall was able to weather the storm before Wilson, Edwards, and Tubman were able to get back on the floor. On returning to the game, Tubman responded with three consecutive jumpers and Calvert Hall forced four turnovers that pushed the lead to 64-58 with 2:10 left in the game. From there, the Cardinals were never threatened and came away with a 72-63 victory. Edwards led the team with 18 points, while Ferrell finished with 16.

The victory set up a rematch against Mackin, which was defeated by the Cardinals, 82-77, earlier in the season. This time, the Trojans made 18 of 21 shots from the field but still trailed, 40-39, at the break. The teams continued to trade baskets. Mackin scored six consecutive points and tied the game, 49-49, with 4:24 left in the third quarter. From there, the Cardinals opened up their pressure game and pulled away. Ferrell scored six points in an 8-2 run. Calvert Hall dictated the tempo the rest of the way and won, 85-77. Wilson outscored Johnny Dawkins 22-16. Edwards finished with 24 points and Ferrell chipped in 18. "In any other season, the Mackin games would be considered epic," Baker remembered. "Two talented, well-coached, athletic teams going head to head, start to finish, twice in the same season. Add to that the main event matchup of Dawkins versus Wilson and you've got something special."

"I felt we had just played in the championship game," Amatucci remembered. "It was a big-time match up. I said it was 'the biggest win we ever had' to keep the players loose. We had never gotten past the semis. It was a great feeling."

DeMatha ran past Cardinal Gibbons, 86-68, in the other semifinal, setting up the much-anticipated dream game in the championship. The Cardinals were not intimidated by the Stags' pedigree or experience in the tournament. There was just one game separating Calvert Hall from an undefeated season and a wire-to-wire run as the No. 1 high school basketball team in the United States. The Cardinals players and coaches relished the opportunity.

Following a night out with the coaches and a near-brawl with some local bikers at My Place, Amatucci had to attend the tournament's pre-championship "Coaches' Brunch" the morning of the game. Characteristically, Amatucci attended alone with the rest of his staff choosing to have an extended rest. DeMatha coach Morgan Wootten highlighted the number of Alhambra championships his team had won over the years and how that experience was going to be the difference in the game. He predicted that the Cardinals would be nervous. Wootten tried to be diplomatic, but Amatucci took it as smack talk.

"I'm pretty fired up, I'm going to get this guy tonight," Amatucci said. "We got on the elevator together after the breakfast. Morgan was getting off the floor before me. I patted him on the rear and said, 'Have a good game tonight.' I think I got in his head."

Amatucci's goal was to apply full-court pressure and make DeMatha's players run up and down the floor. Amatucci recalls, "I anticipated that the Stags would make careless turnovers in the back court." Knowing DeMatha's strength, he also did not want to get into a half-court game with them.

Amatucci woke up with his usual pre-game anxiety but his confidence grew as the day wore on. The coaches and players enjoyed a quiet day around town before heading to the arena. While walking through downtown Cumberland, the coaches ran into the Baltimore reporters who had extensively covered the Cardinals' last three championship seasons—Bernie Miklasz, Sue Riemer, Bill Glauber, and Clark Judge. Amatucci said, "We had built a great rapport with them. Beyond just covering the games, they showed a genuine interest in the players and coaches as individuals. It was a unique relationship." The players toured downtown as one big spirited group. The coaches bumped into them as they gawked at the tournament's trophies that were displayed in a storefront window.

All that was left now was to play the game. For the players, the importance of this night was monumental. Winning the Alhambra had always been their goal. Twice before they fell abruptly short. One more win to grab the ring on an undefeated season and a wire to wire #1 ranking. For the seniors, it could be a storybook ending to an amazing run: countless accolades, the epic Dunbar win, three league titles, and a 91-5 record.

Sikorsky remembered, "First, we had a twenty-minute drive from the hotel to the championship game, and, unlike every other trip, the whole ride was very quiet. We usually had guys cracking jokes and talking trash in the van, but not that night. I think we realized more than ever what we had a chance to do, and we wanted to go out the right way for each other."

The team arrived at the Frostburg State arena to a packed house watching the consolation finals. The Cardinals in their signature coat and tie attire were seated along with the Stags in a reserved area. Young fans, carrying the tournament's thick programs, besieged players from both teams anxiously seeking autographs. For the players and coaches, waiting for the game-of-the-year to start seemed like an eternity.

After the opening tip, the Cardinals jumped out to a quick lead behind their transition break and pressure defense. The Cards were executing their game plan perfectly. "Watching us run our transition in that first half was magic," Amatucci said. "It was like poetry in motion. The ball was not touching the floor. We came out ready to play."

Calvert Hall led, 35-33, at the break. There was just one-half of basketball separating the program from an undefeated season. During his half-time locker room talk, Amatucci remembered emphasizing the importance of sticking to the game plan, playing together, taking care of the ball, and not looking too far ahead. One quarter at a time.

DeMatha made a run in the third quarter as adversity began to build for Calvert Hall. Sass, who made a couple of key jumpers in the first half, was forced to the bench with three fouls. Behind Mike Alexander (24 points), the Stags took a 55-54 lead heading into the final eight minutes.

The Cardinals suffered another huge blow when Ferrell fell to the floor scrambling for a loose ball and sprained his ankle with 7:39 left in the game. He had to be carried by endeared Cardinals' trainer John Sanborn and three teammates to the locker room. The Calvert Hall players were dazed, and Amatucci had to call a timeout to get them refocused. He smacked Edwards so hard on the leg that the sound echoed around the arena. Amatucci recalls, "That quickly got everyone's attention." Ferrell eventually was able to watch the rest of the game from the bench. The Stags took advantage of his absence and led, 75-70, with 3:30 remaining.

"We had been there before, being down seven to nine in the final couple of minutes." Kauffman said. "So, we knew we still had a good chance to win the game. Everything came together again."

Amatucci called another timeout and returned to the floor with Kauffman, Tubman, Wilson, Edwards, and Hill. "We knew we would have to play a lot tougher," Eddie Oliver said. "Vernon Hill was able to fill the spot when Duane went down. Vernon and I had to step up our game and we were only sophomores. Coach trusted and believed in us, and we knew that."

The Cards went to their half-court zone trap and were able to rattle the Stags with the pressure. "As soon as we got into the half-court trap, they turned the ball over two straight times," Amatucci remembered. "Kauffman was just amazing."

Calvert Hall also capitalized on the offense end. Wilson stole the ball and threw a long pass to Tubman that tied the game, 75-75, with 2:38 remaining. Wilson then provided the lead on a jumper with just under a minute remaining. Edwards converted on a pair of free throws and Wilson scored a three-point play and a layup. Wilson's final layup came from stealing DeMatha's inbound pass after his made free throw. DeMatha coach Wooten hung his head. The end was lightning quick and decisive.

Calvert Hall took home the title with an 82-76 victory. The Cardinals had outscored the Stags 12-1 in the final 3:30 and finished the season 34-0.

Wilson scored nine of his game-high 28 points over that stretch. Tubman and Edwards scored 11 points apiece. The three of them along with Kauffman went 91-5 in a Calvert Hall uniform. Edwards was named MVP of the tournament. Wilson was the tournament's Outstanding Player. Puzzle completed.

"We never thought about going undefeated," Tubman said. "We just played each game one at a time and all of the sudden we realized we were like 27-0. We had not lost a game. We were just taking care of business. No one sought out to go undefeated. It was not a topic of discussion. It just sort of happened and developed."

The celebration was subdued among the coaches, similar to the way they reacted following the victory over Dunbar the previous year. "We did it," Amatucci said reflecting back on the last three seasons. "I truly did not have the ambition to seek national recognition or a national championship. My ambition was being totally committed to achieving simple goals—play together, play hard, practice hard. With success achieving those goals, our goals became loftier, but we never strayed from the basics. Sitting in my hotel room, it finally hit me how incredible this top of the mountain achievement was and how it impacted me, the coaches, and all our outstanding student-athletes who together got us to the top. It was something I did not think would ever occur again in the history of Calvert Hall basketball."

The Cardinals were celebrities back in Baltimore. The coaches greatly enjoyed the many well-wishers who bought them adult beverages wherever they went. Calvert Hall hosted an assembly for the faculty and students at which time the school was officially presented with the national championship plaque by "Basketball Weekly" that is still proudly displayed in a trophy case today. The team was honored by the Baltimore Orioles at Memorial Stadium prior to one of their games. The team received accolades from the governor, the mayor and a who's who of Maryland dignitaries.

The magical season still resonates with all of the players. Despite the unprecedented success, the overall experience had a tinge of sadness because the seniors would be moving on. While their physical connections would be broken, the personal bonds they had built would last a lifetime. More than thirty years later, Larry Flower recalls, "It sounds cliché, but we did have a lot of heart. Tooch was able to get the best out of all of us, both players and coaches. He was the right man at the right time. Taking a bunch of teenagers who had lost their friend and teammate only a few months before and turning them into national champions less than one year later is an amazing accomplishment."

"We loved and cared for each other," Wilson said. "The 1981-82 season was special and is still special. I see teams today win championships on the men's and women's side, and I still think of our championship season and how special it was. For some of us it would be our final season together. For Pop Tubman and I, it was the last time we'd ever play together since we were 10 or 11 years old. We grew up and played together at every stop during our youth. Then, we came together with Paul and Darryle Edwards, Duane Ferrell, who grew up with us at Madison, to form one of Maryland's best high school basketball programs and a nationally ranked team as well."

"What I remember most about that team was the friendships, especially with Duane, Eddie and I," Hill said. "We played together growing up. So, it was great just playing ball with your friends."

"Starting off the season, we were excited that we were No. 1," Hill continued. "For me coming in as a sophomore, the magnitude of that ranking didn't really register. It wasn't really something we concerned ourselves about at the start. We liked the fact that we were recognized as the No. 1 team in the nation. But the goals for that year were to win the Baltimore Catholic League regular season, the tournament and then go to Alhambra and win that. We weren't really talking about being the No. 1 team in the nation and going undefeated. Winning the Alhambra was big, especially for the seniors because up 'til then we had not accomplished that goal."

"I knew we were good," Oliver said. "We dedicated a lot of games to Paul Kinney. There was a lot of pressure on us, especially as the season wore on. But we played with a lot of heart. We had played together even before we got to Calvert Hall, so everyone knew one another really well."

Tubman also looks back fondly on that championship season. It's a moment frozen in time.

"What I remember most about the last game, when we won the Alhambra tournament, is that during the trophy presentation, it hit all of us at once that it was the last game we were all going to play together," Tubman said. "We all started crying on the bench. It was bittersweet."

A special era at The Hall had come to an end.

8

THE GREAT ONE

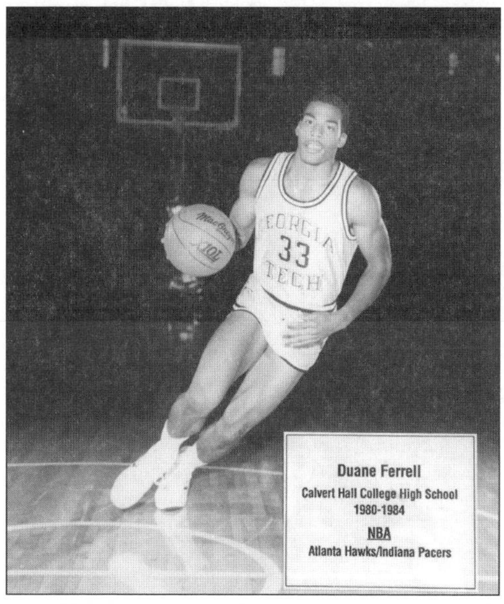

GEORGIA
33
TECH
Duane Ferrell
Calvert Hall College High School
1980-1984
NBA
Atlanta Hawks/Indiana Pacers

"Baby all the lights are turned on you. Now you're in the center of the stage and everything revolves on what you do."

- BILLY JOEL

In the spring of 1980, coming off of a championship and nationally ranked year, going 28-3, Amatucci was again hot on the recruiting trail in East Baltimore. In the fall, he had set his eyes on who he thought would be the most recruited player in the entire city. Now he was putting on a full-court press to persuade a 6'4" eighth grader who reminded him of the great Elgin Baylor to bring his game out to what was now being called "the school on top of the grassy hill" — Calvert Hall. With the trusted support of coaches Henry Powell and Andrew Boston of the famous Madison Buccaneers, Amatucci had the inside track to snatch his prize recruit away from Dunbar and Cardinal Gibbons. That eighth graders name was Duane Ferrell, who would become a legend in his own time.

Amatucci liked to call Ferrell, "The Great One."

Indeed, Ferrell was a larger than life player from the first day he stepped on the basketball court at Calvert Hall as a freshman.

Big, talented, and confident, Ferrell was a smooth player destined for the NBA. He had all of the intangibles that could not be taught. More importantly, he was excited to join the Edwards brothers, Marc Wilson and Pop Tubman at The Hall.

As a child, Ferrell spent most of his time playing in the back alleys and street courts in Northeast Baltimore. One day, a neighbor named Frederick Grady suggested he play in the leagues at Madison Square Recreation Center.

This is where Ferrell first met Marc Wilson, who was shooting around by himself and invited Ferrell to join him. That led to a competitive game of one-on-one, prompting the impressed Wilson to ask his coaches to get Ferrell on his team.

"He was scrawny at the time, so I would muscle him a little," Wilson remembers. "But he went away for a summer before Pop Tubman and I went to Calvert Hall. He came back a man. Country Strong!"

While Wilson doesn't remember mentioning anything to Amatucci, he knew Calvert Hall would get most, if not all, the players from the Buccaneers because he and Tubman were going to the school. Besides, the coaches had an affinity for Amatucci.

"Bee and Sarge liked Tooch," Wilson said.

Ferrell developed a tight relationship with Wilson and Pop Tubman, both of whom paved the way for Ferrell at The Hall. Another influential figure was John Baker, a dedicated history teacher at Northern Parkway

Middle School who graduated from Calvert Hall. Baker set up a meeting with Amatucci and the school's principal to discuss Duane's academic profile and how he would fit into Calvert Hall's program of study. Amatucci said, "The principal and John were educators who were invested in their students, including Duane, on a personal level. They definitely had Duane's best interests academic and athletic at heart." Baker told Ferrell The Hall would be the best choice for him because of the quality of the curriculum and the high profile of the basketball program. Baker would continue to be a mentor and friend to Ferrell, long after he graduated from middle school.

Amatucci regularly attended Ferrell's games at Madison, providing more opportunities to interact with Duane and create a comfort level between the two of them. Amatucci said, "When we made eye contact at games, I could feel a connection between us. We were building a sense of trust."

Ferrell chose to attend the private school over traditional basketball power, Dunbar. The decision provided a power boost to the rising Calvert Hall program. "When Duane made his decision to join us at Calvert Hall," Amatucci remembered, "It was like a shot heard around the world."

Ferrell added: "It was almost an easy fit. I wasn't really familiar with the Dunbar players because I had only played against them. I did know how stacked they were as a team. I knew with situations like that, you had to share time with other talented players. Wilson and Tubman said we should start our own thing at Calvert Hall in the Catholic League. They talked about it and the next thing you know, Tooch starts showing up to a lot of my games."

The Ferrell train got derailed when Duane was not accepted on his initial application to The Hall. Amatucci said, "Duane had consistently good grades and recommendations, but his entrance test score was short of the acceptance level."

An amicable discussion of Duane's academic strengths with Calvert

Hall's assistant principal turned into a verbal free for all where Amatucci may have slammed his fist on the desk to make his point. Amatucci guaranteed that academic support and supervision would be a priority. The academic guarantee and his ability to deliver on it would serve Amatucci well for years to come. It would be the bargaining chip that tipped the scale in his favor on a number of admissions discussions. The Ferrell train was back on track.

Ferrell was confident that he had been seasoned in the rec leagues to make an impact at Calvert Hall in his freshman year. He was prepared to be the sixth man behind Paul Kinney and some of the other forwards. Amatucci told The Baltimore Sun, "Duane's the most talented 15-year old I've ever seen." The biggest challenge for Ferrell was the amount of running required in practice.

"I had to get used to the conditioning," Ferrell said. "The strategy was to get that ball down the floor in a matter of seconds. That's what made us so talented. We could rebound and start the fast break without the ball touching the floor. Teams had trouble guarding us because they could not keep pace. It was just a magical time when we had things rolling."

However, that fateful day at Parkville high school changed everything. Ferrell still remembers being subbed in for Kinney prior to the incident.

"How'd I do?" Kinney asked Ferrell as they passed one another.

"You did great," Ferrell responded, slapping hands with Kinney.

As he ran down the court in transition, Ferrell glanced at the Calvert Hall bench and noticed a commotion.

"It looked like a bolt of lightning just hit him from behind. It was a scary sight," Ferrell remembered. "We ran over there and it was just an emotional moment for all of us. We were just trying to wrap our heads around what was happening."

When Kinney passed away a few days later, the players and coaches were devastated. Eventually, the team decided to rally around their fallen teammate. They were determined to honor Kinney's legacy.

"Afterward, we just galvanized and dedicated the season to Paul,"

Ferrell said. "We knew what kind of player he was and what he would want us to do. He was an inspiration to push ourselves even harder and we came closer together as a family."

The Cardinals rolled through that season, finishing 29-2 and winning the Baltimore Catholic League regular season and tournament championships. Ferrell was in the starting line-up the entire season. He was named the MVP of the WARMland tournament.

The year was highlighted by the showdown with Dunbar at the Towson Center. Even though Ferrell was a freshman, he had confidence and swagger. He wasn't remotely nervous about the game or playing on the big stage in front of more than 5,000 fans.

"You felt the buildup all season," Ferrell recalled. "As players, we knew we were having a special year. We would look at the rankings and see both of us were ranked pretty high. We would beat a team by 10, then Dunbar would try to beat them by 20. It went on all year long. People just kept talking about it.

"Most of us lived in the inner city, so we would hear all the time how we couldn't beat Dunbar. When the time came to play, you just knew the whole city was going to be behind this game. It was like a Muhammad Ali versus Joe Frazier kind of build-up. You didn't often see that type of talent in a high school basketball game. Two of the top teams in the country that were familiar with one another."

Ferrell came up big, tying the game, 83-83, on a layup with twenty-three seconds remaining that set up a third and final overtime. The Cardinals eventually won 94-91, which was the catalyst to the national title the following year. Amatucci remembered, "Duane had a great game, but there was one point in the game when he and Paul Edwards decided on their own to do some ill-advised coaching. Dunbar had the ball on their own baseline with seconds remaining in regulation, looking to go the length of the court to win. Duane and LP decided in advance that they would switch on a screen across, something we never did. As the play unfolded, the screen took place and LP forgot to switch. As a result, Dunbar's Kevin Woods had a chance for an open layup. Fortunately for the Cards he missed and the historic overtime periods followed."

"We had no idea the impact the game would have on both schools," Ferrell said. "I had never played in front of that many people at that point. When you play in a game like that, you don't even think about being tired. You're just competing so hard and you want to win so bad. You know it's about bragging rights. We were very confident. It was an emotional game that we would not allow ourselves to lose."

Ferrell also was able to excel because he was never bothered by Amatucci's intensity. He was able to quickly adjust to that type of coaching style. "Duane rarely expressed any emotion whether things were going well or poorly," Amatucci recalled. "He took criticism in stride. No rolling of the eyes, no hanging his head, he just played." Practices were a challenge, but the players saw the results. Ferrell believed that Amatucci was always going to look out for his players on and off the court. The coach was hard on them because he wanted them to succeed, not just in basketball, but in life."

"Tooch's yelling was different and was more encouraging than degrading or demeaning," Ferrell said. "He was trying to get you to play at the highest level in pressure situations. He was always pushing us to a higher level. It was never that type of yelling that would get you down. You could tell he cared about you. Tooch was a guy you went the extra distance for because he did so much for all of us beyond basketball."

Amatucci's relationships with his players lasted long after they graduated from Calvert Hall. Amatucci would come down hard on a player in practice but made sure to have a personal conversation with that player in school the following day. In his travels to Georgia Tech and around the NBA, Ferrell said Amatucci was unique among the coaches he encountered because of that close bond. As a result, players would run through a wall for him.

Ferrell explained, "When you have a relationship with a coach that cares for you off the court especially when you really need support-whether it's talking about family stuff or whatever is going on in your life-you will pay him back by doing anything he demands on the court and in the classroom."

As a sophomore in the 1981-1982 season, Ferrell had the most fun of his high school career being part of the national championship team. The players were tight-knit and exuded confidence. The Cardinals believed they could win every game, regardless of the circumstances. That proved to be true several times that season when they pulled out unlikely wins, especially against St. Bernard in the Nike Prep Holiday Classic in Las Vegas when Wilson scored in the final seconds to seal the win. The Nike Classic championship cemented Calvert Hall's status as one of the most elite programs in the entire country. Ferrell's performance at the Classic earned him MVP honors, becoming the first sophomore to win the award in the tourney's history.

"We knew we were good," he said. "We didn't know how good, but we knew we were good. Everything was clicking for us. We were so familiar with one another, we could cover each other's weaknesses and put guys in position to succeed. Start to finish, I didn't feel like we would lose a game.

"Sometimes, if the game was on the line, we'd give the ball to Marc and get out of the way. We wanted to play all of the best teams so there would be no doubt we were No. 1. We accepted that challenge. Nationally, we were getting so much coverage that it was bringing attention to the school and the city of Baltimore. It was a great time."

As a sophomore, Ferrell began to emerge as a prime recruit for nearly every elite Division I college program in the United States. He received additional exposure because the Cardinals were playing a national schedule and coaches from schools throughout the U.S. had an opportunity to either see them play or read about them. Ferrell eventually became the center of that attention. Amatucci said, "Duane was coming in to his own. His outstanding freshman season was just a preview of what was to come his sophomore year. His movements were so smooth, some questioned his effort. In reality, he was a natural and made the difficult look easy. He was a human highlight film."

However, it did take some time for his mother and father to catch on because they didn't really understand basketball. Finally, one of the neighbors told them, "Your son is pretty good. You probably want to see him play." That's when they started attending games at Calvert Hall where Ferrell was destined to take his game to the highest level. College coaches certainly were paying close attention to him.

"It was a great feeling," Ferrell said about being recruited. "A lot of colleges were coming to see Marc, but it was also an opportunity to show that I could play at the D1 level. When you saw all of those top coaches at games, you just couldn't wait to get out there. You wanted to impress them. When I was a kid, all I wanted was a letter from their school. Later, my brother used to collect the letters I received from colleges and we would hang them up. My whole bedroom had nothing but college letters on the wall. My brothers were so happy. It was exciting for my family."

Ferrell never begrudged Amatucci for leaving Calvert Hall for Loyola College following the 1981-82 season. He fully understood his coach's ambition. "You have to take advantage of those opportunities," Ferrell said. "At that time, I was mature enough to see the landscape of college basketball. As a high school coach, you don't get a chance that often to go to the next level. The timing was right. All we could do was support him. It was a goal for him."

In his final two years at The Hall, Ferrell played for head coach Charlie Reif. Reif, an outstanding educator and basketball tactician, said, "I remember Duane as one of the most unselfish and unpretentious young men that I have worked with. He never went out of the way to draw attention to himself. Throughout the college recruitment process, he remained himself: quiet, unassuming and team oriented. He led quietly, made the game seem effortless, and used his skills to make his teammates better. He was mature beyond his years. Teammates and adults enjoyed being with him."

Under Reif's tutelage, Ferrell's game continued to reach new heights. As a junior he averaged 22.9 points and 11.5 rebounds per game, earning first team BCL and first team All Metro honors. The Cardinals finished the year 21-13 losing to Cardinal Gibbons in the BCL Tournament final.

His senior year, The Cards captured both the BCL regular season and tourney championships. They finished with a 29-4 record and were ranked #17 in the nation. Ferrell average 23 points and 12 rebounds for the season and was chosen as a Street & Smith's All-American, a McDonald's All-American, first team All Metro, and MVP of the BCL. He would leave Calvert Hall as the school's all-time leading scorer and rebounder. His 2,511 points set a high bar for future Cardinal hoopsters.

By the end of his Calvert Hall career, Ferrell's abilities had reached mythical proportions. Jim Gring of The Baltimore Sun wrote, "If there was a Greek god of basketball, his body would be like Duane Ferrell's 6'6" frame. He has powerful legs for great leaping ability, a strong upper body to muscle under the boards, and soft hands to shoot his jumper. He's the complete package."

Even though Amatucci left the program, he and Ferrell stayed in touch. Amatucci later recruited him to play for Loyola, but Ferrell was looking for a bigger program. After a high-powered recruiting process, Ferrell narrowed his college selections down to Villanova University, Syracuse University, and Georgia Tech. He chose to attend Georgia Tech. The Yellow Jackets were coached by Bobby Cremins, a Bronx, New York, native who landed his first Division I coaching job at age 27 for Appalachian State.

On signing Ferrell, Cremins commented, "Getting Duane was a real bonanza for us. We are very delighted."

Cremins' animated coaching style was not like Amatucci's. While Amatucci liked to crouch in front of the bench, Cremins would scream and jump up and down during a game. Cremins was not averse to calling out players in the media. He and Ferrell butted heads several times during his time on the Atlanta campus.

"Duane is a fine young man and we're delighted with him," Cremins said in the February 1, 1985, edition of The Baltimore Sun. "But there are times he needs to become more aggressive. I know Duane's type; he's very cool. But he has to change his personality some, and it's a tough thing to do. He sort of has to overcome himself, and it's something he has to do himself. We can give him guidance, that's all."

Amatucci remembered, "Bobby was a great coach, but I think he misread Duane. Publicly criticizing Duane was not necessary or effective. For me, Duane always responded well when we discussed things one-on-one."

Despite that early criticism, Ferrell was named the 1985 Atlantic Coast Conference Rookie of the Year. Meanwhile, Cremins was also developing a solid track record, leading the Yellow Jackets to the ACC tournament title that season and reaching the NCAA tournament final eight, where they lost to Georgetown, 60-54. The Hoyas later lost to Villanova in the title game.

Cremins and Ferrell continued to have their ups-and-downs. After Georgia Tech beat Louisiana State, 87-70, on December 16, 1987, Cremins told Washington Post columnist John Feinstein, "I really got on Ferrell at halftime. We need him to play well and he wasn't."

In four years at Georgia Tech, Ferrell averaged 9.1, 12.1, 17.9, and 19.6 points per game. By the time he left the school, Ferrell was the Yellow Jackets' third all-time leading scorer with 1,818 points (14.3 points per game) and finished with 680 rebounds. Despite that success, Ferrell acknowledged he could have been an even better player at Georgia Tech. However, he does not second-guess his decision to play for Cremins.

"I didn't play to the level I thought I could with Coach Cremins," Ferrell said. "I didn't develop each year as I should have, partly because of me tuning him out sometimes. It was different from Coach Tooch getting on you, as opposed to the way Bobby was doing it. To this day, I thought I was the missing piece for Georgia Tech to win a national championship. It was very similar to Calvert Hall. You had two guys at

Georgia Tech—Mark Price and John Salley—and I saw them as Pop Tubman and Marc Wilson.

"Mark and John's games went well with my game," Ferrell added. "All we needed was a couple of more pieces. Georgia Tech was up and coming. They were not one of the big teams in the ACC. I thought I could go in and have an impact right away just like Calvert Hall. I just feel as though I left something out there. I wish I was more mature and handled the whole situation better. I should have been a better player."

Following Georgia Tech, Duane Ferrell signed with the Atlanta Hawks as a free agent in 1988. Ferrell played six seasons in Atlanta, and averaged a career high of 12.7 points per game in 1991-92. Ferrell also played a season for the Topeka Sizzlers in the Continental Basketball Association and averaged 24.3 points per game in 1989-90. He was named the league's Newcomer of the Year.

Ferrell later spent three years with the Indiana Pacers, appearing in 172 games and averaging almost five points per game. He and Erick Dampier were traded to the Golden State Warriors for all-star veteran Chris Mullin on August 12, 1997. Ferrell played two seasons at Golden State before retiring in 1999. Overall, Ferrell played 11 seasons in the NBA, totaling 3,704 points, 1,132 rebounds and 509 assists, and went to the playoffs five times.

"Mentally and physically, I was prepared for the NBA," Ferrell said. "I had thick skin. That gave me an edge because I came into camp not in awe of the players. I always had a good work ethic where I pushed myself. It worked out for me. When I go back and look at the picture of the McDonald's All-American team and see all of those guys that went onto the pros, I played longer than about eighty percent of them in the NBA."

Over his long, impressive career, Ferrell still savors his time at Calvert Hall. Today, he stays in touch with many of the players. In 2011, Ferrell was inducted into the Baltimore Catholic League's inaugural Hall of Fame class with teammates Marc Wilson and Paul Edwards.

"It was such a family feel to it," Ferrell said. "We did a lot of stuff together off the court. We eventually went our separate ways, but when we get back together, we never miss a beat."

After finishing his pro career, Ferrell worked in the Atlanta Hawks organization in player relations and broadcasting. Today, he is a successful entrepreneur and lives in the Atlanta area.

"What often is missed in focusing on Duane's outstanding basketball talents is that he was a great teammate," Amatucci noted. "He always had a smile on his face. He never allowed all the attention or accolades to go to his head. He cared about his friends. Even today, he is very unassuming and stays in touch with his best Baltimore friend and Calvert Hall team mate, Eddie Oliver. I always joke, if you are having trouble getting in touch with Duane, call Eddie."

GOING TO EXTREMES

SPORTS/BUSINESS

THE SUN, Tuesday, September 14, 1982 — Section C

C 6

The Sun / Jed Kirschbaum

New coach, new home

Mark Amatucci, who achieved spectacular success as basketball coach at Calvert Hall, was recently named Loyola College's new coach, and yesterday decided to check out his team's home court on Evergreen campus.

Tooch becomes a Greyhound.

"Too high or too low there ain't no in-betweens ..."

\- BILLY JOEL

"Athletes aren't the only ones who have the eye of the tiger. There are a lot of coaches with that hungry look that says, 'I want to be the best.' Calvert Hall's Mark Amatucci has that look and the record to back it up."

- BILL GLAUBER
The Baltimore Sun

Even with returning players Duane Ferrell, Eddie Oliver, Vernon Hill, and Ted Frick, Amatucci's goal was to reload for the 1982-83 season. The Cardinals lost four starters—Wilson, Edwards, Tubman, and Sass, in addition to the multi-purpose Kauffman. Empty holes needed to be filled. Amatucci was focused on adding new recruits to keep the momentum going. "How do you replace those seniors?" Amatucci pondered. "We had to regroup. It was a huge challenge and we had a lot of work to do. The point guard spot was the position I was most worried about."

The Cardinals pulled a coup by locking up Kirk Lee, a top AAU player from right out of Dunbar's backyard; Lee lived a stone's throw from the famed East Baltimore high school. They also added Bobby Graves, a quick, slashing guard to the roster. Amatucci was thinking the combo provided excellent potential to fill Pop Tubman's shoes.

As the summer began, Amatucci put basketball on hold for his wedding to his wife, Pat, and their honeymoon. Not long afterward, he was back in the gym at Calvert Hall laying the groundwork for the following season. In mid-August, he had just finished a coaches' meeting when his friend and former roommate, Jim Fitzsimmons, told him that Loyola College athletic director Tom O'Connor had called.

"I would call him back right away," Fitz told Amatucci.

The previous year, Amatucci had put out some feelers to major Division I college programs about a potential position as an assistant coach. He was just kicking the tires on opportunities and possibly new challenges. "I know I had told Brother Rene that I was staying put," Amatucci said. "Realistically, it would have to be a special situation to consider a move. Because of our success over the past few years, I received some encouraging responses, but nothing to the level I was looking for. Loyola was one of those schools who replied informing me at the time there were no openings."

That changed when Greyhounds coach Billy Burke unexpectedly left after just one season. He guided the team to an 11-16 finish in Loyola's first year as a Division I program. Burke decided to change careers and took a position in the investment industry.

"I took Fitz's advice and made the call," Amatucci remembered.

O'Connor was interested in talking to Amatucci about the Loyola head coaching vacancy. They decided to meet for dinner at a restaurant in Timonium. After exchanging a few pleasantries, O'Connor got to the point and asked Amatucci if he would be interested in the position.

The caveat was Amatucci had to make a decision within twenty-four hours. Amatucci had been unaware of the opening and that the interview process was already moving ahead. Nonetheless, it became obvious to him that O'Connor had set his sights on the Cardinals' coach. O'Connor later revealed in the press conference that Amatucci was chosen from a field of sixty-two candidates.

More than thirty years later, O'Connor is still confident that Amatucci was the best man for the job. In 2014, after serving for many years as the athletic director at George Mason University, O'Connor was named vice president of collegiate sports at Snodgrass Partners, a specialized executive search and leadership development firm headquartered in Kansas.

"It was not a gamble," said O'Connor about hiring a high school coach to take over a Division I college program. "Mark has a terrific basketball mind, and I was impressed with his passion. He had great contacts for recruiting in the Baltimore area. If I had the opportunity to hire Mark again, I would do so without hesitation."

Amatucci was interested in the position, and he and O'Connor began working out the details right away. Amatucci was surprised the salary for a Division I basketball coach at the school was only $19,000, which was still a significant raise from his current salary. There was also only enough money in the budget for one, full-time paid assistant. There was no booster club. Overall, Loyola's financial investment in Division I basketball was significantly below that of their competition. Despite those initial challenges, Amatucci was confident in his coaching acumen and did not see the financial situation as a deterrent.

Still, Amatucci had just one day to make one of the biggest decisions of his life. "If I had to do it over, I would have said I needed a little more time," Amatucci recalled. "I would not have jumped into it so quickly."

Returning home, Amatucci discussed the situation with Pat, who certainly wanted more than twenty-four hours to process the proposal. Time was not on their side because O'Connor needed an answer. Not considering Pat's input, Amatucci decided to take the chance and accepted the position. His tenure as the head coach at Calvert Hall was over, at least for the time being. He had gone 117-27 in four years. Now, at age thirty, he was the youngest head coach in Division I basketball.

"It was a surprise; we had just gotten married in June," Pat Amatucci said. "They were coming off a great year at Calvert Hall and there was a lot of prestige. I was there for all those events. Then, we got married and it was the first time I had left home. It was a big adjustment. I don't remember him even saying anything about Loyola until he took the job. He made the move and I was a little bit fearful, but I thought it was something new and would be better for him."

Charlie Reif took over the reins of the Cardinal program, and Joe Baker became head JV coach.

There were mixed emotions among the Calvert Hall players. Ferrell, who was entertaining more than 200 scholarship offers from colleges, understood the decision and wished his coach the best. "It's a step up," Ferrell told The Evening Sun. "Mr. Amatucci sat down with us and asked how we felt about the move. Everyone on the team felt the same way—we understand why he's moving up, but it's a big letdown for all of us."

Vernon Hill, who later played for Amatucci at Loyola, also understood the decision, but was worried about the impact on the Calvert Hall program.

"We had a team meeting where Tooch informed us that he was leaving," Hill remembered. "There was some surprise at the decision. We had Coach Reif who was going to take over. He was already a part of the coaching staff, and we were comfortable with him. We were okay.

With Tooch, there was a sense of 'you're leaving now?' Duane, Eddie and I never really discussed it. We were kind of happy for him, but there was some shock he was leaving at that particular point. We never really thought that was going to happen. I assumed he would be there for my entire three years."

Oliver also was taken back by Amatucci's decision. In the end, however, he was happy his coach was able to secure such a big opportunity and predicted Amatucci would turn Loyola into a perennial winner, just like he did at Calvert Hall.

"It was shocking, but we knew coach Amatucci had to do what he had to do," Oliver said. "We understood that and wished him well. We continued to play hard for Calvert Hall. All of the guys were close with Coach Reif, especially me, Duane and Vernon."

At the formal press conference to introduce Amatucci as the new head coach, O'Connor said the new hire met two main criteria for the job: he had local roots for effective recruiting and a track record for leading a program to success. "I feel we hit the nail right on the head," O'Connor told the media.

Amatucci was hoping to get the Greyhounds rolling within two or three years. He had already developed that successful timeline at Calvert Hall. This time, the hurdles were even bigger at Loyola.

"I didn't really do much research," Amatucci said. "I didn't have a sense of where the program was and where it needed to go. I saw the record. They had a decent year for their first season as a Division I program. The bottom line is I should have done more hands-on analysis. But I was a high school coach getting a Division I job. Those opportunities are extremely rare."

Amatucci continued to teach at Calvert Hall until late September to help with the transition of his teaching duties. During that time, Amatucci left Calvert Hall in the afternoon to head down to Loyola until late in the evening to get acclimated to the new position. His first hire was Pat Dennis, who was an outstanding player at Loyola Blakefield and

Washington & Lee, as the top assistant. He had previously been on the coaching staff at Towson State College. The two had once gotten into a scrum during a pick-up basketball game, but there was no lingering animosity. "He winds up being my assistant," Amatucci said with a laugh.

The amenities at Loyola were challenging. The coaching staff was relegated to one office in the basement of the antiquated Evergreen Gymnasium built in the 1920s. Dave Cottle, the new head lacrosse coach, was about ten feet away in an adjoining space.

"It was not an ideal situation, especially not being full time until late September," Amatucci remembered. "Pat Dennis was extremely beneficial to me because he knew the college ropes and was a tenacious recruiter. Coach Dennis had an excellent basketball IQ. But it was just hard. It was not your typical Division I program."

On the court, the current group of Greyhounds' players would not adjust to Amatucci's hard-nosed coaching style. He wanted to play transition basketball the same way he did at Calvert Hall, but the players competed at a much slower speed. From day one, the team's intensity never reached Amatucci's expectations. Amatucci was vocal in practice, which rankled some of the players, many of whom came from schools in New York.

However, there were some highlights.

David Urban, a Pottstown, Pennsylvania, native, thrived under Amatucci's system and had two solid years after averaging just one point per game as a sophomore. Steve Rossiter, a 6-foot-6 center from Staten Island, brought a blue-collar work ethic to practices and games. Amatucci quickly recognized the efforts of "Urbs" and "Ross" and built a solid connection with them. Amatucci recalled, "There was mutual trust and respect; I could count on both of them."

There were only two Baltimore players on the roster—Todd McClendon, from Cardinal Gibbons, and Bob Selby, a Loyola Blakefield alum—but neither made a positive impression. The rest of the roster would have struggled to get playing time at Calvert Hall.

Loyola lost 17 consecutive games to open the season, which was an ignominious start to Amatucci's college coaching career. The frustration rose to a level that Amatucci had never experienced. Amatucci explained, "In my mind, being 34-0 and national champs set a high bar I was expected to duplicate, realistically or not."

At one game during that tough stretch, the Loyola students wore paper bags over their heads. Amatucci went directly to O'Connor's office and vented about the spectacle. Amatucci called it an "embarrassment," and at one point, swept everything off O'Connor's desk onto the floor. The athletic director just looked at him patiently.

"I understand. We're going to get through this Mark," Amatucci remembered O'Connor saying. Amatucci had found a true ally in O'Connor, noting, "He never raised his voice or lost his composure."

"Tom was very supportive of me," Amatucci said. "He was fantastic, just an outstanding and terrific guy to work for. O'Connor was smart, classy and had the head coaching experience to empathize with the team's struggles."

Still, Amatucci grew frustrated with the state of the program and a massive overhaul was needed for the Hounds to be successful. Slowly, the program began to evolve. McClendon left the team because of injuries, and Amatucci began to tire of Selby's antics—poor work habits and divisive attitude. Selby had been late for several practices and was pulled from a few others for not playing hard.

Amatucci benched Selby for a February 5 road game against William & Mary, and Selby became disruptive on the bench during the blowout loss. He spent much of the time talking to the W&M student section and wearing a towel over his head. Looking down the bench during the second half, Amatucci observed Selby drinking a Coke and eating a sandwich provided by that same group. It was the last straw for Amatucci, who dismissed Selby from the team the following day.

"That was as bad as it gets" Amatucci said about Selby's behavior. "It was insulting to me and the team."

From that point on, the Hounds began to show some fight, and that would become a trend throughout the rest of the season. Furthermore, the year was not a total washout. The Greyhounds snapped the 17-game skid with an 82-75 victory over the University of Baltimore at the 5th Regiment Armory downtown. Finally, this was an encouraging sign. It was a much-needed boost of confidence for Amatucci, who remained fully committed and confident about turning around the program despite the adversity.

Interestingly, the win came without the aid of the talented Mo Hicks. He had violated Amatucci's classroom attendance rule and was suspended for the game. Hick's suspension definitely got the attention of his teammates. In Amatucci's system, everyone was required to follow the team rules. There was no star system. Winning without Hicks was a defining moment in the development of the program.

Prior to a February 12 game against St. Francis (N.Y.), a heavy snow swept through the Baltimore area, shutting down roads and cancelling school. Amatucci walked more than five miles from his apartment to the Loyola campus to hold a 3 p.m. practice. Following the session, Amatucci made the cold, long hike home, including a stop at Harford Road's infamous Dutch Mill for a beer to warm up. The following day, Loyola beat St. Francis, 76-69.

"You go to extremes," Amatucci said. "I do what I have to do. It was a great opportunity to show the team that the commitment I expected was about actions and not words. We won."

The Greyhounds then beat Wagner, 77-76, for their second win in three days. Another signature victory came later that month against cross-town rival, Towson, coached by Vince Angotti, 92-84, in Loyola's home gym.

"The Towson win was a really good one. The Towson Tigers under Angotti were a traditionally strong program featuring local talent. The win provided bragging rights for the guys." Amatucci reflected.

At this point in the season, the Loyola students were back to using their paper bags for lunch.

Amatucci adjusted to his personnel by playing more zone and running a four corners offense led by Hicks, who had gotten his act together. At that time, there was no shot clock. When Loyola held a lead, the team went to the four-corners to run time off the clock. Amatucci recalled, "In addition to using the clock to our advantage, the four corners opened up the floor for Mo to create one-on-one opportunities. Mo excelled in attacking the hoop."

The season ended with a thud as the Greyhounds lost, 81-60, to Robert Morris in the Eastern Collegiate Athletic Conference tournament. The Greyhounds finished just 4-24, and more house-cleaning was in order. Amatucci began to put his full stamp on the program. As a result, he retained just three players from that inaugural team—Maurice Hicks, Dave Urban, and Steve Rossiter.

Throughout the season, Dennis had been working non-stop on the recruiting trail. Amatucci and Dennis were focused on recruiting student-athletes who would instantly buy into Amatucci's style. He wanted student-athletes who would play hard, play together, and represent the high standards of Loyola College. The best place to find the type of players they wanted, the coaches believed, was in the Catholic Leagues of Washington, Baltimore, and Philadelphia. Amatucci and Dennis implemented their recruiting plan effectively and ended up with a top incoming class.

David Gately of Mount St. Joseph in Baltimore was a top priority. He was a ferocious competitor who brought instant offense to the lineup. "Gates utilized the entire floor," Amatucci said. "He was a master at using screens and getting open without the ball. One-on-one he had a tremendous ability to set his man up and get to the basket. For us, he was our Chris Mullin (St. John's University, standout NBA player)." Tom Gormley, a left-handed point guard from Monsignor Bonner in the Philadelphia suburb of Upper Darby had impressed Amatucci when his Cardinals played them in the Alhambra Tournament. Gormley could handle the ball, had good range, and was a defensive stopper. He had the mental toughness to deal with the high expectations Amatucci had of his point guards.

Aubrey Reveley played for Joe Gallagher at Washington's St. John's College High School. Reveley brought versatility, confidence, defensive toughness and a winning attitude. Tommy Lee from famed Roman Catholic in Philadelphia was a hidden gem. At 6-5 he played like he was 6-8. Lee was a bull on the boards, loved to compete and was a player very loyal to his team and his coach.

There was one glaring glitch to this outstanding recruiting class: Lee was initially not admitted to Loyola. The news sent Amatucci into a rage, which included threatening to resign. O'Connor went to bat for Lee with Father Sellinger, the president of Loyola. Lee was given a second review by the admissions office and was admitted. Four years later, a proud Lee graduated from Loyola with a 3.4 GPA.

In May, while attending a summer league game in Annapolis, Dennis unexpectedly found the 6-foot-5 Kevin Carter, who had graduated from St. Mary's High School Annapolis. He had started his college career at Niagara University but wanted to be closer to home. Dennis called Amatucci while at the game and said, "You are not going believe it. I've found the other big guy we are looking for."

Carter was strong, could leap out of the gym, completely unselfish, and played with tremendous heart. He visited Loyola and instantly felt a connection to his future teammates and loved that he would be getting a chance to play right away. After sitting out the first semester, Carter brought instant leadership and an outstanding work ethic to this talented recruiting class. With each passing day, Amatucci had more confidence in the direction the program was taking.

As the 1983-1984 season grew closer, Amatucci expectations began to rise even higher. The Greyhounds were a completely different team with a new spirit. The players worked hard each practice, which regularly lasted about three hours. In addition to the returners and recruits,

Mike Savage and Phil Lazzati earned spots on the roster as walk-ons. Amatucci said, "Mike and Phil were two competitive guys with great attitudes and excellent basketball IQ's. They made us better by pushing their teammates in practice. The difference in the preparation showed on the court. The coaching staff was enhanced with the addition of two of Amatucci's Calvert Hall assistants, Chris Devlin and Steve Misotti. Most importantly, the players embraced Amatucci's intensity.

"Tooch would just get into your face and just yell," Gormley said. "You couldn't even wipe the spit off your face. He taught us a lot."

Loyola opened Amatucci's second season with a resounding 124-79 win over Lebanon Valley. The 124 points is still an all-time Greyhound scoring record. The Greyhounds started four freshmen and Urban. Hicks, the talented sophomore, started the season on suspension for violating team rules. Fortunately, Gormley stepped right into the point guard slot without missing a beat. "After this game, I had a great feeling for the real potential of this group," Amatucci recalled.

That was followed by a 78-50 loss to Villanova, which won the national championship two years later. One of Gately's best friends went to Villanova and was a team manager. He bet another Villanova student that the backcourt of Gately and Gormley would outscore Wildcats' guards Dwayne McClain and Harold Jensen. Gately (15 points) and Gormley (10) scored 25, while McClain had 19, but Jensen could not make up the difference. The beer was delivered cold.

"We hung for a while," Amatucci remembered. "The kids played hard, and we we're not intimidated. I was not unhappy."

The Greyhounds were making some serious noise, and Amatucci finally had the players running up and down the court just like his days at Calvert Hall. This was a recipe for success.

"It's the new Loyola College," Amatucci said. "We're going to run. We're going to trap. We are coming at you for forty minutes. No one in the ECAC could play that way. We were going to take teams out of their game. Practices were intense, and I did not create a whole lot of love during practice. The crucible of practice created team bonding. We were a tight group, and it showed on the court."

Despite the hard practices and his animated personality, Amatucci had actually forged solid relationships with all of the players. They were "his guys." Amatucci allowed the seniors to grab a beer in the hotel bar when they were on the road. Underclassmen were allowed to socialize without many restrictions. The players knew they had to act responsibly and not get into trouble, or there would be dire consequences, such as running around a large lake across the street from the campus.

"He's a no nonsense guy," Gately said. "Those practices lasted for three hours with no water. They were tough. But Tooch stood by his players. He pushed you, and pushed you and pushed you in the classroom and on the court. Those practices were so competitive, but we wanted to win. He turned the place around. It had been a disaster."

One time, Gately was out drinking at a Loyola mixer to the early hours of the morning. He even jumped onto the stage and sang a few tunes with the band. The following morning, he received a call at 6 a.m. from Amatucci who had gotten word Gately was crooning at the dance. That meant a trip to the lake for a morning run.

Loyola finished the regular season 16-11 and was the most improved team among NCAA Division I basketball programs that year. Amatucci was named ECAC Coach of the Year. The Greyhounds finished 11-2 on their home court. The winning record was just part of the overall progress. Amatucci was changing the culture.

When he first arrived at Loyola, the team traveled by bus on the day of the game, even long distances. Travel was not much different than high school. The bus driver was making the itinerary—when to stop, where to eat, etc. After the second road trip, Amatucci squashed that strategy and assigned travel planning to Coach Dennis. The Greyhounds began leaving for road games the prior night, having team meals and study hall on the road. He scheduled a shoot-around the morning of the game at the opponent's gym, budget be damned. That routine became an absolute priority for away trips. Amatucci raised his own funds for travel and hired a new bus driver to take the wheel.

"It was a great bonding experience for us," Amatucci said about the road trips. "The players got more opportunities to know each other beyond basketball. The trips allowed the coaches more time to interact individually with the players. On these trips the team found that, unbelievably, Amatucci had another side to his personality. The players all got along. It was starting to be fun. We were winning some games and starting to believe in ourselves."

The season had another milestone as the Greyhounds played their final game at the old Evergreen Gym on February 25, 1984, beating Siena, 82-62. The game was highlighted by a lively skirmish between the teams that included Ross stepping in to pull a swinging Amatucci away from the fray. The team's new on campus home, Reitz Arena, opened the following December beginning a new era for Loyola basketball.

There was reason for even more optimism leading into Amatucci's third season. The Hounds had their second consecutive outstanding recruiting class. Pop Tubman transferred to Loyola from Oakland University in Michigan and was now eligible to play. Vernon Hill from Calvert Hall also opted to join the Hounds. Besides his outstanding transition ability, Hill had developed into an effective scorer on the block.

Glenn Rogers, 6-6 from Metuchen, N.J., and Brad Meyers, a 6-7 swing player from Reading, Pennsylvania, rounded out the class. Rogers was athletic, a strong post player and could also be a weapon facing the hoop. Meyers had a consistent jumper and the versatility to be a threat in the paint. Amatucci finally had a complete roster that could excel in transition, trap full court, and wear teams down.

Realizing the potential of this squad, Amatucci wanted to push this group to the extreme. He had a smile on his face when he thought about that. He was determined to continue to develop the family mentality of the players. Push them to the limit, let them take their anger out on him, and drive them closer together.

To accomplish his goal, Amatucci continued to develop his coaching staff. With Pat Dennis taking an assistant's job at the University of Richmond, Amatucci was concerned about finding the right person to fill Pat's void. He hired Jeff Nix to replace Dennis. Nix had a great career as a player at Canisius, had been an assistant at St. Francis (Pa.), and had a Notre Dame connection. Amatucci remembered, "Notre Dame coach, Digger Phelps called me, and bluntly said, 'You better hire him now.'" Nix proved to be a great addition to the Loyola basketball family. He immediately fit right in with the kids and staff. "We all embraced the big guy," Amatucci said.

Nix would go on to spend thirteen years as an assistant coach on the collegiate level, including stops at his alma mater Canisius (1979-81), St. Francis University (1981-84), Loyola (1984-85), Xavier (1985-87) and Notre Dame (1987-92). As a result, he knew many of the top Division I coaches and possessed that big-time mentality. Later, Nix was an assistant coach for the New York Knicks, and also served as assistant general manager. Currently he is the assistant general manager for the Detroit Pistons. Thinking back on his time at Loyola, Nix commented, "The most important factor in winning at schools like Loyola is the player development program. We were not going to get the four- or five-star players in recruiting, but with hard work on and off the court we could make one- to three-star players into three-or four-star players during the course of their collegiate career. In all my years of coaching, working for some of the best coaches in the game, nobody was better than Mark Amatucci in practice planning and execution. I have never seen a coach maximize the use of a practice floor like Mark. He utilized every basket and every available space to provide a constant laboratory of action. He was a master in developing players and making the game fun for them through all of the hard work. Mark not only developed the players' skill level, but he improved their mental capacity to work and to believe that their effort would pay dividends for them down the road—not only in basketball, but in life too."

After hiring Nix, Amatucci, added another trusted and familiar face, bringing back Doc Reif to specifically improve the Hounds' overall defense. "The guy was a defensive aficionado," Amatucci said about Reif. "He was extremely creative and detailed." The two would spend hours discussing defensive footwork and situational game adjustments.

Reif, however, was not a welcomed sight by some of the players. They mumbled to themselves and stomped their feet when Reif entered the gym. They knew the toughest part of the day was still ahead even after two hours of practice. Gately especially hated seeing Reif sauntering through the gymnasium doors.

"After two hours of practice, I see Coach Reif walk in and I say, 'This is fucking bullshit,' as loud as I could," Gately remembered. "After practice, Reif told one of the assistants to take me out to the lake and keep me running. It was snowing. When Coach Reif came in, you knew that it was sixty minutes of defensive hell."

Gately estimates the Greyhounds played five possessions of zone defense over his entire four years. "We played full-court man for forty minutes for four years," Gately said. "We never changed. We were in great shape, I'll tell you that."

The hard work paid off.

"The footwork was important because we wanted to force everything to the side, and not allow penetration in the middle of the floor," Amatucci said. "From there, we would talk about utilizing the full court run-and-jump and applying it in the half-court. We would work on different rotations in the trap. When we were playing straight man-to-man in the half-court, if the ball went to the low post we had a wing jam the ball. If the post player kicked the ball back out, the wing needed proper footwork to return to his man."

Most teams in the ECAC, with the exception of Fairleigh Dickinson, were similar to Baltimore Catholic League teams, running a half-court offense built on utilizing the high post and using little full-court pressure. Amatucci was ready to take advantage of their style and wear teams down by the second half. Skip Prosser, who later would coach Loyola (1993-1994), Xavier and Wake Forest, and Dino Gaudio, who coached Loyola (1997-2000) and later Wake Forest, used to visit Amatucci's workouts and were impressed by the offensive and defensive continuity. There was never any standing around. It was a mental commitment to detail ... the little things.

"We did a lot of footwork, a lot of positioning, and also put a lot of emphasis on communication, so that everyone knew what was expected and where everyone was expected to be," Reif said. "We didn't leave a lot to chance. Those kids spent a lot of sweat and time out there trying to get it right. We were doing some good stuff. They didn't need the ball once I got to practice."

For the coming season, Amatucci had put together a difficult schedule with games against Virginia, Maryland, Notre Dame, Navy, Richmond, Delaware, and Holy Cross. The Holy Cross game was the inaugural contest in Loyola's Reitz Arena. The Hounds soundly defeated the Crusaders, 87-73, before a full house. Mo Hicks had a great night, scoring 18. Holy Cross head coach George Blaney told reporters after the game, "We just couldn't control Hicks. Not one time were we able to stay in front of him." Amatucci was proud of the way the Hounds attacked their tough out-of-conference opponents. They pushed teams to the limit. Amatucci had no fear of the big stage and his players embraced his swagger.

"This was the best group of guys I had in my entire time at Loyola," Amatucci said about that 1984-85 team. "Some coaches in town got upset when I said we wanted to be Baltimore's team. Those coaches were pissed off. I asked myself, 'What's wrong with wanting to be Baltimore's team?' If they didn't want to stick their neck out and promote that idea, so be it. I didn't have that problem."

Towson coach Terry Truax told Baltimore Sun columnist John Eisenberg: "I respect him. I think he says some stupid things. But it's funny. You tell him you disagree with what he says, and he says, 'Aw, yeah. I know.'"

The Greyhounds ran past Truax and the Tigers, 81-73, in the opener.

"After the decisive win, I wondered who was feeling stupid now," Amatucci quipped. Loyola then played in the Virginia National Bank Tournament hosted by the University of Virginia Cavaliers. In the opening game, the Greyhounds trailed Virginia, 41-33, at the half. The Cavaliers struggled against the press. "We felt, as a team, we had a legit shot to pull the upset," Amatucci said.

Loyola pulled to within 60-53 with 6:38 remaining in the game. Virginia, led by Tim Mullen (16 points), was able to pull away down the stretch for a 72-60 victory. Hicks led Loyola with 23 points. In describing the Hounds' tenacious effort against Virginia, Bernie Miklasz of the News American wrote: "Pop Tubman, a sawed-off guard dog who is one of many molecules in a maniacal swarm that Amatucci summons from the bench to leave knee flesh and sweat on the lane paint, buzzed across the baseline and lunged after a lazy dribble. The Spalding became a free bird, and another frenzied molecule, Mo Hicks, raced up court with it on a mad, coast-to-coast dash to two points. It was life as a video game."

"The days of us being a sacrificial lamb are over," Amatucci said. "If teams want to play us, they'll have to prepare."

In the consolation game, the Greyhounds ran past the University of Tampa, 73-59. Gormley went nine of twelve from the field and led the Greyhounds with 24 points.

"Tooch didn't play around with those non-conference games," Gormley said, "so, you had to be ready to play."

After losing a tight game to Delaware, the Greyhounds had a showdown with Maryland and Len Bias before an announced 6,102 at the Civic Center in downtown Baltimore. Once again, the Greyhounds hung tough and trailed just 43-38 at the break, despite playing without Gately because of a knee injury. The Terrapins regrouped and opened the second half with a 17-6 run en route to an 88-74 victory. Bias finished with 22 points.

"We were all ticked off, Amatucci said. "Being close was not acceptable anymore."

Navy, led by future NBA star, 6-foot-11 center David Robinson, also posed a stern test for the Greyhounds. Robinson had led the Midshipmen to a 41-33 lead before picking up his fourth foul midway through the second half.

Amatucci remembered, "At this point, with Robinson on the bench, I'm thinking we have the Middies." However, the Greyhounds could not contain his backup, Vernon Butler, who dominated inside the paint. Butler finished with 20 points, Robinson scored 18, and Navy came away with a 63-54 victory. Again, no satisfaction for the Hounds.

"These players regularly performed above their talent level," Reif said. "They were good kids and hard workers. They competed and played with confidence and enthusiasm."

Later that season, the Greyhounds had a chance to beat Notre Dame and coach Digger Phelps on the road. The game was set up by Loyola assistant coach Jeff Nix, who had worked at Phelps' basketball camps for a number of years. With sixteen seconds left in the game, Gately missed a short jumper. Carter missed the put-back before Hicks missed a short floater. The ball went out of bounds off a Notre Dame player. Gately took the inbounds pass, missed another jumper and Carter's tip in follow up missed as time expired. Amatucci recalls, "I'd still love to get my hands on that guy who put a lid on the basket."

Final score: Notre Dame 61, Loyola 60.

After the game, Phelps locked eyes with Nix during the handshake and told him, "Don't ever call me again." The Greyhounds had that effect on teams that season.

"We wanted to win the game, not just stay close," Amatucci said afterward, "Our body language confirmed that we could play with anybody. It was Notre Dame. The significance of pulling off the upset would have been transformational to the program."

Gormley remembered: "That was the only game in my four years that I did not score. I had a guy named David Rivers on me and I couldn't get a shot off. But we had a bunch of chances to win at the end. That ball just kept rolling around that rim."

The tough schedule had Loyola battle-tested for the ECAC, where no team ran away with the regular season.

"We didn't have a real center, so we just had a bunch of guys that could run," Gormley said. "Because we were so small, we had to pressure. We didn't have the talent of most teams, but we had the heart. That's how we were taught by Tooch and Pat Dennis. You better be ready to go through a wall or dive on the ball."

The players showed that toughness on a regular basis. Gately suffered a torn meniscus, but was back in the starting lineup after missing just seven games.

"Tooch did not want you going to the trainer. He hated trainers," Gately recalled. "He knew I could swim. So, he would go down to the pool and have me swim. I told him that something was not right. I had an X-ray, and they cleaned up the tear with surgery. I came back in just over three weeks. One day, I was just watching practice with a huge knee brace on and Tooch asks me if I could run a little bit. I was able to jog. Then, I did some shooting drills. Two days later I was in the game against Wagner. Unless I couldn't walk, I was going to play. I understood and agreed with Tooch's rule—If it ain't broken or falling off, be ready to practice and play."

Somehow, Gately did not show any ill effects from the injury, scoring 16 points, including the game-winner, with seven rebounds and three assists in a 65-64 victory over the Seahawks. Amatucci marvels at Gately's perseverance to this day.

"It just shows you the mentality of that class of kids," Amatucci said. "That was the kind of commitment they all were giving. It's pretty unfathomable that a kid comes back from that type of injury and not only starts but finishes with those impressive stats."

Loyola finished the regular season 14-13 and 8-6 in the ECAC, earning the No. 4 seed for the conference tournament, being held at Loyola's Reitz Arena. The Greyhounds breezed by No. 5 seed St. Francis,

85-71, in the opening round. It was Loyola's first win in the tournament's four-year history.

This set up a showdown in the semifinals with top-seeded Marist. Adding to the build-up for the game was that Marist's coach, Matt Furjanic, Jr., and Amatucci had a history of bad blood between them. Wagner coach Neal Kennett put it plainly, "Amatucci hated the SOB."

Over the years, the Greyhounds had developed an intense rivalry with Marist, led by 7-foot-3 center Rik Smits, who was the second overall pick in the 1988 NBA Draft by the Indiana Pacers. Defensively, the Hounds game plan was to pick Smits up full court on made baskets and mid-court on misses. The goal was to keep him off rhythm and to push him off of his favorite low post spot. Take him out of his comfort zone. This strategy was implemented each time Loyola played against Smits.

Loyola opened a 14-point lead in the first half and appeared to be cruising toward a victory. However, the Red Foxes chipped away and managed to take a 50-48 lead with 3:14 left in the game. The teams traded baskets the rest of the way, sending the game into overtime.

Neither team could take control, which set up a second overtime period. Mark Shamley gave Marist a 55-52 lead with fifty-three seconds left. Loyola pulled to within one on a pair of free throws by 6-foot-7 freshman Brad Meyers. Drafton Davis then missed the front-end of a one-and-one free throw for Marist. Carter grabbed the rebound for Loyola. Hicks took the outlet from Carter and jetted across half court and nailed a 22-foot jumper with three ticks remaining on the clock, providing the Hounds with a 56-55 miracle victory.

"When Mo got into his zone, he was unstoppable," Amatucci said.

Tommy "EZ" Lee and Kevin Carter did not allow Smits to be a factor in the game. The strategy worked to perfection.

Loyola then faced No. 2 seed Fairleigh Dickinson in the championship game for a spot in the NCAA tournament. The teams split their regular season games. Over the spirited rivalry, Fairleigh Dickinson coach Tom Green had become Amatucci's arch nemesis. Green had put together a huge roster with most of the players ranging from 6-foot-5 to 6-foot-7 and playing hard, physical basketball.

"Offensively, Green loved to go inside," Amatucci remembered. "The team was unselfish. They only ran on turnovers. They just methodically wore you down and beat the hell out of you. Tom was in my head every time we played them. And Green really practiced getting into my head before a game."

Amatucci rarely addressed the media on game day. The cutoff to speak with coaches was around 6:30 p.m. before a 7 p.m. tip off, according to league rules. Amatucci mandated that any interview had to take place before 5:30 p.m., and even then, there were no guarantees he would cooperate. The focus was on winning the game, and he didn't want to deviate from his normal routine.

Earlier that season, Amatucci was sitting in the stands prior to playing Fairleigh Dickinson when Green sat right next to him. As Green was making small talk, Amatucci was trying to find a way to tell him to "get the hell away" so he could clear his head for the game. Green had executed his mind game to perfection.

In the conference championship, the Greyhounds had no trouble focusing and led, 54-46, with just under three minutes left in the game. Green usually had a quiet demeanor on the sideline, but this game he became more animated with each possession, almost aping Amatucci's style of coaching. This aggravated Amatucci even more, because the Knights appeared to be getting away with fouls at both ends of the court.

"Every time down the floor, he is screaming, yelling at the officials, while jumping up and down," Amatucci recalled. "I said to myself, 'That SOB is trying to get a technical foul,' but the officials would not call one. In fact, they would not call any fouls even though they were mugging us at both ends of the court. I'm convinced he was deliberately imitating me. I think it worked."

Fairleigh Dickinson rallied and tied the game, 55-55, on a ten-foot jumper by Larry Hampton with sixteen seconds remaining that sent the game into overtime. The Greyhounds missed four one-and-ones in the final minutes, which proved to be costly. It was new ground for Amatucci. He was used to closing out these types of games at Calvert Hall and now at Loyola.

In the extra period, Loyola missed several critical layups and free throws. As a result, Fred Collins made a pair of free throws with twenty-one seconds left to give Fairleigh Dickinson a two-point lead. Carter then missed the front end of a one-and-one with fourteen seconds remaining and FDU held on for a 63-59 victory. Vernon Hill remembered, "Of all the games I ever lost, that was the one that sticks with me most. We had the best guards out there, but we lost because we could not convert free throws and made some bad decisions. The one thing I wanted in my college career was to experience the NCAA tournament." The Greyhounds finished the season at 16-14. Despite the deflating loss, it was another successful year for Amatucci. Truthfully, Amatucci felt the Hounds had a let a golden opportunity get away from them, but he knew this group would use the defeat as incentive to get back to the championship game the following year.

Much of the Greyhounds' success derived from the camaraderie of the team. "We did everything together," Gately remembered. "We partied together and we practiced hard together all season. We worked our asses off. We were a close-knit group." Tooch agreed. "That was a key ingredient to our success," Amatucci said. "We had great kids that were athletic. They were all hard as nails and busted their ass. They had no problem with my aggressive style of coaching. And when the players did get angry with me, it just drew them closer to one another. Off the court, everyone got along."

Getting along was not only a hallmark of team, but was also an absolute for the coaching staff. Prior to the ECAC Tournament at Loyola, Nix rented a suite for the coaches at the local Marriott Hotel for three days. The room was larger than the first floor of Amatucci's house at the time. After beating Marist in the semifinal, the coaches hit the town with

Nix and Penn State assistant and good friend Jeff Bower, who would later become the head coach at Marist and the New Orleans Hornets in the NBA. "Bow-man," as he was called, is currently the general manager of the Detroit Pistons. "It was not bad having a little star power to celebrate the huge victory," Amatucci said. The celebration lingered to the wee hours of the morning.

"Building a successful program—practices, games, recruiting trips, study halls, travel—requires countless hours from the coaches. Our guys never went off the clock. For us, It wasn't a job; we enjoyed it, we were passionate about it, and most importantly we all got along. When we got some free time—we made the most of it," Amatucci said.

A creative bunch led by self-appointed social director Doc Reif celebrated "Rocktober" during the preseason, which included "international night" each Friday after practice. Doc would choose a different ethnic-themed cuisine from the various restaurants in Towson. Those eateries included Italian, German, Mexican, and French fare to name a few. The adult beverages paired with the entrees complimented the meal and were plentiful as expected. "We typically were the last customers to leave the restaurant," Amatucci recalled.

Saturday practices usually ended by 1 p.m. and were followed by a little tour of the Towson drinking establishments for afternoon strategy sessions. Amatucci said that by 4 p.m. the married members of the staff were making a hurried getaway to stay in good graces with their better halves. That left Nix on his own, which usually led to a long and adventurous evening. "The good times kept us loose," Amatucci said. "Getting away from the game was a good distraction. We never looked at the job as life and death."

After his third season at Loyola, Amatucci's commitment to "going to extremes" had the Greyhounds on a roll. Unfortunately, Amatucci was about to realize that considering "going to extremes" as an absolute can have negative consequences—especially when dealing with the NCAA Committee on Infractions. To be continued....

10

BEING CLOSE ONLY COUNTS IN HORSESHOES

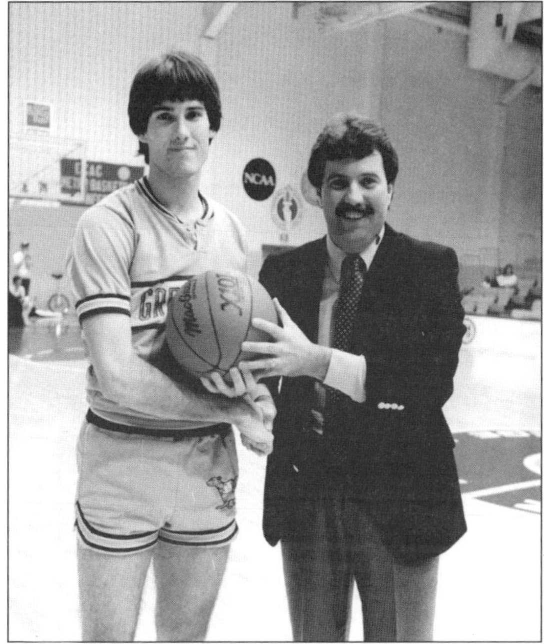

David Gately and Tooch.

"They just keep coming back this year. People counted us out twice and they responded once again. They are a great bunch of overachievers that work their butts off. In the big picture, that is what matters most. These guys are winners."

\- MARK AMATUCCI

Loyola had ten returning players for the 1985-86 season. The team suffered a setback with the loss of Glenn Rogers, who left because of academic reasons. Rogers was a powerful, 6-foot-7 forward who gave the Greyhounds an effective inside presence. "That was as big of a blow that you could have at that time because he had an entire year of experience. We were expecting it to be a break out year for him," Amatucci said.

The departure of coaches Reif, Misotti, and Nix was another distraction to the anticipated smooth start for the year. Defensive guru Reif moved out of the area. Misotti left to fulfill the obligations of his full-time job. Nix left to take a job at the Xavier University. Nix was replaced by Rich Zvosec, who later coached at University of Missouri–Kansas City, Millersville (Pennsylvania) University, North Florida and St. Francis (N.Y.) College. Amatucci also hired Mike Edwards as the part-time assistant coach. Edwards had been a head coach at Towson Catholic High School and Dundalk Community College and became one of Amatucci's best friends.

"Despite these distractions, we are hitting our prime now," Amatucci recalled. "Coming into that season, we were confident that we could win the league and make the NCAA tournament. We are solid, confident and experienced on both ends of the court. I'm thinking this is our year to put it all together. The Hounds had earned respect within and outside the conference."

All five starters—Reveley, Gately, Gormley, Carter, and Lee—returned and would be playing their third year together. Key reserves Pop Tubman, Brad Meyers and Vernon Hill were starting their second year with the team. Highly recruited Mike Morrison, a 6-3 shooting guard, and the versatile Jeff "Goose" Nattans from Calvert Hall were expected to make an immediate impact.

Nattans was a different type of student-athlete because he played both basketball and soccer. He performed at a high level in both sports while also carrying a 4.0 grade point average. One of Nattans' goals growing up was to play two Division I sports, and he succeeded. Both soccer coach Bill Sento and Amatucci were open to the idea, and Nattans rewarded them for the confidence.

"I am extremely grateful to Coach Tooch and Coach Sento for believing in me and giving me this incredible opportunity, because many others schools that recruited me told me I would have to pick one sport," said Nattans, who is head of mergers and acquisitions and business development at the investment firm of Legg Mason. "The Loyola Athletic Department provided excellent academic resources and structure consistent with the Jesuit mission and commitment to educating the whole person. My professors were also willing to work with me. Both basketball and soccer coaches would monitor your grades and your attendance."

"The basketball team also had mandatory study hall for two hours a day on Sunday through Thursday," Nattans noted. "In classic Coach Tooch fashion, if you missed a study hall, you were 'on the baseline' to do extra conditioning at the next practice. He made it very clear that you did not want to miss study hall. Tooch's goal was for his players to learn how to set priorities, utilize time management and develop a strong work ethic—all valuable life lessons that I benefit from using every day."

The Greyhounds showed their experience in the opener with a convincing 71-53 victory over Division III Dickinson College. Coming off the strong win over Dickinson, the Hounds were ready for their Reitz Arena league opener versus the always tough St. Francis (Pa.) Red Flash. The student "Dog Pound" section was treated to a physical, back and forth game with the outcome not decided until the final minute. Loyola pulled out the victory for its second win of the season.

Not only was the team winning, the infrastructure of the overall program was stronger.

Amatucci finally had the program on par with other Division I schools as far as academic resources, travel planning, and player development. The Hounds were consistently receiving as much media coverage as the big boys from Maryland and Navy. Progress was also evident on the court.

The practices were intense as ever.

"We would practice for four hours, and back in those days, you had no time limits," Zvosec said. "Of course, there would be no water breaks. You say that nowadays and coaches would get fired for not giving players water. What I found out very early was that I would be on the sidelines and Tooch would be subbing guys in and out. The guys would come to me and ask if they could go to the bathroom. I said, 'Go ahead, just hurry up.' They were going out to the hallway to sneak a drink. They thought that Tooch didn't know that. He did, but he was not going to bend his rule of no water jugs because he thought it made them tougher."

In his own defense, Amatucci commented, "We wanted practices to be high intensity and extremely competitive start to finish. Extended group stretching and team water breaks kill the momentum of the workout. Practicing our way developed mental toughness and physical stamina. Basketball-wise it created game-like focus. In reality, I was paying attention. If I thought somebody needed a break, I subbed him out for a breather. As far as needing water at practice, I would tell them, "You gotta be a camel.'"

Prior to Christmas, Loyola traveled to DeLand, Florida, for the Hatter Classic, a competitive tournament that included challenging match ups for the Hounds. The Hounds clicked on all cylinders in the tourney opener, running past Hardin-Simmons University, 89-73. No contest. The Cowboys took Loyola lightly and were not prepared for the full-court pressure. The Hounds dominated the entire game, showing off their lightning quick transition game and smothering full-court defense.

In the finals, the Hounds faced a strong Stetson team on its home court. Amatucci quipped, "I was feeling a little anxious about the welcoming we would get in the finals from the gentlemen in the striped shirts. The Hatters rarely lost on their home court, and if it was going be seven on five we were in trouble."

A fired-up Greyhound five again played two complete halves and stunned Stetson, 69-62, to win the tournament championship. Loyola's strong performance in the early season led opponents to re-work their game plans.

"Teams tried to get smarter when they played us," Amatucci said. "They would attempt to take us out of our transition game by sitting in a half-court zone. With our lack of size, their plan was to take away our inside game and force us to beat them from the perimeter. What I had to do was get away from a traditional zone offensive attack—perimeter passing to stationary shooters. What I created was a lot of motion in our zone offense to free up our strengths, which were getting Gately open anywhere we could or getting Aubrey, Morrison, and Gorms free off of back screens. Once we were able to get our perimeter game going, that would open up an inside presence."

The Greyhounds also utilized 6-foot-7 forward Brad Meyers, who had consistent three-point range. "He wasn't overly physical, but he was an effective threat in the zone offense," Amatucci said. "Kevin, 'EZ,' and 'Joe' unselfishly set solid screens which opened up a number of perimeter options." A week after the tourney championship, Stetson coach Glen Wilkes payed Amatucci a big compliment by calling him and asking him to share the zone offense that took down the Hatters.

After winning the tournament, players and coaches went their separate ways. Zvosec organized a meal for the coaches at one of DeLand's finest restaurants. The owner congratulated the coaches by picking up their tab. The players were on a twelve o'clock curfew and had been warned by Amatucci not to get into any trouble. Later that evening, the players all congregated in Amatucci's room and the hotel manager knocked on the door when the gathering got too loud. The players hid in the bathroom while Amatucci dealt with the manager.

"It was really neat," Amatucci remembered. "Why would players want to go to hang out in the coach's room? But, they did. It was a great night to celebrate with our hoop family. I'm thinking if we consistently keep the intensity at this level we are going to do some serious damage. Still undefeated."

The Greyhounds returned home and disappointed Amatucci with a flat performance, losing 69-62 to their nemesis Delaware. Frustrations boiled over when Loyola center Tommy Lee went after a Blue Hens player in the tunnel after the game and tumbled down the stairs. "I was really pissed off and the kids were too," Amatucci said about the loss.

Still fuming from the Delaware loss, Amatucci and his squad travelled to California to face the USC Trojans. Relying on Coach Zvosec's regularly dependable scouting report, Amatucci did not expect to see any zone defense, but that is exactly what USC had implemented. Their strategy was effective. The Hounds had to waste an early timeout to get organized, but found themselves down by 21-points at half-time. Loyola finally made the proper adjustments and started playing its brand of basketball by turning up the pressure. The Hounds eventually cut the lead to ten, now forcing USC's Coach Stan Morrison to use a timeout. Morrison's adjustments proved successful as time ran out on the comeback and Loyola lost, 89-79. In Amatucci's post game comments he lamented the fact that it took the Hounds an entire half to make effective adjustments to the Trojans' strategy.

"You can't win many games going down 21 in the first half. There was no consistent effort on either end of the floor," he said.

Displaying the emotion and intensity Amatucci expected, the Greyhounds then pushed Rutgers deep into the second half in an 82-74 setback. Once again, Loyola struggled against the Scarlet Knights 3-2 zone and was hampered by missing one-and-one free throws. Late in the second half with the game's outcome still on the line, Kevin Carter missed five free throws in a row, sealing the game for Rutgers. The Hounds were developing a bad habit of letting golden opportunities get away from them.

After beating a very talented Drexel five, the Greyhounds endured the hardest stretch of the year. The team lost to Wagner, 65-63, on the road. The Seahawks were led by Terrence Bailey, the leading scorer in the nation. Making matters worse, Loyola's bus got stuck in a snow drift after the game, and the team had to wait an hour for a replacement. The already gloomy mood on the bus was only exacerbated by the wait.

Two days later, the Greyhounds were unable to stop their slide and fell, 67-57, at Fairleigh Dickinson. The only bright spot was Gately's 26 points, taking him over 1,000 points for his career in less than three full seasons. However, the losing streak was a huge disappointment. The focus and leadership the Hounds desperately needed from the veterans was nonexistent.

"Driving up I-95, I'm thinking we are going to win those two games," Amatucci said. "If we are going to win the conference, that is an absolute. It was a bad weekend and a worse trip home." On their return to Baltimore, Amatucci called a late-night coaches meeting to identify what needed to be done to get the Hounds playing to the level they were capable of. It was a long meeting.

The Hounds bounced back with a pair of decisive wins over Long Island and St. Francis (N.Y.). Gormley surpassed 1,000 points for his career in the victory over St. Francis. Loyola demonstrated renewed vigor winning six of eight games to end the regular season at 15-11. A loss to long-time rival Mount St. Mary's took some luster off of the late season wins. The Mountaineers were led by Jim Phelan, one of the all-time winningest coaches in NCAA history.

"Jimmy Phelan was just a great coach," Amatucci said. "They were comparable to a mid-major Division I program. Losses to the Mount were always hard, especially for the basketball alumni."

Amatucci was confident his team still had the talent and depth to win the ECAC conference title and advance to the NCAA tournament. The talented and reliable backcourt of the Hounds created matchup problems throughout much of the season. The passing and leadership of Tubman, Gately's offensive versatility, Gormley's quickness to the hoop and consistent jump shot, Morrison's size and power and Reveley's ability to create off the ball gave their defenders all they could handle. In addition, Loyola was wearing teams down because the Greyhound players had the stamina to go hard for forty minutes. Amatucci boasted, "Intensity until the final buzzer is the reward earned from countless hours of high-powered practice. Nobody outworked us. Nobody."

Some of the success during the latter part of the regular season provided the Hounds with momentum heading into the opening round of the conference tournament game against host Robert Morris. Loyola had beaten the Colonials twice during the regular season, but knocking them off a third time on their court would not be an easy task. Nonetheless, Amatucci was looking ahead to playing Marist for the title and for a spot in the NCAA tournament.

Robert Morris implemented an unexpected twist to their game plan in the second half. Coach Jarrett Durham used a box-and-one defense against Gately, the Hound's leading scorer, to stymie Loyola's flex offense. Amatucci was caught off-guard by the strategy. The Greyhounds players had not seen that type of defense all season, and they struggled to adjust.

Amatucci remembered, "We had to call a timeout. I calmly told them to be patient. We would run our flex offense and keep Gates on the block to set back screens and then find an open spot in the paint to catch and score."

Despite struggling against the box-and-one, Loyola was in position to win the game. Gately uncharacteristically missed the back end of a one-and-one in the final seconds that forced an extra period with the score tied 60-60. "After I made the first one to tie it, I felt okay," Gately said after the game. "Usually, that's the tough part. Then in overtime, I missed all of those jump shots. I started pressing, lost my confidence, and was forcing shots."

In overtime, Robert Morris junior Ron Winbush set the tone with a pair of perimeter jumpers that provided a 68-64 lead. Carter managed to make the front end of one-and-one to pull Loyola to within 71-69 with thirty seconds remaining. However, he missed the second shot, and Gately was forced to foul Mike Brunson, who converted both free throws. Robert Morris held on for the 75-69 upset.

For the second year in a row the Loyola players and coaches were devastated. They could not believe the season had such a sour ending. Expectations were not meeting reality. Talent, spirit, effort, attitude were all there, but they couldn't get over the hump. There was no satisfaction in being close.

"I get emotional win or lose," Amatucci said. "But after that game, I went back to the hotel and stood in the shower and replayed the game over and over. The onus was on me. I didn't have us ready to play. I was looking ahead. We were not ready for the box-and-one. We had loyal fans that did not bother attending the game because they were anticipating travelling up for the semifinals and championship game. Instead, we were getting on the bus the next morning and heading south."

The first order of business for Amatucci and Zvosec when they returned home was to implement a new offense to counter the box-and-one. Amatucci ensured that debacle would never happen again.

As the Greyhounds headed into the 1986-1987 season, Amatucci was focused on more than practice planning. There would be a huge void when the talented group of seniors graduated the next June. Amatucci was also dealing with roster issues in the present. Brad Meyers transferred for reasons Amatucci was never able to ascertain. Glenn Rogers had left the previous year. Perhaps, the biggest blow arrived when Vernon Hill left school for personal reasons. It was as if dark clouds were beginning to form over the program.

"It was tough when Tooch and I met back up at Loyola," Hill said. "At the college level, you have to operate differently with the players and all of the politics. He had made that adjustment, but I still saw him as Tooch from Calvert Hall and the relationship we had in the past. We would clash sometimes.

"The biggest thing for me was I didn't know how to lose," Hill explained. "People used to patronize us telling us we played real well, like we used to do to our opponents when I was at Calvert Hall. I lost more games as a freshman than I lost in three years of high school. I was used to playing in front of big crowds. It was a lot of things that I wasn't used to that kind of wore on me. I also had to deal with the personal issues with my mom, who passed away after the end of my freshman year. Going into my sophomore year, I didn't really want to be at Loyola. It was a rough time for me. Tooch did everything he could to support me through that difficult time. That's the reason why we have such a strong friendship to this very day."

To offset the losses, Zvosec and Edwards aggressively recruited high-caliber players. They were able to land Marquis Hamwright from New Jersey, and Derek Campbell, a stout defensive player from Bishop McNamara in D.C. Both played hard with enthusiastic attitudes. Amatucci also nabbed Byron Allmond from Mackin.

Amatucci and Reif traveled to Toronto to recruit Mark Kovinsky, a 6-foot-7 player who had three-point range. For the home visit, they arrived at 10 a.m. and were promptly offered a beer from Kovinsky's father. Amatucci and Reif shortly sealed the deal to land Kovinsky. Amatucci remembered, "Doc and I spent the rest of the afternoon and evening actively enjoying the sites of Toronto. It was one of our better road trips."

"We still didn't have that blue-chip guy," Amatucci said. "We're consistently neck-and-neck with the mid-majors. I honestly didn't think anyone was out-recruiting us in town with the exception of Maryland and Navy. However, we were not getting that game-changing player. It was frustrating. "

The 1986-87 season started on a high note with a 74-70 victory over Penn State. Loyola trailed by eight points at the break. Amatucci recalled, "At the half, I told the guys to be patient, they cannot handle the pressure, stay with the game plan." The Greyhounds were then able to take over the second half with their signature, fast-paced pressure game, forcing twelve turnovers that they turned into 30 points. "Sometime we looked like we were running in mud," lamented Penn State head coach, Bruce Parkhill, "Loyola played exceptional defense, and they stuck it to us all afternoon. Their strength was that defense." Sophomore Mike

Morrison led the Greyhounds with 20 points, while Hamwright scored nine of his 10 points in the final six minutes off the bench. It was a signature win against a high-profile opponent.

"This one has to rank right at the top, especially on the road and beating a school with the tradition Penn State has," Gormley said after the game. "This one has to really help us." We went to Notre Dame and USC, got close, but could not finish. But this time around, our experience was the deciding factor."

Loyola then took down St. Francis (Pa.), 96-84. The game was marred by an altercation between the coaches. St. Francis coach Kevin Porter and others carried a grudge against Amatucci because he had talked about leaving the ECAC for the Metro Atlantic Athletic Conference. Amatucci took some extra satisfaction in the lopsided result that night. "What's wrong with wanting to move up?" Amatucci thought at the time. "Mind your own business."

From there, the Greyhounds hit a tough stretch.

Towson finally got a measure of revenge with a 98-82 victory at Reitz Arena. After the game, Pam Truax walked into the post-game interview room and said, "I'm looking for Baltimore's best coach," alluding to her husband, Terry Truax, who had taken umbrage about Amatucci's earlier comments about being Baltimore's team.

"If Loyola wants to be Baltimore's team, they can have the title," Terry Truax said after the game. "I'll just settle for being an improved team."

Amatucci remembered, "Terry was really insecure about the success our program was having. He had a fixation about us. With this win, which he greatly enjoyed, he was still 1-5 against the Hounds."

The Greyhounds were not ready for the game. Some of the players were looking ahead to the team's upcoming trip to California. Following the loss, Gormley approached Amatucci and asked him why he was so quiet during the game. Amatucci responded, "I had purposely coached that way because I wanted the seniors to assume bigger leadership roles." Gormley countered that the players, however, fed off of Amatucci's energy and intensity and that they needed him to get back to being his animated self on the sideline.

Feeling the performance against Towson was more about player preparation than coaching style, Amatucci held a no-ball practice the following day. The players regretted their performance against Towson. Amatucci even had a timed duck walk, where the players assumed a squatting position while walking forward in a low stance. Gately was the first player to vomit, followed by several others. To add to the misery, Reif arrived and the team practiced defense for sixty consecutive minutes, no water, no rest.

The season got worse when the Greyhounds arrived on the West Coast. They were manhandled by the University of San Diego, 87-60, in their first game. "They played our style offensively and defensively." Amatucci said. "They ran up and down the floor. They dove on the floor. They took charges. They beat the living hell out of us. There were a lot of bad losses in my time, but that one was the worst. I asked myself, 'What the hell am I going to do now?'"

Amatucci decided not to berate the team. However, he made it clear to the players that he was not going to accept being embarrassed like that again. He took away the players' free time and told them they needed to meet among themselves to straighten things out. The next game against Loyola Marymount was not going to be any easier.

The same problems began to surface again.

During the warmup for the Marymount game, Amatucci was infuriated by the team's lackluster effort. Amatucci responded by banishing the entire team back to the locker room with twelve minutes left in the warmups. "If you're not sweating during warm ups, you're not playing" was one of Amatucci's absolutes. Back in the locker room, after a few pointed comments. Amatucci stormed out. The Hounds returned to the court with just a minute prior to the start of the game. The players managed to shake off the poor pregame and make it a contest.

Loyola Marymount, coached by the notable Paul Westhead, played a run and gun offense called "The System." Westhead had been a college and NBA head coach prior to coming to Marymount. The Hounds were not intimidated by the up tempo play and led the Lions late in the game, 98-97, with under a minute to play. The Lions managed to escape with a 103-98 victory.

"There are no moral victories," Amatucci said about the possible upset. "I would have loved to have said I was happy with that performance, but I wasn't. Close only counts in horseshoes. For three straight games, I had put extra effort to motivate the team. Things were not looking good. It was a long flight back East."

The Greyhounds returned home and breezed past Wagner, 95-80. However, the game was followed by a disappointing 78-53 loss to Fairleigh Dickinson. Once again, the Knights were able to control the game because of their physical, inside presence. The downturn continued when Gately missed a shot that would have put the Hounds up by four leading to a 72-70 loss to Bucknell, which went to the NCAA tournament that season. This was followed by a discouraging 83-78 setback to Long Island.

Loyola had lost six of seven games and the season was spiraling downward. "The players were not responding to me," Amatucci said. "We're in trouble."

The frustration boiled over in a 75-57 win over Robert Morris. Amatucci was assessed three consecutive technical fouls by referee Mark Moser just 4:40 into the game. The first came when Amatucci protested a touch foul against Lee. He was then given a second technical foul when he loudly asked why he couldn't get a further explanation on Lee's foul. Moser quickly assessed Amatucci a third technical foul, resulting in an automatic ejection. An incredulous Amatucci became irate and had to be restrained. He was escorted back to the locker room by five of his players. Coach Zvosec and Coach Edwards took charge of the team and the players responded to the challenge and played one of their best games of the year. Amatucci recalled, "I was incredibly proud of the guys. Unintentionally, it was the spark we needed to get us going."

Amatucci was given a simple reprimand by ECAC commissioner Frank Szymanski, who said: "Mark Amatucci has had an excellent record with officials. There was no indication of past problems of this sort. He has already apologized to the officials, so as far as we are concerned, the matter is closed."

Years later, Amatucci admitted he might have gotten off a little easy: "It helped having Frank Szymanski as the commissioner. He and Tom O'Connor were good friends."

Amatucci traveled back to Calvert Hall following the win over the Colonials to get advice from his mentor, Coach Binder. Amatucci was worried about losing the team just as he did during his first year as the coach for the Cardinals. Binder suggested backing off. He told Amatucci to clearly define the team's goals and share with each player his expectations for that player.

"Don't let your emotions get out of control in practice. Avoid the no ball practice," Binder told him. "Work on what you need to do to make the team better. Focus on the next game. Make it clear what you expect and leave it at that."

Amatucci followed his advice. However, there were still challenges that were becoming too big to overcome.

"I think the expectations were really high, especially after the Penn State game," Amatucci said. "Realistically, the personnel losses were catching up to us, including a season ending injury to Marcus Hamwright. You lose three quality returning players who would have been our first three guys off the bench, and it's tough to overcome. Basically, we were relying on six guys—Pop, Gorms, Gates, Tommy Lee, Mike Morrison, and Aubrey Reveley. We would give Goose and Robert Tucker, a transfer from the University of Richmond, a run and try to get some help from the freshmen Campbell and Allmond. It was at this point of the season that I began to believe the seniors were starting to tune me out." Amatucci added, "The seniors had accomplished a lot on the court and for the program but had hit a wall. The challenges, personnel issues, and disappointments were taking their toll on the players, the team and their coach."

After a 59-55 loss to Marist, the Greyhounds rolled past Monmouth, 94-81. That was followed by another disappointing 84-83 loss to Mount St. Mary's. This time, Loyola went on a 23-6 run to take a 79-74 lead with 3:36 left in the game. The Mountaineers recovered, and a key basket by former Amatucci pupil Paul Edwards provided the Mounties with an 84-81 lead with 1:24 remaining. Tubman answered for Loyola with a jumper to pull within one. The Greyhounds had two chances to win the game in the final fourteen seconds, but a pair of shots by Morrison clanked off the rim and time expired.

From there, Loyola won four consecutive games over Monmouth, St. Francis (N.Y.), Robert Morris and St. Francis (Pa.). However, that run was followed by four straight losses to Richmond, Marist, Wagner and a Seton Hall team that was coached by P.J. Carlesimo. The Greyhounds cut a 17-point deficit to four in the second half against the Pirates. However, the rally ended with a 92-85 loss. The game was played at an ice rink called South Mountain Arena because Seton Hall's basketball court was being renovated. Amatucci was underwhelmed by the venue. Carlesimo was impressed with the Greyhounds.

"They upped the defensive pressure, and we couldn't handle it," Carlesimo said after the game. "If they had big people, we'd have been in trouble. Honestly, they outplayed us, but usually talent wins out."

Amatucci did not take any solace in the close defeat. He noticed the players were also getting physically tired. "Trying to be positive heading into the league tourney, Amatucci told the team, "Anybody can win this thing."

The Greyhounds recovered with another four-game winning streak against Long Island, St. Francis (N.Y.), Monmouth and Winthrop. However, the regular season ended with a solid whooping, 78-58, by the Knights of Fairleigh Dickinson. Amatucci recalled, "I was starting to believe we would never beat FDU. No matter what we did, nothing worked."

The Hounds regrouped for the ECAC tournament and knocked off St. Francis (Pa.), 77-69, in the first round. Before the game, St. Francis coach Kevin Porter's commented that his team could not win the game. The highly competitive Amatucci found Porter's statement to be humorous. Amatucci says, "I said to coach Z and coach Mike, is this guy for real." The victory set up another meeting with Fairleigh Dickinson in the semifinals, which was not an opponent the Hounds were looking forward to facing.

The St. Francis game was the last home game for the seniors. Reveley commented to The Baltimore Sun, "It just really hit me when I was sitting alone up there (after scoring a career high 30 points). It will all be over in a few weeks."

"I don't think the guys thought they could beat Fairleigh Dickinson, especially when you lose by twenty the week before," Amatucci said. "We lost 78-53 the first time we played them. I did not have a good feeling going in to it. A feeling I was unaccustomed to."

Indeed, the Knights starting five put together a dominant 75-50 victory, ending the careers of Loyola's seniors—Gately, Gormley, Lee, Reveley, and Tubman. That group had managed three straight seasons with sixteen wins and won fifteen more games in their final year playing a tough schedule that featured some of the nation's top programs. Gately scored more than 1,600 points; Gormley more than 1,400 points; Reveley more than 1,200 points; Lee played in all 112 games during his career and finished with 781 points and close to 600 rebounds; and Tubman had more than 100 assists in each of his final two years. Except for a brief time apart, Amatucci and Tubman had been together for eight years and 169 games, with 126 of those games being victories. Sue Reimer of The Baltimore Sun wrote, "There will always be a special bond between a coach and his point guard."

"If those kids did not know how much Tooch cared about them, they would have bolted," Zvosec said. "They would have just laid down in practice. But they didn't. The one thing they all understood was how much he cared for them."

Amatucci was numb, and he didn't have much to say to the players in the locker room after the game. He remembered the bus ride being "silent as a morgue" during the long ride back to Baltimore.

It was the end of an era.

"It was a sad night. It was our last game ever," Gately recalled. "I remember sitting in the locker room, and a couple of other guys and I were crying. When you put so much into something and you know it's over, that hurts, especially playing for Tooch. I loved it. We butted heads because we both wanted to win. But he would let you speak your mind. That's why he was great for our group. We were outspoken and we told him what we thought. We all loved playing for him."

Amatucci lamented, "The next couple of months were difficult ones. Separation anxiety set in. Pop, Aubs, EZ, Gates, and Gorms had become the cornerstone of the program. I deliberately avoided dealing with the fact they were graduating and moving on to their next life challenges. As with our Calvert Hall group moving on after the 1982 season, I felt like a father coming to the realization that his sons would be leaving the nest. It was a bittersweet reality. Together as a family we had accomplished so much more than anyone connected with Loyola could have expected."

Adding to Amatucci's melancholy mood, after three years the issues with the NCAA were coming to a head.

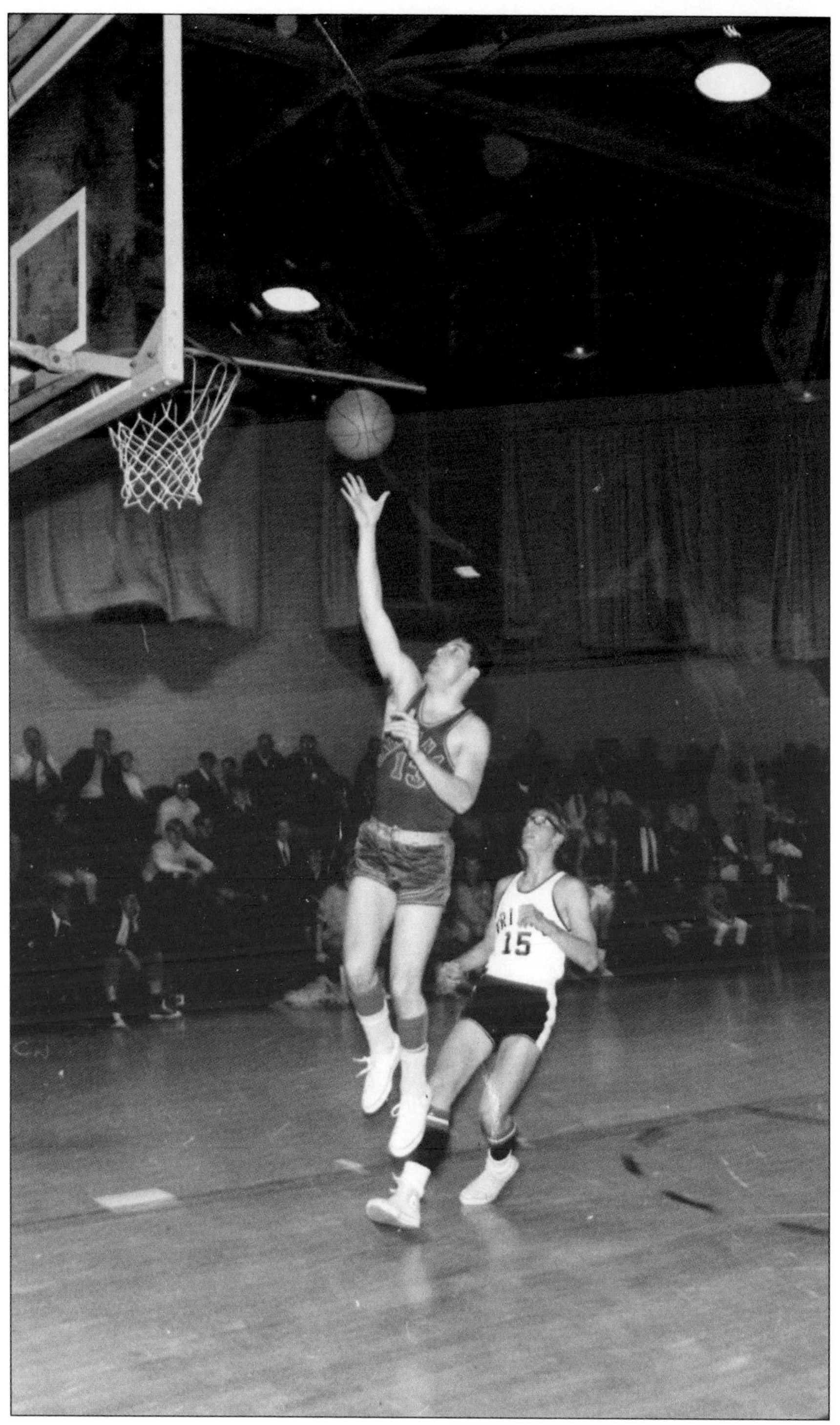

Tooch going to the hoop.

Tooch's first varsity squad – 1977-1978 Cardinals

Marc "Money" Wilson finishing the famous Calvert Hall fast break.

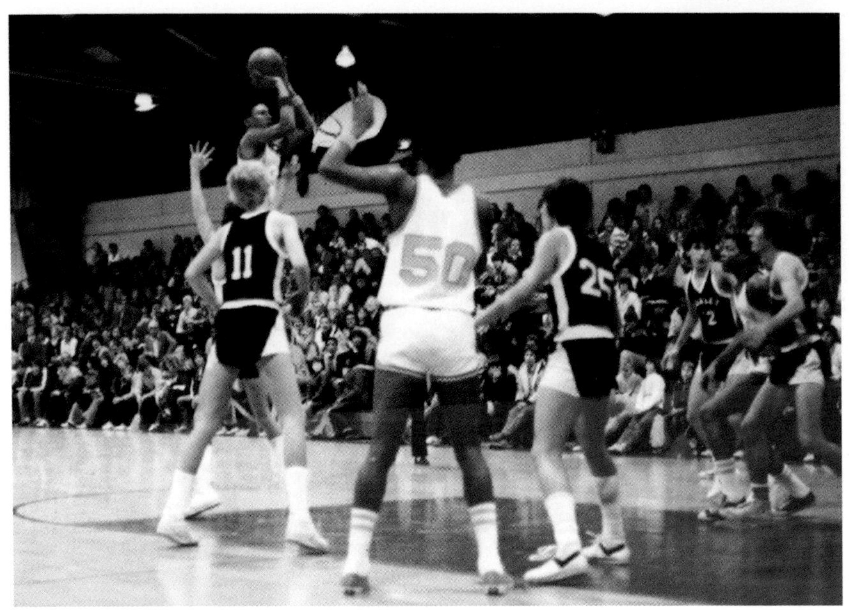

Darryle Edwards rising with the J versus Archbishop Curley. His brother Paul hopeful for the pass that is not to be.

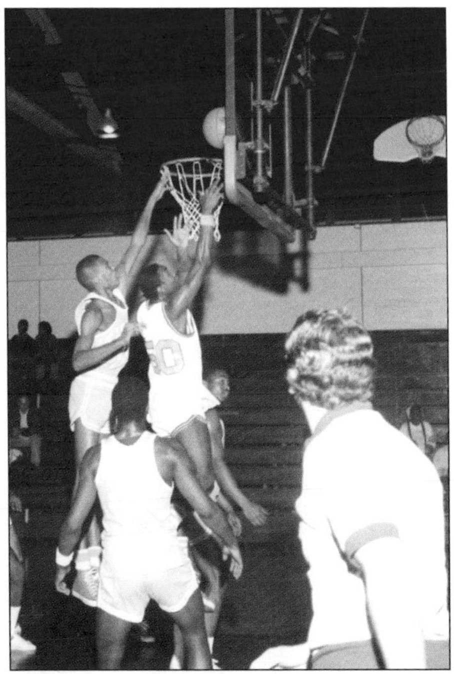

Paul "LP" Edwards III always tough on the glass. He made a living off other player's misses at both ends of the court.

Duane Ferrell and Marc Wilson (kneeling) in a All Metro team photo.

Huddling up for some wisdom from Tooch.

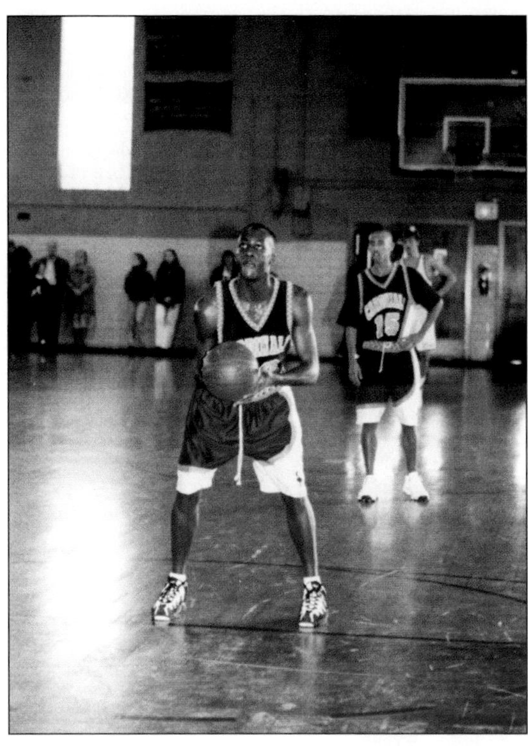

Delbert Randall finishing a three-point play versus Loyola.

Juan showing his stuff converting a steal.

Calvin Wise dunks for St. Mary's College.

Tommy Rose's Wedding Reception –
Vince, Del, Tooch, Tommy, Tavar, and Jon.

1982 Pepsi Challenge, The Spectrum, Philadelphia, PA, championship medal. The Cards took down national power Camden, featuring Billy Thompson and Kevin Walls, in the final.

"Team for the ages"
Original artwork by Stephen Morton.

The Amatucci Family –
Michael, Stephanie, Jamie, Pat, Tooch, Jacquelyn and Dennis

Mom (Pat) and the girls all smiles at the Tooch court dedication.

Jackie and Dennis' rehearsal dinner at Jerry D's Saloon.

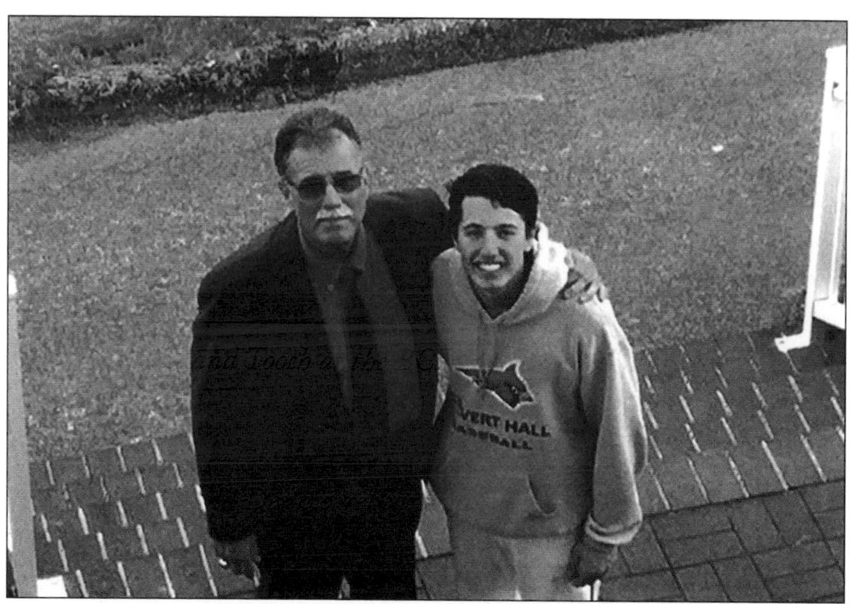

Mike and Tooch at the BCL Hall of Fame dinner.

Tooch and Mike, two proud Hall grads –
Mike's graduation June, 2015.

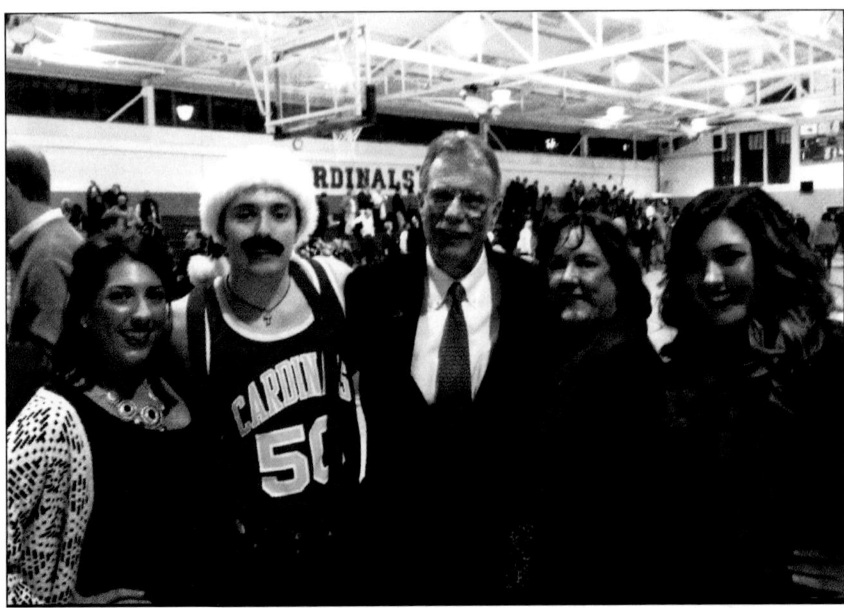

The Amatucci family enjoying the moment – Tooch Court dedication.

"Tooch and Kitty"

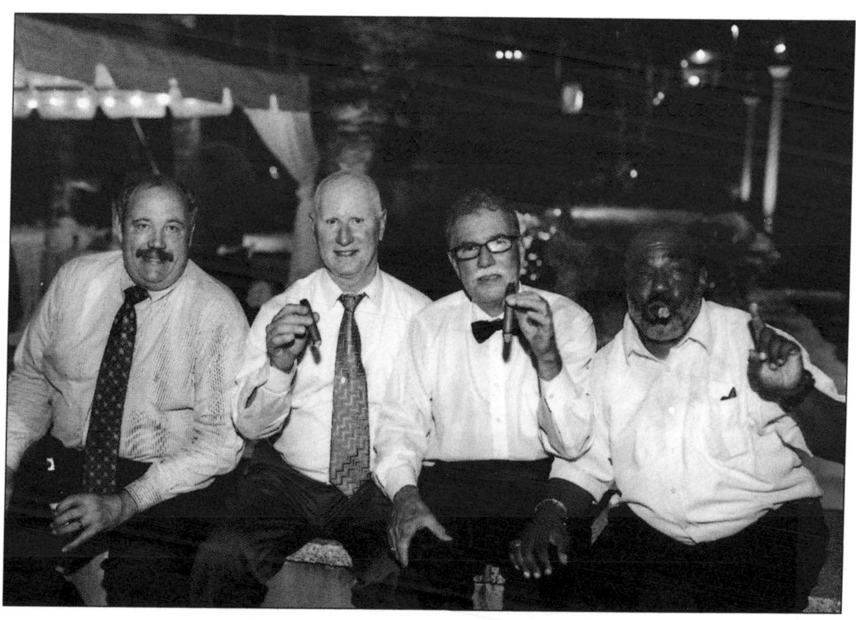

Baker, Eckerl, Amatucci and Rodgers celebrating Stephanie and Jamie's wedding.

25th reunion of the National Championship team.

The Cardinals' coaching staff reunion at Tooch's court dedication. Recreating a classic picture from the 80's.

The Cardinals' coaching family celebrates Tooch's Hall of Fame induction.

Three BCL Hall of Famers – Paul Edwards III, Mark Amatucci and Marc Wilson

Hoop alumni Steve Morton captures Tooch in action.

WEIGHING THE SCALES OF JUSTICE

Tom Gormley and Tommy Lee celebrating their Loyola College graduation.

"Looking back on it and if I was a little bit smarter or wiser, I probably would have been more contrite. Back then, I wasn't going to back down."

- MARK AMATUCCI

For three years, Amatucci had to deal with potential NCAA sanctions hanging over the program. These infractions stemmed from the summer after his first season as the head coach when he helped organize practices and weightlifting sessions outside the allotted time allowed by the NCAA. All of the returning players and incoming freshmen, Gormley, Reveley, Hicks, and Lee who were taking summer classes, gathered a number of times to practice under the supervision of Steve Misotti, Chris Devlin and Mark Healy. Even though Amatucci was not present at the sessions that took place at Calvert Hall and Loch Raven Elementary School, it was still against the NCAA's regulations.

"I sat down with Pat Dennis and we talked about what we were going to do in the off season, especially since we were going to have the entire incoming class here," Amatucci remembers. "Pat made some suggestions on what we should do as in terms of playing and lifting. Obviously, under the NCAA rules, you were not allowed to have any interaction with players on the court or in the weight room."

"In my mind, I planned on having the players practice. I wanted to have somebody there to supervise the workouts because I didn't trust having them do this on their own. I didn't want unproductive, half-assed sessions. I naively or subconsciously blocked out that these sessions would be a rules problem because I was not actually watching them or giving instruction."

While the sessions made a huge difference in the team's performance on the court, they also led to an NCAA investigation as a result of a complaint filed by a former player in 1984.

The investigation identified several other potential infractions:

Amatucci loaned some of the players $25 during summer school in 1983 for groceries because the dining hall was closed.

Amatucci loaned players other small amounts of money, ranging from fifty cents to $5.

A group of players used Amatucci's credit cart to rent a car to travel home. They had given Amatucci cash up front for the payment.

Amatucci allowed Tommy Lee to borrow his car in order to get to tutoring sessions.

The NCAA sent a letter to O'Connor about the pending investigation. The NCAA sent representatives to the Loyola campus to conduct interviews with the players and coaches. By May 1986, the NCAA finally held a formal hearing on the violations at its offices in Scottsdale, Arizona. Amatucci attended the meetings with his attorney as did O'Connor and counsel for Loyola. At this time, Loyola had distanced itself from Amatucci and was ready to deal with the potential infractions independently. LSU and Texas El-Paso also had hearings in the same office that day involving their potential violations.

"Why it took three years, I don't know," Amatucci said. "I guess it took them that long to decide whether it was worth pursuing. It was a tough time."

Amatucci did not like being characterized as a cheater. He was prepared to defend his actions. Amatucci was confident the NCAA would take into account he was a 29-year-old coach that made a novice mistake. The other programs having a hearing that day were accused of much more severe infractions. He believed Loyola's mistakes were minor in comparison.

"At the end of the day, I didn't appreciate the way the committee was addressing me," Amatucci said. "I felt like they were talking down to me. If it had been Jim Boeheim or Jerry Tarkanian, they would have used a different tone. It was something I resented."

On May 30, 1986, the NCAA initially rendered a mild reprimand for the infractions. Loyola was placed on one-year probation without sanctions. This meant the Greyhounds were allowed to participate in the NCAA tournament and did not lose any scholarships.

Surprisingly, two months later, the committee decided to increase the penalties. Amatucci is convinced the NCAA made him pay for his arrogance. This time, the NCAA Committee on Infractions changed the conditions of the probation.

"The committee determined that the penalty in this case is meaningful and appropriate in that it affects the college's head coach, who was directly involved in the violations," Frank Remington, chairman of the infractions committee, said at the time. As a result, Amatucci also could not recruit for an entire year. Loyola was required to develop a "rules-education program" for the athletic staff.

"When it came time for me to comment I believe the committee was looking for me to be apologetic and repentant, Amatucci said. "Looking back, if I was a little bit smarter or wiser, I probably would have been more contrite. Back then I wasn't going to back down."

The decision had a destructive impact on the program. The team was already losing a talented group of seniors the following year. Hill, Rogers, and Meyers had already left the program, leaving a huge void. The Hounds were going to be gutted for the 1987-88 season. Amatucci being confined to campus was devastating for recruiting.

Zvosec and Edwards were forced to do most of the recruiting with Amatucci dealing with the sanctions. The two of them had some initial success. The Greyhounds were able to land a key player, Tracy Bergen of DeMatha, who decided not to enroll because of personal reasons. Bergen later enrolled at Loyola and played under Skip Prosser.

"If Tracy Bergen plays, it's night and day, because you're replacing Gormley with a kid out of DeMatha that had the same potential," Amatucci said. "Losing him hit me right in the gut. The recruiting had gotten more difficult because of the sanctions, and we were losing athletic director Tom O'Connor, who had accepted the position of athletic director at Santa Clara University."

The new AD was Tom Brennan, who almost immediately clashed with Amatucci. Amatucci saw Brennan as controlling and hung up on bureaucratic procedures. Brennan did not play collegiate sports, which also did not enamor him to Amatucci. His background was primarily in fundraising. Brennan had a Ph.D. from Syracuse and preferred to be called "Dr. Brennan." Amatucci simply called him "Tom." In an article from the Baltimore Sun, sportswriter Bill Tanton wrote, "When it came to people skills, Brennan couldn't have passed kindergarten. Athletic department members, almost overnight, became unhappy."

"Going from Tom O'Connor to Brennan was a disaster" for him personally, Amatucci said. "But I didn't help things. My reluctance to cooperate did not bode well for my future at Loyola."

Loyola finished the 1987-88 season 8-22, which included losses to Maryland, Hawaii, Santa Clara and San Francisco. The freshmen were not prepared for the rigors of the schedule and the program struggled to recover from that challenging season. The stress surrounding Amatucci continued to build. He scrambled to find answers.

"Mentally, I started to come apart. I could see where this was going," Amatucci admitted. "It started to affect my home life. It was tough on Pat because she got thrown into this without any warning. When we met, I was a high school coach and teacher that didn't lose any games. It's a whole different scenario when you're losing, your job security is dependent on the performance of 18-year-olds, you have outside distractions, and players are injured or leaving the program. Pat didn't know how to deal with that. There was no sense in me coming home right away after a loss because it was going to lead to a battle. That was all on me. It was a hard time for her and the kids."

The team was improved the following year, but lacked the athleticism and depth needed to be successful in Amatucci's aggressive, high-tempo playing style. The Hounds were limited by a slow front court and a back court that was not committed to playing Amatucci's style of defense.

A highlight of the season was the arrival of Dunbar guard Kevin Green, who had the outstanding talent to make an immediate impact. Amatucci said, "Kevin's scoring ability, physicality, and court sense reminded me of Mike Morrison."

"The basketball program had never had a Dunbar kid at that point," Zvosec said. "I'm not even sure the university had a student from Dunbar. Kevin came in and became one of the all-time leading scorers and graduated on time. He is a great ambassador for the program."

The season proved to be a challenging one. The Hounds finished 11-18. Despite the struggles, Nattans said the team never stopped playing hard for their coach. "Coach Tooch was going to push you and your teammates to your limits … and the only way to get through it was to be in it together," Nattans said. "No one could do it successfully on their own. You needed to go through it together as a team and pick each other up. It is an extreme example of a bonding experience. It is like Outward Bound … but for an entire season."

Looking back on that season, Amatucci reflected, "Had there not been so much disruption going on—the NCAA restrictions, the transition in athletic directors, near misses on recruiting, and my stubbornness, this group had the potential to keep the program moving forward."

As the season progressed, Amatucci began to see the writing on the wall and knew his days at Loyola were coming to an end. His frustration and anxiety boiled over several times during the season.

There was a clash with a professor interrupting practice to set up for a film shoot. A dispute over the distribution of NCAA Final Four tickets further eroded the already tenuous relationship between Amatucci and Brennan. On the court, Amatucci was ejected during a frustrating loss to Mount St. Mary's.

Following a four-game road trip late in the season, Brennan called Amatucci into his office and told him the school was going to make a change with the coaching position. Instead of getting angry, Amatucci remembered, "I said OK and ended the discussion. I left, went to PJ's Pub, and even though the future was unclear, I started thinking about my next move. The first item on my list was to meet with the players."

The players took the news hard and responded with two straight wins over St. Francis (N.Y.) and Long Island University at Reitz Arena. The Hounds, though, dropped their final two regular season games on the road.

Amatucci's seven-year reign at Loyola ended with a 79-66 loss to Long Island in the first round of the Northeast Conference Tournament. The players were devastated that they could not send their coach out a winner.

"We have a lot of mixed emotions," Allmond said after the game. "We were out there together playing. Now, it seems like the breakup of the family. It's seems like everyone was kind of waiting and waiting for it. It's over, and it really hurts a lot. We feel very sorry that Coach Amatucci is leaving. Everyone was very upset. Personally, I think he should be the coach."

Amatucci remembered, "It was tough to walk out of Reitz Arena for the last time. Being surrounded by my family and the players took some of the pain way."

Amatucci pondered his next move. His family was concerned about the future. Would they be forced to move? If so, would his girls, Stephanie and Jackie, be able to adjust to new schools. The uncertainty weighed on the family, especially Pat, who was wary of leaving her close-knit family behind.

"It was a very dark, sad time," she said. "He was upset and I was literally scared at that point. We had two daughters. It was a disheartening period because of the time we had spent there and all of the good things we had accomplished. I felt like they just turned their back on us and that was the end. It was all very abrupt."

Even though he was no longer the coach at Loyola, Amatucci continued to stay in contact with Morrison, who was selected in the second round of the 1989 NBA draft by the Phoenix Suns.

"That was the highlight, sitting at home that night and watching him get drafted," Amatucci said.

Morrison had come a long way as a player and student. In his freshman year he lacked stamina and strength. He was once carried from the weight room by his teammates because he had passed out while completing a less than strenuous session. Amatucci remembered telling Gately and Gormley, "Drag his butt out of the weight room." Four years later, he was getting ready to run up and down the court with the best players in the world. It was a dream come true for the Washington, D.C., native.

"I came to college with the goal of playing in the NBA because I went to high school with Len Bias," Morrison said, "I grew up with guys like Len, Johnny Dawkins, Tommy Amaker, Tyrone Jones, who went to UNLV and played in the NBA for a while. I was able to see Adrian Dantley on a regular basis, along with Dereck Whittenburg and Thurl Bailey.

There were a lot of guys from my neighborhood that went onto the pros. We saw that playing in the NBA was a realistic dream."

Morrison was another success story during Amatucci's time at Loyola. He attended Northwestern High in Hyattsville, Maryland, the same school as Len Bias. During his freshman year Morrison struggled with his academics and worked closely with tutor Susan Luchey, who was the academic advisor for the basketball program. Amatucci believed academic support was essential to student success and had enthusiastically lobbied for the creation of the advisor position. Luchey told Amatucci there might be a bigger problem behind Mike's struggles. In response, Amatucci arranged to have Morrison evaluated by local specialist, Dr. Leo Otterbein. The evaluation determined that his processing and focus were impacted by ADHD. From that point on he was given appropriate academic support and accommodations. With his strong work ethic, determination and effective tutoring, Morrison thrived academically and put himself in position to be successful after college.

"When I first got there, I didn't think I could do it," Morrison remembered. "Tooch was able to show me I could, if I was willing to put the work in. He assured me nobody was going to do the work for me. It wasn't going to get done unless I did it. On top of that, all of those NBA dreams I had were going to go right out the window. He put me in position to be successful."

Morrison said Amatucci, Luchey and other academic advisors were willing to work with him even on Saturdays. Morrison was grateful his tutors were willing to put aside valuable family time on weekends to help the players. It was literally the difference between staying at Loyola or having to go elsewhere. Luchey also had a tutoring style that resonated with Morrison and other teammates. She certainly did not do the work for them, but helped them understand the process and closely supervised their work.

"It was one of the best experiences of my life," Morrison said about his time at Loyola. "You learned to understand the important things that allowed you to get your dreams fulfilled. It was a community created by Tooch that was so much more than playing basketball. He was a big part of our lives."

Luchey said it was common practice for Amatucci to take a proactive role in the education of his players. That was a key ingredient for the program's stellar graduation rate.

"We addressed things like time management, goal setting, note taking, reading textbooks, etc.," Luchey said. "I had three tutors who worked under me and we worked with the team members on courses they found difficult. Mark required the guys to attend tutoring sessions and work with us on study skills. He was the driving force and did not really give the guys any choice in the matter."

Each of the players was required to attend a one-hour study period during the day Monday through Friday. There was a two-hour study session supervised by an assistant coach on Sunday through Thursday from 7 p.m. to 9 p.m. All freshmen were required to attend study skills classes one night per week and they were joined by any player with a grade point average lower than 2.5.

"Having those study halls was absolutely, positively necessary," Morrison said. "You had to be somewhere, and there were consequences if you didn't show up. I couldn't go back home to D.C. and just hang out with my friends whenever I felt like it."

Gately and Gormley went from being placed on academic probation to having a 3.0 GPA. Tommy Lee also progressed each semester, eventually earning a 3.4 GPA before graduating.

"Tooch developed trust from the administration and developed trust from the kids," Zvosec said. "When I started at Loyola, the school had stringent admissions requirements with minimum leeway. Most Division I programs had policies that would allow exceptions to admissions requirements. At Loyola, academics came first. Mark proved to the Loyola leadership that student-athletes who did not meet the regular admissions qualifications could be successful at Loyola.

"So, when Mark went in and told the AD that this kid will be successful at Loyola academically, they trusted him. The record speaks for itself," Zvosec added. "Tommy Lee was the first basketball admission exception recruited by Amatucci. He graduated in four years and made the dean's list."

Amatucci expected his players to work just as hard during these study sessions as they did on the court. If they struggled academically, they were not going to play. That was a firm, steadfast rule of the basketball program that was never compromised, regardless of the skill set of the player. Amatucci had even established a study hall when the team was on the road for games. Luchey traveled with the team to conduct these academic sessions.

"On the road, study halls were planned around practice, game and travel times," Luchey said. "I had an infant during part of the time I was in this position, and I frequently brought her on road trips with me if my husband was also traveling. So study hall became quite a family affair."

"For the time, academic advisors for athletics were not a typical position in an athletic department, so as far as being on the cutting edge of something, yes the program was a success. I was new to higher ed at the time, and goodness, if I knew then what I know now about learning styles, leadership, motivation, teaching study skills based on personality types and strengths, it would have been so much better! But the guys knew we had their success as our goal, and they knew they would be held accountable for doing their work and putting time in," she said.

However, Amatucci's interest in academics was not just limited to Loyola. In 1989, there was an uproar about Proposal 42, which would have denied scholarships to freshman athletes who met only part of the standards of Proposition 48. Loyola supported Proposal 42 and Amatucci did not have any issues with the school's stance. However, he said the NCAA needed to adopt more common sense, rather than more rules, when it came to a student's academics and recruiting. There should not be a need for either Proposal 42 or 48, Amatucci contended.

"I don't think it's necessary to have either rule," Amatucci said. "Too many coaches lie to these kids, promise them the moon. Then, you have a kid with an ego as big as a large pizza, adding to the problem. If he doesn't make it in school, then the coaches leave him high and dry."

For Amatucci, it was always about the players and their well-being. He even wrote a commentary for The Evening Sun titled, "College Athletes: They need a support system ...." In this opinion piece, Amatucci lauded the merits of the mandatory study halls for student-athletes. Amatucci contended colleges and universities needed to be more proactive in supporting student-athletes and putting them in position to succeed. He said college coaches must be held accountable if players do not perform as well in the classroom as they do in athletics. Loyola's basketball academic support program was recognized in an NCAA publication. Both the Baltimore Sun and the Baltimore News American published articles highlighting the program.

Amatucci had concrete proof to support his claims. In his first five years at Loyola, the GPA for the Loyola basketball players increased from a 2.2 to a 3.1. Amatucci lauds that milestone and the graduation rate among his players. All of Amatucci's four-year players graduated on time with the exception of Mike Morrison. Following his professional career, Mike completed his degree. Under Amatucci, hoop players with averages above 3.0 and dean's list recognition were the norm not the exception.

Amatucci's players at Loyola are grateful for the stringent requirements he placed on them. The habits they learned at Loyola as far as effort and time management translated into life after school.

"Tooch is a great leader," Nattans said. "He is one those special individuals that gets his team to buy into his vision and then pushes them—kicking and screaming—to the limits. He believes in his players and believes they can accomplish more than they think they can ... through practice, hard work, commitment, accountability and teamwork. We knew that there was no way the other team was going to work as hard as us or had gone through all that we went through to get there. Nobody worked harder than we did."

"He made me a captain my senior year," Nattans said. "It was notable as I was one of the only captains in our league that was not a starter. Coach Tooch is very thoughtful and that was his way, I believe, of rewarding me for my hard work and commitment throughout the journey, and it sent a powerful message to the younger players."

"It was not easy and his methods are a little crazy, but the results speak for themselves. As we get older, we appreciate more and more the impact that he has had on us and the valuable life lessons that he taught us."

Phil Lazzati, who, like Nattans, also played both basketball and soccer, carries a close bond with his Loyola teammates this very day. He has been in three of his teammate's weddings and works professionally with another. Lazzati said the whole experience—the athletic, social and academic aspects—made him realize that "the more you put into something and prepare for something the more successful you become."

Lazzati said: "Playing basketball at Loyola changed me and affected me significantly. It gave me confidence that no matter where you start, you are only at the beginning of your journey or challenge. If you accept your position in life, you will remain there, stuck there. If you choose to be the best, prepare, work hard, and do not place limitations on your ability, you will build confidence and maximize your talent.

"I owe this all to Coach Amatucci. Coach Tooch saw some hidden talent in me and asked me to walk-on when he saw a skinny gym rat shooting hoops alone in Loyola's musty old gym on a gray day in 1983 after soccer practice."

Amatucci had certainly left the Loyola basketball program in better shape than when he arrived. The team received as much media coverage as higher Division I schools such as Maryland and Navy during his tenure. The Hounds were a dynamic story for local readers as the team traveled around the country to take on top-tier opponents. The Hounds also opened Reitz Arena to much fanfare. The students went from wearing bags on their heads to establishing the spirited "Dog Pound" section, giving Loyola a definite home-court advantage. Fans could now anticipate conference championships and potential berths in the NCAA tournament.

Other upgrades included the establishment of a basketball booster club, extending academic offerings into the summer for student-athletes, creating a professional team travel plan for road trips, and better staff resources. Amatucci remembered, "We started out with the bare minimum. We had to rent cars for the assistants to recruit. We only had one full-time assistant and the part-time assistant was being paid less than a high school coach's stipend. Our recruiting budget had little room for overnight stays or even meals while on the road."

Amatucci's seven-year tenure as the head coach is the second longest in the school's Division I history. His team's four-year string of winning fifteen or more games each year has not been equaled. Amatucci ranks third all-time for Loyola's winningest basketball coaches behind Jimmy Patsos (145 wins) and Lefty Reitz (129). Five of Amatucci's players rank among the top ten scorers in school history. Gately, Gormley, Hicks, and Nattans are members of Loyola's Athletic Hall of Fame.

Leaving Loyola at the age of thirty-seven, an age when many Division I head coaches' careers are just beginning, Amatucci was forced to question his legacy. Loyola was an experience that included overcoming challenges, exceeding expectations, and creating new cultures, mixed with poor judgment, disappointing loses, and wavering institutional commitment. Amatucci wondered, "At the end of the day, which way does the scale tip—was my tenure more success or more failure?"

ABSOLUTES

Tooch and "Doc" Reif on the sideline at Loyola.

"I am not afraid of an army of lions led by a sheep; I am afraid of an army of sheep led by a lion."

- ALEXANDER THE GREAT

Amatucci won eighty percent of his games in thirty-two years of coaching. He learned many valuable lessons in his first stint at Calvert Hall and then at Loyola. In 1989, when his time at Loyola ended, Amatucci was able to step back and reflect on his experiences as a coach and teacher. He honed in on the beliefs that were fundamental to his success in building teams and developing players.

Critical to these beliefs are a series of "absolutes"— absolutes which were never debated and were applicable at all levels:

• Don't accept limitations from players. The team must go into every game prepared strategically, physically, and emotionally to win.

By game time, Amatucci's teams never went on the court thinking anything less than, "Let's beat someone's butt."

• Hold players accountable. Personally, academically, and athletically, players were held responsible for their actions. "I told my guys because I love you, I can't turn my head," Amatucci said. "If I turn my head, I am not doing my job. When you're doing something well, I am going to reward you. I am going to make sure you understand that in a positive way. When you're not doing well or what is expected, there are going to be consequences because I'd be letting you and the team down. If you don't go to class you, don't play. If you don't give your maximum effort, you don't play. I don't care who you are. I wasn't hard to figure out."

• Be decisive. Amatucci explained, "Most people don't like being put on the spot. I learned from my dad that in life you have to be direct. If you believed in what you were doing, and you've worked at it and practiced hard, then being decisive is an easy choice. If you can't make decisions, you're always going to be stuck in the middle and continually second-guessing yourself."

• Have a plan. The coach and players must be prepared to effectively attack an opponent and make necessary adjustments. Don't stray from the plan and attempt to make changes on the fly. The plan must reflect the strength of your team. Amatucci referred to his plan as, "The Four Ps – Passion, Practice, Patience, Productivity"

PASSION

Have total commitment, don't take days off; don't cheat the game.

"Passion was the first thing I looked for in a recruit," Amatucci said. "How hard did he play? Did he do the little things? How did he react when his team was down by twenty? For my staff, passion was the most critical of the absolutes. I wanted guys who didn't punch a time clock, loved to teach, challenged me, and who cared about the players."

Joe Baker recalled, "Coaches' meetings could get pretty heated. We had a great staff determined to help our teams be successful. I'd like to say cooler heads always prevailed, but that might not be completely correct."

Passion drives a leader's ability to articulate his vision and inspire and motivate a group to work toward a common goal. Ted Frick, a member of the 1982 Calvert Hall team remembered Coach Amatucci saying, "Just give me your best every day. That is all I ask." Frick added, "Now, as a husband and a father of five, this touches home. . . . and being a business owner and operating golf schools for the last 27 years, I can truly understand and respect (those words). I can remember coach using this statement on me often because I was the guard playing behind Pop and Money, so playing time wasn't in the equation. What Tooch asked of me was to bring it to every practice, to push Pop and Money to become better players! (I hope I didn't let him down.)"

PRACTICE

Getting on the floor early and staying late. Practice with a purpose. What's tired? An excuse.

Amatucci always ran a competitive practice. As a result, the players were ready and determined to close out a game. They were not going to run out of gas because of all of the conditioning they did day in and day out. They were mentally and physically tough because of the hard work. Amatucci said, "If I could practice seven days a week, twelve months a year, I would. I loved every minute of it."

Juan Dixon remembered, "Once at the Eastern States Invitation in

Trenton, New Jersey, we weren't able to get gym time on an off day. That didn't bother Tooch. We got in the van, found an outdoor court not being used in late December and had practice. When the sun began to go down, we put the van headlights on the court. When it comes to practicing, Tooch is crazy."

"Doc" Reif and Tooch discussing the meaning of life.

Amatucci recalled, "All of that man-to-man, all of that half-court work, all of Coach Reif's drills and all that conditioning was going to pay off in the last two minutes of a game. In crucial game situations, when the team needed a defensive stop, I would say, 'Go back to your basic man-to-man principles that we work on every day. Stop the ball. Stop penetration. Get it done.' It was built on the confidence the players had developed through practicing these situations every day. We believed."

Amatucci paid close attention to the tiniest of details. During conditioning, he did not want any players bending over after a sprint or when lined up for free throws because it was a sign of weakness. He also wanted the players standing still and looking directly at him when he was speaking. During games, Amatucci directed, "Don't ever look over at me on the bench, if you do you will be taking a seat next to me. Execute screens correctly. Use proper technique for defensive and offensive skills." Amatucci also demanded during conditioning that players finish each sprint and not pull up before reaching the end. "Run through the baseline. Don't stop, or you will run it again," Amatucci would bark.

Players were expected to arrive early for practice to get themselves prepared because there was no standing around once the session began.

There was constant movement and no water breaks. Amatucci also did not constantly interrupt the flow by talking to the players. There would be two minutes of demonstrating the drill and then the players had to execute. If they made a mistake, Amatucci would stop the drill briefly to correct them, and then it was back to the drill. If there were careless mental errors or lack of effort, then all of the players would run.

"In a five-on-five drill when we were emphasizing defense, that didn't mean the offensive guys were allowed to go through the motions," Amatucci said. "You can't make us better if you're not getting after it as hard as you can to challenge the defense. If I am focusing on denying the ball and breaking down support D and you are not busting your rear on O, we are definitely not getting better as a team. Everyone has to constantly push their teammate on both sides of the ball."

PATIENCE

Don't expect instant gratification. Brick by brick, one step at a time. Shortcuts are not going to get us anywhere. Don't think ahead, don't be satisfied until the job is 100 percent complete. Get better at one thing every day at practice. Celebrate a team win, not your individual performance. Execute the little things necessary for the desired result. Don't allow distractions to interfere with your performance. Maintain focus.

PRODUCTIVITY

Productivity is putting all the pieces together effectively. This facet is critical to success and earning the accompanying rewards. The foundation of productivity is time-management. Amatucci believed, "Time-management is the key to life."

"The absolutes serve as a blueprint for team and individual growth," Amatucci said. Growth involves going beyond what is accepted or expected. He added, "I asked my guys to push their limits. In the classroom, on the practice court, and in games, I was relentless. There was no status quo. We wanted guys to be accountable and independent."

The absolutes were not an edict from Amatucci but rather the framework for effective and productive teaching. Amatucci did not want his players to follow the absolutes robotically. He wanted them to understand the benefits of buying into his philosophy. Amatucci explained, "Implementing the philosophy was a fine balance between holding their hands and kicking them in the ass. In practice, there would be days where I wanted to have one of the infamous 'no ball' practices, but I knew on that particular day I might lose them. The absolutes are more than a list of mandates applied thoughtlessly."

"People get too hung up on winning," Amatucci said. "Winning does not define you, preparation and effort do. The challenge is getting the kids to do things they don't want to do. Collectively, once they buy into the philosophy, team productivity will happen," he said. "With our guys, starting with Calvert Hall, a lot of them were coming from tough neighborhoods. We put them into a positive, productive and challenging environment. I believe they were able to embrace the opportunity and take advantage of the education and athletics."

Building relationships is critical to implementing the absolutes and to having players trust the process. Relationships are more essential off the court than on. "I think our commitment to teaching life lessons defined our programs," Amatucci stated. "The success we had at Calvert Hall and Loyola occurred because I had a special connection with the players. I could not have gone to extremes on the court and be as demanding as I was unless I had their confidence and trust off the court. The door was always open. Making time for my guys was an essential."

Not everyone bought into what Amatucci was selling. Amatucci shared, "I can be patient waiting for a player to commit to the system, but at some point, if you aren't on board, I'm not keeping you around. I used to tell the guys, 'I'm only working with the living, not the dead.'"

Amatucci's absolutes are not all about basketball. He reflected, "I've always been a crusader for the needy, supporting cultural and social change—never backing down when confronted with an obstacle. If I needed to stretch the rubber band as far as it would go, I did. I never gave a second thought to starting five black student-athletes. For that matter, I never considered going into predominantly black East Baltimore as something dangerous. I didn't see black or white. I always took the position that, 'There are good people and bad people. There are people who are in need and those who are not. There are people deprived of equal opportunity and those who are not.' I've always lent my support to the have nots. Was I a crusader or just a guy who liked to push the limits? Funny, I never knew a crusader who didn't push limits."

Over the years, Amatucci would be relentless fighting for his student-athletes to be admitted to high school or college. Duane Ferrell, Juan Dixon, and Tommy Lee all had been initially rejected for admission by Calvert Hall and Loyola College. Amatucci recalled, "I practically held administrators hostage absolutely refusing to take 'No' for an answer. Papers were swept off desks, voices raised, and fingers pointed." Ultimately all three were accepted and proved Amatucci's instincts were correct. Amatucci said, "I did my best imitation of Kitty McNeal. Ability is not all about test scores and numbers, it's a lot about determination and character."

Amatucci asserted, "So without me going to extremes for Lee, Ferrell, and Dixon, do they end up achieving the enormous amount of success they have accomplished? Tommy Lee—Dean's List, Division I player, Loyola College grad, high-profile professional career; Duane Ferrell—Georgia Tech graduate, major DI player, NBA pro for thirteen years, highly successful businessman; and Juan Dixon—graduate University of Maryland, arguably Maryland's all-time best player, eight years in the NBA, DI head coach. I don't know for sure, but I can tell you, all three bought into the four Ps and used the absolutes to their advantage."

Amatucci is most proud of the leadership he provided his students, players and teams in supporting opportunities, fostering success, and overcoming challenges. His leadership style is well-defined. There is "always a way". He exhausted options and sought opportunities in search of a pathway to follow. Amatucci boasted, "I looked people in the eye and made them feel uncomfortable. I refused to back off until I got the result I thought was the correct one."

Trust and loyalty are essential to lead, and his players knew that Amatucci always had their back. Vince Williams, Calvert Hall class of 1995 noted, "After graduating from Goucher College with a degree in business, I was uncertain in which direction to go. I called Coach Tooch for advice and guidance; through this conversation, he helped me develop goals and an action plan to start my career in the financial services industry. Fast forward to years later—through his guidance and counseling, I have now been in the industry for over eighteen years and have been very successful in my career. Coach Tooch stills calls to check in on me and offer his support. I am a proud example of his commitment, loyalty, and passion to his players not only on the court but also after graduation"

Having reflected through the summer of 1989—Amatucci realized he still believed in his philosophy, he still loved basketball, and was determined to stay in the game. The story continues. …

13

BACK IN THE GAME AND LIVING ON RITCHIE HIGHWAY

Del Chambers and Tooch

"The fight is won or lost away from witnesses behind the lines, in the gym, and out on the road, long before I dance under those lights."

\- MUHAMMAD ALI

After leaving Loyola, Amatucci pondered his next move. He was offered opportunities in insurance and financial planning that were more lucrative, but his heart was still in coaching basketball. He had taken odd jobs and worked camps to make ends meet, but he still believed in his basketball philosophy and was confident he could find a way to get back in the game.

Following up on a tip from a close friend, Amatucci applied for the head coaching position at Anne Arundel Community College (AACC). Rumor was Norm Ambrose, an assistant coach from the Naval Academy, was the front-runner for the job. The athletic department was expanding and the new coach would also be an assistant athletic director. After making the initial call, Amatucci was contacted by Buddy Beardmore, AACC's, newly appointed athletic director, and interviewed for the position. Beardmore had been the long-time head lacrosse coach at the University of Maryland and was a member of the National Lacrosse Hall of Fame. After an extensive interview process, Amatucci was offered the position in August 1989. Amatucci commented, "I felt very comfortable with Buddy. We had similar personalities and coaching philosophies. This seemed to be a great situation to build another successful program and get back on track. So here I am, picking up the pieces as I make the 1½-hour commute to AACC daily. Ritchie Highway became by best friend."

Once again, Amatucci had the daunting task of completely overhauling what he inherited. The amenities were subpar, even worse than many high schools. The bleachers in AACC's gym obstructed the entrance to Amatucci's office when they were pulled out. Nonetheless, Amatucci was happy to be working and to be feeling productive. Off the court, there were other obstacles. The physical education department and athletics had a tenuous relationship. A number of AACC supporters were upset of the selection of Amatucci over Ambrose.

In addition to coaching, Amatucci's responsibilities entailed overseeing the maintenance for athletics and coordinating the academic support system for all AACC athletes, an area in which he had experience and great success. In addition, Amatucci served as the compliance contact for the NJCAA. That entailed filling out an inordinate amount of paperwork at the end of each semester. A new challenge for Amatucci was that the rules for junior college were dramatically different from those for NCAA Division I programs. The eligibility rules were very complicated, and it was not always easy to interpret confidently a player's eligibility status.

Amatucci would later find that the eligibility issue would become more than a paperwork headache.

The PE department had previously held these responsibilities and resented them being moved to athletics. As a result, PE faculty made little attempt to help orient Amatucci to existing programs, especially compliance. Not being discouraged, he implemented his familiar and acknowledged academic support system. He provided bi-monthly academic evaluations for the athletes, initiated mandatory study halls, and demanded class attendance.

"The one thing I was truly worried about was the compliance stuff because I had no experience in that area and was receiving little support," Amatucci remembered.

He walked into a situation where the basketball team had consistently struggled and was averaging about six wins per season. The players were not attending class, and the program was like a rudderless ship. Amatucci immediately began conducting individual meetings with the players. Another priority was to become a regular face in the crowd at nearby Truxtun Park where some of the area's most talented players would gather to play games in a local summer league.

"It was a big-time atmosphere," Amatucci said about the Truxtun league. "It was outside and drew raucous crowds who knew the players and the game. It was the Madison Dome on a bigger scale. It was just like the famous outside courts in Philly, New York, and D.C. There were great players passing through there. The word got out that I was looking for players and the program was getting a fresh start. There was a little buzz growing about AACC's new coach."

Amatucci held a formal meeting with potential players in the early fall. The team would open the season against nationally ranked powerhouse Allegany College of Maryland on the road. There would be no easing into the regular season. Mark Healy, his former assistant at Loyola College, joined Amatucci at AACC.

"At the community college level, strong athletic programs are really driven by the athletic director and strong, veteran coaches," Healy said. "Without them, it gets really transient, and you get coaches in and out. There's no consistency. We definitely walked into a bare cupboard to start."

About 25 prospects showed up for that first meeting. In the back of the classroom, one player wearing sunglasses, a baseball cap turned backward, and chains around his neck showed little interest in attending the meeting. Also attracting Amatucci's attention was his shirt that said, "It's a Black Thing. You wouldn't understand." Amatucci told him to sit up, take off the sunglasses, and remove the cap. That player was Del Chambers, who was warned by Amatucci to never again bring that display of body language to a meeting or he would be gone. At this point, there was no indication that Chambers would become the face of the program and Amatucci's most trusted and loyal player.

Amatucci and Healy hosted two open gyms to make cuts. Amatucci kept 13 players for his inaugural season and was impressed with the overall talent. Tommy Rose, a slightly built, 6-foot-3 swingman who brought a tough, no-nonsense mentality to the court, had played at nearby South River High School. Jason Sigler attended Broadneck and was

Tommy Rose (center) at his wedding reception.

a deadly sharp shooter. Mike Davis was 6-foot-5, 235 pounds, but was nimble, could play inside, and step out to shoot the J. Tremaine Walker was a talented player from Severna Park who would be effective in the transition game and with pressure defense. Chambers was starting to show his potential as a difference maker and as the team's unequivocal leader on and off the court. It took some time for the players to buy into Amatucci's tough coaching style, however they soon began to see the fruits of their labor.

"It was physically and mentally draining," Chambers said. "I did question how much I wanted to play basketball. But over time, you just became a more confident basketball player. It was good for us, but very tough initially."

Ronnie Wade from Annapolis Senior High was working hard to earn a degree while supporting his young son. Wade could consistently knock down shots from three-point range in transition and he would make an impact against zone defenses. Amatucci quickly realized the world of a junior college player could be more complex and required creative flexibility on his part. One of Amatucci's first rule adjustments was to allow Wade to bring his child to practice on the weekends. No limits.

"That first day we walked in, it was sort of like the Bad News Bears," Healy said. "I tried to be a buffer and run interference ahead of time. I told them, 'Do not be late for a meeting because someone is going to be made an example of. And, make sure you're paying attention because Tooch is going to lay the law down quickly.'"

Amatucci mandated the academic rules he had at Calvert Hall and Loyola. The players had to attend class, work hard, and make academics a priority. They were required to show up on time and realize they were going to be held accountable for their actions. The practices were also equally as hard, but the players thrived in the structured environment. They responded to Amatucci's demand for aggressive fast-paced basketball.

"I didn't really know much about him," Rose said. "When he first got hired, the Annapolis Capital had a couple of big articles about him getting the job. When we met him at that first meeting, he came in and set the tone right away. He told us how things were going to be and there were not going to be any exceptions. For me, it was great, because if you did what you were supposed to do, you were going to get an opportunity."

AACC lost to Allegany in the opener by almost 50 points, but Amatucci was encouraged by his players' heart and perseverance. The second time AACC played Allegany at home, the margin was down to 25. Amatucci and the players were happy with that type of progress.

"By that time, they were buying into the system," Amatucci remembered. "They liked the competitiveness and being challenged. They appreciated going out there and feeling like someone cared about them. A lot of them were castoffs and they had no other place to go. I truly believed they reveled in our family-oriented atmosphere. From the git-go, if the attitude wasn't right or you didn't want to play together, then you were out of here. That problem never arose."

AACC finished the season 22-11. Chambers had emerged as a legitimate Division I prospect and was often the best offensive and best defensive player on the floor. Amatucci also founded a booster club and raised money for uniforms and travel. He forged a strong bond with Beardmore, who was also the lacrosse coach. They would discuss strategies during lunch at Beardmore's waterfront home. Amatucci, like his players, was very happy with his new family.

"It was so prophetic that I was in the same situation like I had been at Calvert Hall and Loyola in relation to being able to bring in a bunch of guys who bonded so well right off the bat," Amatucci said. "I thought this was going to be another rewarding chapter in my career. I can honestly say Buddy and I changed the culture of that athletic department."

The second year at AACC brought even more optimism. Amatucci landed several key recruits. Jay Mouzon was a huge catch who solidified the point guard position, but had to sit out the first semester because he was academically ineligible. Butch Williams, 6-foot-7, 220 pounds, and James Sharpe, who was 6-2 and could jump out of the gym, also entered the fray. Ray Osborne, another blue-collar, versatile player with a team-first mentality would solidify our deep and talented rotation. Amatucci was confident he had a championship caliber team.

"We had a great recruiting year," Amatucci said. "We could get to the hole, knock down J's on the perimeter, rebound and play defense. I could envision us being a very dangerous team."

With Mouzon sitting out, Chambers unselfishly moved to point guard. It was a role that Chambers embraced.

"It was a big adjustment," Chambers said. "I tried it in high school and it didn't go well, mainly because I wasn't a strong ball handler at the time. It went much better at Anne Arundel because Tooch trusted me to do it. That gave me confidence. He worked me through the ups and downs."

Wade played the two spot, Rose and Osborne could each play at the three or four positions. Big Butch Williams solidified the center position. Sharpe started at the four and gave Amatucci the flexibility to play him at all three frontcourt positions. AACC was deep and rolled through the early part of the 1990-91 portion of the schedule.

"Once we got going, we were as good as any team I ever had," Amatucci contended.

By January 1991, AACC was 11-3 and ranked seventh in the National Junior College Athletic Association poll. Amatucci and Healy implemented the same system that had been successful at Calvert Hall and Loyola. Opponents struggled against the constant pressure, which regularly resulted in double-figure turnovers by the opposition.

"We were doing things defensively in JUCO that ninety percent of the teams never did," Amatucci remembered. "Most teams were playing zone, which never was a deterrent to us. It never slowed us down because we were so quick in transition. Nobody could run with us. Furthermore, nobody practiced like we did. We went six days a week, while other teams practiced Monday through Friday for ninety minutes. We were going close to three hours. You were going to have to be conditioned for the type of game we were committed to play. You can't run up and down the court for forty minutes, or play man-to-man for forty minutes, if you're not mentally and physically fit. They were as athletic as any team I ever coached."

Rose said the players embraced the hard work because they were seeing the results. They knew there was a method to Amatucci's madness.

"He was big on hard work," Rose recalled. "But, you felt you were getting better by the way he was pushing you. You didn't look at it like this was crushing you. You looked at it as a way to become a better player. We had a good group of guys that wanted to work hard, and it matched his personality."

Amatucci noted, "Tommy was not the greatest athlete, but compensated with a relentless work ethic, competitive nature, and an uncanny ability to make big plays in crucial situations." Rose admitted he wasn't exactly a leaper. A fact that was highlighted whenever the Pioneers played at Cecil Community College, which had a rubber basketball surface. Rose's feet seemed to stick to the floor when AACC played at Cecil. "It was like watching someone wearing weights in their shoes," Amatucci remembered with a laugh. "He couldn't jump and get off the floor. It pissed me off, but at the same time, it was hilarious."

The Pioneers continued their early season success, picking up an important 96-64 victory over Essex Community College on February 4, 1991. The win avenged a 70-66 loss earlier in the season. Chambers and Wade had 25 points apiece. Amatucci believed the team's success was a combination of excellent talent and great chemistry. He explained, "A strong connection between team members magnifies the value of planning and practice. Getting on the road has always been an effective method to grow positive relationships, and this was no exception with the Pioneers." On one particular road trip to Cumberland, Amatucci was making his routine bed check when he came upon Ronnie Wade's room. Amatucci knocked on the door and Wade told him to enter. Amatucci scanned the room, but did not see Wade, who called out from the bathroom. Amatucci opened the door and found Wade immersed in a bubble bath with a bottle of champagne and a big smile on his face. By breakfast, everyone had heard about Ronnie's bubble bath which provided a source for hours of comic exchange for the rest of the season."

AACC played Frederick Community College in a late February regular-season game. Frederick was led by Derek Shackelford, who later starred at George Mason University. The games between the two schools were always intense and physical. The gym was packed each time they played. AACC had run Frederick off the court in their first encounter earlier in the year, so the Frederick players were looking for a measure of revenge on their own court. The hotly contested game went back and forth.

Overcoming foul trouble, AACC took the lead late into the second half before Frederick tied it in the final seconds to send the game into overtime. Shackelford had collected his fourth foul going into the overtime period. Amatucci was aware that Chambers knew Shackelford off the court. During a timeout before Shackelford was to go to the free-throw line, Amatucci told Chambers to say something to agitate him.

"I know exactly what to say," Chambers told him.

When play ensued, Chambers whispered something to Shackelford, who became irate and went after him. Technical foul. Shackelford was out of the game, and AACC pulled away for the victory, gaining a momentum boost going into the league tourney.

Amatucci approached Chambers after the game and asked what he said to Shackelford. In short, Chambers made what some might consider a derogatory comment about his sister. Shackelford learned that keeping his cool might have been a better option for his team.

AACC played Frederick again in a regional tournament semifinal and was up by double-digits at halftime. However, Amatucci wanted to keep his team focused so he told Healy to stay clear of the water cooler in the locker room because he was going to toss it. In the locker room at half time Amatucci went on a blistering tirade and ended the talk by tossing the water cooler. Healy . . . who didn't pay attention to Amatucci's instructions, spent the second half drenched.

AACC finished the season 29-7, was ranked as high as No. 2 in the nation (Division II) and advanced to the Region XX Division II final, one game away from the national tournament in Michigan. Rose was named All-Region XX. "We were three points away from being a team that makes it to the Elite 8 in Division II," said Rose, who also played lacrosse. Amatucci reflected, "JUCO basketball gets a bad rap. Individual play, no structure, and no heart. This was absolutely not the mentality of this team. This was a special group of guys and a special moment for them. They played unselfishly and were relentless in their effort. I was as proud of this team as any that I have coached. Not making it to the Elite Eight was disappointing, but we all realized we had put Pioneer basketball on the map. We got together the evening of our last game and this time Ronnie was not the only one drinking champagne."

Chambers earned a scholarship to Division II Bloomsburg State College in Pennsylvania. After a standout career at Bloomsburg, he played professionally in Ireland and toured with the Washington Generals/Harlem Globetrotters. He later coached at Archbishop Spalding and is now the head coach at East Bay High School in Florida. Rose was recruited and played at Goucher College. He helped lead the Gophers to two NCAA Division III tournament appearances. He later reunited with Amatucci as the freshmen coach at Calvert Hall. He went on to be the varsity coach at Mount Carmel High School, winning three Maryland Interscholastic Athletic Association championships. Currently, he is the head coach at Goucher College.

After the season, Amatucci and the team were on a high. However, trouble began to arise in February 1991 when a staff member at the school violated federal and state laws by sending a student's academic records to a reporter without permission. Amatucci recalled, "I misinterpreted the guidelines and certified a player who was in fact ineligible. The staff member made no attempt to notify Buddy Beardmore that there was a question of eligibility."

The 1991-1992 season started out under a dark cloud. Amatucci was unhappy with how the ineligibility issue had been presented and was handled. "We lost our momentum. I was distracted by all the off-the-court issues. We had a player who couldn't pay his tuition. A couple of guys were becoming ineligible at mid-year. I sensed everything unraveling."

Amatucci resigned following an 85-71 victory over Harford Community College. "There were a lot of people around here who didn't want us [he and Beardmore] around. We represented change they didn't want," Amatucci said at the time.

Amatucci had grown tired of a "circus" atmosphere and the constant battles with the physical education department. Even though Amatucci fully cooperated with the NJCAA investigation, there were constant rumors surrounding the program. Amatucci and Beardmore were being made scapegoats, according to an article by Pat O'Malley in the January 15, 1992, edition of The Baltimore Sun.

O'Malley wrote, "There is no question that the two high-profile men have more than their share of haters at Anne Arundel. In times of crisis, the haters crawl out of the woodwork and throw fuel on the fire—if they didn't help start it.

"It was discovered during an internal investigation that a faculty member had initiated the investigation into Amatucci's hoops program by sending transcripts without the student's permission to the NJCAA," the story added. "That was just another example of someone from the old athletic department regime attempting to smear Beardmore and Amatucci."

Healy stayed on as the coach for the rest of the season to support the remaining players. However, the school opened a search for a new coach the following season, and Healy declined to apply.

In the end, Amatucci was proud of what he had accomplished at AACC. He developed a strategic recruiting plan. Making home visits became a part of the process. Media coverage drastically improved. Amatucci was the default communications director for athletics. He implemented a media day for each season. The media events were well attended by the local journalists, including radio, and TV outlets. The athletic budget grew from $30,000 to $200,000, helping teams to be better prepared and more competitive. Amatucci said, "Buddy and I were a good team. I enjoyed working with him. We got things done."

"What we were doing with those guys was something they had not experienced before," Amatucci said. "We were successful not only playing ball, but also in the classroom. Guys became serious about their education. Winning made it easier, but they all bought into the four 'Ps' and the absolutes. Same blueprint. Same success."

Chambers added: "It was disappointing that he had put AACC on the map and it ended the way it did."

Reflecting back on the AAAC experience, Amatucci said, "Being relentless, not accepting limitations, stretching the rubber band, really defined me and had been very effective in the success of my career. Unfortunately, my failure to realize that there are times when you need to change speeds, change directions, and take a more compromising approach had once again bit me in the ass."

Amatucci made the difficult phone call to his wife, Pat, and let her know that he was looking for work again. Amatucci said, "Having been through this before, I realized this call would not be as graciously received as was the case with Loyola." He picked up a variety of odd jobs as he sent resumes to numerous schools. Amatucci was getting responses from Division III athletic directors, but not the response he wanted to hear. The usual refrain was that Amatucci was overqualified and they could not pay him a suitable salary. Despite the setbacks, Amatucci was not ready to go in a different direction. He said, "I might be in the ground, but they haven't buried me yet."

In the spring of 1992, Amatucci secured an interview at Division I, St. Francis of New York, a team the Hounds routinely beat while he was at Loyola. Former assistant and close friend Rich Zvosec had coached at St. Francis before being hired at the University of North Florida.

"There was no doubt that I was going to get that job," Amatucci said.

"It was supposed to be a slam dunk."

Amatucci connected well with athletic director Carlo Tramontozzi, had a strong recommendation from Zvosec, and was well respected by the athletic department. It didn't hurt that Loyola was in the same conference as St. Francis.

Amatucci interviewed, met with the selection committee, and athletic director, and it appeared he was going to be offered the position. The interview was on a Thursday. After the interview, Carlo told Amatucci the committee would meet on Friday, and he implied a favorable decision would be made by Monday. However, the call that followed was a disappointing one; Amatucci was not selected. Amatucci is convinced that members of the committee called Loyola for a reference, and the job fell through.

Amatucci also secured interviews at Rider College in New Jersey and Roanoke College, a Division III program in Salem, Virginia. Both opportunities looked promising. The interviews went well, and once again Amatucci had a positive interaction with the selection committees and school staff. Amatucci even met with the players at Rider. Maryland basketball coach Gary Williams made a call to Roanoke on Amatucci's behalf. However, Amatucci contended, both programs decided to move in another direction after conferring with staff at Loyola.

Finally, Amatucci landed an assistant coach position at Washington College, a Division III program in Chestertown, Maryland. The Shoremen were coached by the acclaimed Tom Finnegan, who was a three-sport athlete at the school and is a member of its hall-of-fame. Amatucci had used Finnegan as a reference and received a call from the coach when the position opened. Amatucci and Finnegan had known each other for many years. Finnegan had consistently recruited Baltimore Catholic players to serve as key contributors to his successful teams.

"Tommy is a true teacher of the game," Amatucci said about Finnegan. "He is a passionate, driven coach. He is also brilliant with Xs and Os. Even at this point in my career, it was a great learning experience working with him. I learned a lot, especially about the details of running an effective and productive half-court offense."

Amatucci was paid $1,500 for the position. He commuted back and forth to Chestertown so he could be close to his family. Finnegan found him a rent-free room close to the campus to use when games or trips ran late. On the court, Amatucci was given the freedom to implement his pressure defense, which included man-to-man and zone half- and full-court traps. He also told Finnegan the benefits of visiting recruits in their homes. Amatucci also built a strong relationship with assistant coach Mike Hart, a Chestertown native.

"I had never been an assistant coach and I was eager to do well," Amatucci remembered. "I appreciated the opportunity and didn't want to screw it up. It was really a fulfilling and fun time again. I think God was looking out for me, being in the right spot at the right time."

Finnegan was optimistic about the prospects for the season. As the season played out, the upperclassmen did not develop as he had hoped. Younger players where not yet ready for impact roles on the team. The Shoremen finished the year 14-11, losing their final game in the conference tournament at Widener College.

"I thought he was a very good coach fundamentally," Finnegan remembered about Amatucci. "I had watched his teams play, and they were always very aggressive on defense. He liked to pressure as much as possible. Mark also had a very competitive outlook throughout the whole game. You had to earn things against his teams."

Finnegan added, "Overall, he was a terrific coach. I always thought you had coaches who were into helping their players and other coaches who were just looking to take the next step to go somewhere else. I always thought Mark was there to help his players. He was not driven just to see what the next door was going to be open."

One of the highlights of the season was the intense rivalry with Goucher College and their coach Leonard Trevino. The players fed off the animosity between Finnegan and Trevino. "Those games were out-

and-out brawls," Amatucci remembered. "You couldn't have asked to see better basketball. Both teams were highly competitive. It was just really invigorating being involved in that."

Amatucci enjoyed the experience. The players respected his philosophy and understood the repercussions for not playing hard. Washington would often open games with high-end pressure, a new strategy for the program. The strategy caught a number of opponents off-guard.

Finnegan had planned to go on sabbatical for the 1993-1994 season. If Amatucci stuck around for another year, he would have the opportunity to take over the program as the interim coach during Finnegan's hiatus. Ultimately, Amatucci would be in line to become the full-time head coach when Finnegan retired.

Amatucci and Pat went as far as to look at homes in the Chestertown area as he considered whether to remain at the school. At the same, time he continued to look for other head coaching opportunities with no success. When an opportunity opened at his alma mater, Juniata College, Amatucci was told he was overqualified and the school could not pay him enough money. Amatucci reflected, "I'm not sure how much I believed the reasoning. To me, the rejections all led back to Loyola, and I sensed people there were actively working against me."

In late April, Amatucci landed a phone interview with the United States Merchant Marine Academy in Kings Point, New York. The athletic director invited him to do a second interview this time on campus. Amatucci told him: "Look, I'm driving because I can't afford to fly. Is it worth my time to drive all the way up there for the interview? He said, 'Yes.' I think if I take that interview, I get the job."

However, fortunes changed quickly.

Amatucci had decided to attend the Calvert Hall versus McDonogh playoff baseball game at Gilman the afternoon before he was scheduled to drive to Kings Point. Joe Binder was still the head coach and was assisted by Lou Eckerl, who was also the athletic director. Calvert Hall had an opening for the basketball position. Eckerl asked Amatucci if he was interested. Amatucci responded in the affirmative and was told that assistant principal Lou Heidrick would call that evening.

"I can't guarantee you a teaching position right now," Heidrick told him.

"It doesn't matter. I am interested," Amatucci responded.

When Amatucci finished speaking with Heidrick, he called the Merchant Marine Academy to respectfully decline to travel up for the interview.

Amatucci would be making a trip, just a much shorter one.

YOU CAN GO HOME AGAIN

The Cardinals in the huddle.

"I'll be back in the high life again
All the doors I closed one time will open up again
I'll be back in the high life again
All the eyes that watched me once will smile and take me in."

- STEVE WINWOOD

Amatucci met with Calvert Hall principal Brother William Johnson, who was heavily invested in the basketball program. He then met with a committee that would decide whether to offer him the job. There were lingering concerns over the issues at Loyola and Anne Arundel. Amatucci's track record overrode some of those potential challenges, but he was not taking anything for granted. He had previously interviewed for a job in Calvert Hall's admissions office just after leaving Loyola.

Because of his strong relationship with the then principal, Brother Rene Sterner, Amatucci was confident that he would land that job. While anxiously waiting to hear back from Brother Rene, it was leaked to Amatucci that he was being passed over for the position. That experience left a bad taste in his mouth because in the end he had not even gotten a phone call about the decision. It took a few years to get over the slight. Amatucci recalled, "Not hearing directly from Brother Rene that I would not be hired was shameful. I deserved better."

This time, fate was working in Amatucci's favor. At the end of the school year, Brother DiPasquale, a Calvert Hall guidance counselor, was transferred to another school, creating the opportunity for Amatucci to fill that role. Following the interview and vetting process, Amatucci was indeed offered the job. He reunited with former assistants Mark Healy, Chris Devlin, and Mike Edwards. Newcomer Jon Capan joined the staff as the junior varsity coach, and Anne Arundel alum Tommy Rose became the freshman coach.

The job, however, came at a personal cost. Joe Baker was no longer the head coach after nine seasons, finishing 139-122 with a Baltimore Catholic League regular-season title in 1989.

"Brother William Johnson, principal of Calvert Hall, has dismissed me as the head basketball coach," Baker said in a statement. "An evaluation of my performance by Lou Eckerl, athletic director, states, 'Team academic performance, team conduct and behavior, good sportsmanship, dedication, hard work and program organization were all maintained as usual.'"

Calvert Hall had gone 18-10 and finished ranked No. 14 by The Baltimore Sun in Baker's final season. The Cardinals also reached the tournament semifinals.

Amatucci commented, "It seemed like there was some fuzzy math involved."

Itching to get started, Amatucci did not waste any time putting his stamp on the program. He had seen the team play the previous season and knew many of the underclassmen from working Coach Baker's camp. He was not impressed. After having a team meeting, Amatucci met individually with the players before the school year ended. It was time to clean house again.

"My gut told me we had some players who were not committed to the program," Amatucci remembered. "There was complaining among the parents. Their work ethic was suspect. Their attitude and body language didn't win me over. I was trying to determine what each individual would sacrifice to be a part of this team. I didn't care if you started or played one minute. Everyone was equal. It was a clean slate."

He began conducting workouts where his suspicions were reinforced. Those same players were out of shape, played selfishly and with no discipline. In short, they had no future with the program.

However, a number of upperclassmen showed promise. One player that stood out in early workouts was John Bauersfeld, who would become the head basketball coach at Calvert Hall in 2007. Bauersfeld had not played a lot the previous season, but promised Amatucci he would be a difference maker if given the opportunity.

"He was the first one that really impressed me as far as the type of kid I wanted to keep around," Amatucci said. "Bauersfeld did everything I asked him to do. He was a gamer and provided outstanding leadership by example. JB was consistent from three-point range, especially in transition where he had the green light. He would later be named captain of the 93-94 team."

Bauersfeld remembered that the first meeting with Amatucci had been intimidating. Right away the message was clear: either you buy into the new system or you're gone.

Bauersfeld played best in that type of environment. He also remembered how quickly Amatucci weeded out the players who were simply not going to provide the needed effort.

"It was a big change for a lot of people," Bauersfeld said. "It motivated me. I was the last guy off the bench as a junior. When I met with Tooch, I said 'I'm going to start for you. He kind of laughed at me, and I said, 'You shouldn't be laughing at me.' He liked that and respected that. I knew it was going to be hard. I thrived under him because I enjoyed being pushed like that. I like to push my teammates. I became an effort leader for that team."

John Artis was a player who rarely got on the court for the junior varsity. However, he had sprouted to 6-foot-3 and was an outstanding leaper with tremendous athleticism. Artis rarely spoke and eventually earned the nickname "The Chief" after the character in the novel "One Flew Over the Cuckoo's Nest." Richard Black, a hard-nosed scrapper, was the kind of player who could be a contributor off the bench. Rich added to the team's needed depth.

Another solid returning player was Brian Taylor, a 6-foot-5 senior with tremendous upside with the potential to be a Division I prospect. His game needed to become more physical to give Calvert Hall a presence in the paint at both ends of the court. Bunky Grinestaff, quarterback for the Cardinals' football team, had leadership potential at the point guard position if he could play more consistently on the defensive side of the ball.

Amatucci had a solid trio of sophomores—John McKay, Vince Williams, and Tavar Witherspoon—that would eventually play the bigger part in getting Calvert Hall back atop the Baltimore Catholic League. Amatucci says, "These three wowed me early on. They were talented and fierce competitors."

"Vince had played mostly at the three spot [small forward] the previous season, Tavar was projected as a three and McKay was a two [shooting guard]," Amatucci said. "Honestly, only McKay, who was a pure shooter, proved to fit my original instincts. A Division I baseball and hoops prospect, he really understood the mental gymnastics of intimidating opponents. Vince's perimeter game was inconsistent. He didn't talk much. He did mumble a lot. But, I could tell right away that he would run through a wall for me. Tavar stretched out to be 6-foot-3, and he believed his game was all about stepping outside and shooting threes. What I found out very quickly was that he was dreaming. His real game was that he was tough, athletic, a ferocious rebounder, had great instincts and could score around the basket. Tavar became my four man [power forward]. For the rest of his career, I would never allow him to step out of the paint to shoot J's. I envisioned they were the three that were going to take us back to the promised land."

Another player, Tommy Wallace, a red-haired kid who was 6-foot-3, 130 pounds, was cut from the freshman team and rarely received playing time on the junior varsity. However, his tenacity and willingness to make any sacrifice for the team won Amatucci over.

"I just loved his attitude and determination," Amatucci said. "Once we got into workouts, I said this is the kind of kid that I want on my team. The other players needled him, but he was one of the toughest son-of-a-bitches that ever played for me. He never complained."

On the recruiting trail, Gary Williams, at 6-foot-6, was the only legitimate player that Amatucci was able to corral because he got started late in the spring. Williams was also a talented soccer goalie who impressed Amatucci with his quickness and good hands. Amatucci remembered, "Gary was raw and inexperienced but, he was big and strong for an eighth grader and showed great potential." Come September, he would be on the roster.

Players immediately struggled during Amatucci's workouts, especially with conditioning. There was no easing into the transition of the new coach. Amatucci taught how to effectively run the break and to prioritize man-to-man defense. He wanted to see results. Once, when the Calvert Hall gymnasium was closed for floor maintenance, an unfazed Amatucci had the players practice on a tennis court on a blistering hot afternoon. No questions. No problem. No ball.

"It was a rough transition for them," Amatucci said. "I had confidence in the process that had been successful for me in the past. The potential was there. It was up to them to buy into the system."

Amatucci saw further challenges in the team's first game against Dunbar in the Craig Cromwell Summer League. Starting the game like deer in headlights, the Cardinals did not score a point in the first half. Amatucci made it clear during halftime and at the end of the game that this type of performance was not acceptable on any level.

"Obviously, they knew this was not what I was looking for," Amatucci said. "I looked them right in the eye and forcefully made my point."

Starting the second week of September, rigorous team conditioning began that included running and lifting three days per week. The aerobic training consisted of running a series of stairwells, along with longer timed runs and sprints. Amatucci conducted a regular practice in the gym the other two days and occasionally on Saturday. There were no league restrictions on out of season practice, so Amatucci kept the same schedule as his previous stints at Calvert Hall and Anne Arundel. In the conditioning and practice sessions, attention to detail was emphasized. The lessons learned were as much mental as they were physical. Amatucci noted, "The workouts were certainly not something the guys looked forward to."

By the end of the preseason, two players who had been key contributors to the 20-4 junior varsity the previous year did not fit into Amatucci's plans. A veteran varsity player decided the new expectations at Calvert Hall were too much and decided to transfer to Mount St. Joseph. Amatucci was more than happy to help expedite the process.

Anticipating the start of the regular season, Amatucci was cautiously optimistic as the Cards prepared for their home opener against a talented and well-coached Severn team. Using their trademark transition game and smothering pressure defense, The Hall jumped out to an early lead and took control of the contest. Not to be denied, Severn remained patient and by using their own transition game pulled even with the Cards by the end of the first half. Amatucci's message at halftime emphasized the need to take away Severn's transition game and to stop penetration in the half court.

The Cards jumped out in front again in the third quarter only to have the Admirals battle back, and the teams would end up tied at the end of regulation. In OT, with less than thirty seconds remaining the Cards tied the score only to have the Admirals move right down the floor to win with a basket in the final seconds. Amatucci remembered, "We did a lot of good things, played unselfishly with intensity, created turnovers, made crucial shots, but on the negative side, not getting back on D or stopping penetration offset the positives. Tough loss."

Heading to Frederick for a game with Maryland public school powerhouse Thomas Johnson, coached by the distinguished Tom Dickman, the Cards were 3-2 and Amatucci was satisfied with the team's progress.

The Patriots brought more than the Cardinals could handle in an 85-56 blowout, exposing all of the team's weaknesses. Amatucci recalled, "Embarrassing is an understatement. It was time to make some moves; the most prominent being moving Vince Williams to the point." Things did not get better. Next up, the Cards dropped a game to Philadelphia's Archbishop Carroll in a lackluster effort.

Amatucci's temperature was on the rise, "At practice the day after the Carroll game, they came out moping. I quickly threw them out of practice and told them to come back at 7 p.m. Don't be late. I'm hoping that I'm pushing them to come together as a team." Amatucci's tirade proved ineffective. In their next contest, the Cards, playing their worst game of the season, lost 63-61 to a weak and undisciplined Northern High School. Amatucci recalled, "I'm looking for answers."

Next up was the Kennard-Dale Tournament just outside York, Pa.

The Cardinals were matched up against St. Paul's of Baltimore in the opening round. However, a light snow fell in the area and schools in Baltimore County were closed. This meant St. Paul's could not make the trip. Amatucci told the tournament officials that his team was travelling to the tournament despite the inclement weather. The Cardinals won by forfeit in the first round game because St. Paul's could not play. Amatucci and the players stayed overnight to help with team-bonding. The strategy worked as the players dined at Coach Devlin's house in nearby Shrewsbury. The team was well-behaved and avoided any screw-ups. The Cardinals played host Kennard-Dale in the championship game before a packed gym. Calvert Hall prevailed 47-44 with Gerald Spann making key clutch shots in the final stretch.

"Winning that tournament was a turning point in the year for us," Amatucci remembered.

Calvert Hall returned home and practiced twice a day over the remaining days of the Christmas break. The players were not happy about the eye-opening workouts, but the benefits were huge. The Cardinals picked up another impressive win, 66-62, over No. 11 Walbrook, which was coached by Gus Herrington. Amatucci uncharacteristically went to a 3-2 zone, and the players effectively responded to the change. By taking away dribble penetration, they were able to shut down Walbrook's two key playmakers—Travon Broadway and Antwon Jenifer. With six minutes to go in the fourth quarter and having the lead, Amatucci elected to pull the ball out, attempting to force Walbrook out of its zone and play man-to-man. Much to Amatucci's surprise, Coach Harrington's team stayed in their zone until there were only three minutes left in the game. Amatucci looked at his assistant, Mark Healy and said, "This is a gift. When the Warriors finally went man-to-man and tried to trap, we were able to spread the floor, looking for layups or to get fouled. The spread allowed us to run time off the clock and seal the win."

The following game against St. Maria Goretti was cancelled because of bad weather in Hagerstown. That cancellation would eventually lead to some drama at the end of the season. Nonetheless, Calvert Hall kept the momentum going and took down No. 13 St. Frances, 59-55, on a Sunday afternoon at home. The Panthers traditionally struggled in Sunday afternoon games and the Cardinals took advantage of the opportunity. The Cards were well prepared for the St. Frances offense because they used the same game plan regardless of playing against man or zone defense. On defense, Amatucci used the same formula as he did against Walbrook, utilizing the 3-2 zone. St. Frances didn't make adjustments, and that proved costly as Calvert Hall made a key defensive stop and then made its free throws in the final seconds to earn the victory. Most importantly, unlike in their losses to Thomas Johnson or Northern, the Cardinals were focused for the entire 32 minutes, showing tremendous poise under pressure.

At this point in the season, it was becoming obvious that the team was starting to click on both ends of the court. Amatucci recalled, "The wins were a result of total team effort. Witherspoon was beginning to stand out as a big-time defensive player and offensively a major contributor inside the paint. Williams was adjusting to the point guard position, highlighted by his ability to just go out and kick the opponent's point guard's ass. He's becoming a big-time shutdown guy. John McKay, tending toward being lackadaisical on defense, was consistently averaging 20 points a game during the winning streak. The carrot was that McKay knew that if his defensive effort was not there, he would be observing the game from the bench."

McKay was prone to being a distraction off the court and in practice, but Amatucci knew, "I had to have him on the floor for us to be successful." Dealing with McKay required Amatucci to stretch the rubber band.

Seeing the results of their intense practice, the players were beginning to buy into the Amatucci method. Amatucci recalled, "It allowed me to push the envelope even more in practice. The results continued with victories over Eastern Tech (69-44), Towson Catholic (47-45), Loyola Blakefield (72-71, OT), and Bishop Walsh (64-52). The winning streak propelled Calvert Hall into the top 20 of The Baltimore Sun poll.

This set up a key game against powerful Cardinal Gibbons, which was led by guard Steve Wojciechowski, who later starred at Duke and is currently the head coach at Marquette University. Playing at the top of its game, Calvert Hall cut into a 10-point deficit and trailed the No. 6 Crusaders by just two points at the end of the third quarter. With four minutes in the final period, Gibbons coach Ray Mullis went to his spread offense, allowing Wojciechowski to take over the game and score 11 of his 31 points in the final minutes. Gibbons held on for a 70-64 victory. Amatucci, unhappy with the loss, however was quietly encouraged that the mighty Crusaders had to go into their four-corner offense to bring down the Cards.

"I am not into moral victories," Amatucci said. "We showed a glimpse of what was possible, but I didn't want them to think it was okay to lose. I think I gave them hell for the way they failed to defend the four-corners at the end of the game. In my mind, I felt good that Mullis had to spread the floor in the final two minutes to beat us."

Calvert Hall bounced back with a 52-48 victory over Mount St. Joseph on a Friday night. Spann had been late to practice the previous day and was suspended for the game. Nonetheless, the other players stepped up and finally knew they could win without one of their top players. McKay led the Cardinals with 16 points. Amatucci said, "They were starting to believe in one another."

The Cardinals had a budding rival with St. Maria Goretti and its coach, Cokey Robertson. Cokey, Mullis, and Loyola's Savage were part of the old guard of the Baltimore Catholic League. Amatucci was convinced that they were not happy that he had returned to the sideline. Feeling disrespected, Amatucci had even exchanged words with Savage prior to The Hall's home game versus the Dons.

Responding to a sarcastic remark, Amatucci replied: "Jerry, I don't get what's up with you. I've been a Division I head coach and my team won a national championship here at Calvert Hall. I'm tired of your shit."

Amatucci was finding out that Goretti's Robertson was always a tough matchup and a stickler for details. His opponents had to prepare for his teams in every aspect of the game. "To me, he was one of the best coaches in the league," Amatucci said. Similar to Mullis' red towel, Cokey carried a white towel on the sidelines. To make a point to his players or the officials he would often toss it in the air, which irked Amatucci. In a highly charged game at Calvert Hall, the teams went toe-to-toe for four quarters. After Goretti took a 72-70 lead in the final seconds, John McKay had a chance to win the game on a three-pointer at the buzzer. The shot fell short, but Amatucci was convinced that McKay was fouled in the act of shooting. Drawing attention to himself, Robertson threw his white towel in the air to celebrate the win, which did not escape Amatucci's eye. Amatucci could not properly respond to the towel toss antics as he was occupied chasing the lead official, Tommy Reese, into the locker room "to discuss" the perceived missed call. He began banging on the door.

"Tommy, you have to come out of there sooner or later," Amatucci yelled.

Finally, Coach Devlin pulled Amatucci away for the health and welfare of Mr. Reese. This game was just the beginning of a heated rivalry with Goretti. Later in the season, Amatucci refused to make up the previous game with Goretti that was postponed because of the snow. Robertson, looking for the home court advantage and the win, wanted to make the game up after the Catholic League Tournament. Amatucci, with a wink, didn't see any reason to make the trip. This annoyed Robertson, who was confident he could add one more win to his overall record. The bad blood just got thicker.

On the road, Calvert Hall had another showdown with Cardinal Gibbons and led 30-24 at the half. Once again, the Crusaders rallied again behind Wojciechowski (16 points) and prevailed, 62-59. This time, Amatucci took no solace in this loss.

"I'm pissed because we had them," he said. "But that shows how well the kids started to believe in themselves. I was able to get them to come together as a team by incorporating the four P's that made us successful in the past. I was not going to be satisfied with anyone giving less than 100 percent."

Amatucci spent a good deal of time that season explaining to Witherspoon his responsibilities as the four-man, or power forward. Instead of getting to the post on the break, Witherspoon liked to shoot from beyond the perimeter. As a result, he was given an alternative: "If you shoot the ball from outside the perimeter, you're coming out," Amatucci told him. Not until Tavar had been asked to take a seat on the bench several times did he gain an appreciation for Amatucci's lesson.

Witherspoon was known to kid around with the other players in the locker room prior to games, which aggravated Amatucci. On one occasion, entering the locker room and finding Tavar clowning around, Amatucci abruptly told him to exit and go somewhere by himself to get focused on the game. When the team reconvened in the locker room for last minute game instructions, Witherspoon was missing. Amatucci found him in the bathroom propped up against the wall with his hands over his face.

"What the hell are you doing?" Amatucci asked him.

"You told me to go somewhere and think about the game," Witherspoon responded.

For the rest of the season, Witherspoon would spend his pre-games in the bathroom getting mentally prepared. This unique routine proved extremely effective.

Despite all of the positive strides gained in the season, the Cardinals had a disappointing 89-66 loss to Canterbury, a Washington, D.C., prep school. The loss did not annoy Amatucci as much as the lack of effort by his players. He was convinced the players had quit during the game. The team missed an opportunity to demonstrate their potential against a formidable opponent.

Isolating himself after the game, Amatucci was trying to cool down.

The Cards' AD, Lou Eckerl, entered the locker room to let him know that his wife and children were upstairs in the gym waiting for him.

"I know you're upset, but Pat and the girls are upstairs waiting for you," Eckerl told him.

Disrespectfully, Amatucci replied, "Why don't you mind your own business?"

Amatucci regretted the remark. It was his spontaneous, selfish side showing itself again. Calvert Hall travelled to St. Frances for an important league matchup and dropped another frustrating game to the Panthers, losing 53-51 on a pair of free throws by Mark Karcher, a future All-Metro Player of the Year who later starred at Temple. The Cardinals had squandered a 34-20 halftime lead. It seemed like the Cards were going backwards.

A bit of light shining through the darkness of a disappointing loss was that Vince Williams finally became the vocal leader Amatucci had envisioned. Throughout the season, the guard was so quiet during practice that Amatucci made the players run when Williams would not verbalize instructions on offense and defense. "I was an introvert in high school," Williams said. "I didn't talk. I led by example. What he needed was someone vocal on the court. Unbeknownst to me at the time, he picked me. I don't why or how he had the foresight to know I could handle it. If somebody did something wrong in practice or threw the ball away, he turned around and yelled at me. 'Why did he throw the ball away? Why didn't you give him instructions?' So it was very challenging. I got to the point where it was frustrating because I could be out of the game and he was still yelling at me."

That reserved demeanor ended after the St. Frances loss.

Before Amatucci entered the locker room after the game, Williams went off. "You m*#f#@ better get your shit together because I am the one he is going to take it out on," Williams yelled. "I'm tired of him getting on my ass every day in practice."

Standing outside the locker room and listening in, it was music to

Amatucci's ears.

The Cardinals earned another noteworthy victory, 58-55, over No. 2 Southwestern on February 17, 1994. Calvert Hall led by 20 points before the Sabers mounted a furious comeback. Taylor led the Cardinals with 22 points and Witherspoon scored 16. Calvert Hall's high-pressure defense forced 25 turnovers.

After the game, the Southwestern coaches and players chased the game officials into the locker room. The angry and disgruntled Southwestern fans charged onto the floor looking for a fight. Trying to gain control of the situation, Amatucci told the Calvert Hall fans to stay in the bleachers and the players to get into the locker room. As he turned to leave the floor, Amatucci spotted his six-year-old daughter, Jacquelyn running across the court to him. He scooped her up safely and returned her to her frantic mother. To restore order, Lou Eckerl had to call the Baltimore County police to intervene.

After a convincing victory over Mount St. Joe to finish the regular season, Calvert Hall took down Loyola for the third time that year, 63-52, in the first round of the Baltimore Catholic League Tournament. McKay led the team with 18 points, Williams had 12 and Taylor scored 10. Even Savage conceded that Calvert Hall "was playing as well as anyone in the league." The following night in the semi-finals the Cardinals successful run ended with a 73-55 loss to Cardinal Gibbons in the semi-finals. Gibbons would go on to win the tournament, earning a berth in the Alhambra Catholic Invitational Tournament.

Calvert Hall finished the season 17-11. There was great optimism for the future.

Amatucci reflected, "I was impressed with what this team accomplished. They learned the value of working hard. They earned victories over highly ranked teams. They created a strong chemistry. They were primed for greater success."

What started happening was that everyone bought into what he was selling," Williams said. "Things just took off. We played a lot of teams that had more talent than us, but we worked hard and believed in ourselves and everything gelled together."

As the season wrapped up Amatucci realized, "I'm in a familiar place. We are back in the high life again."

GUNSLINGERS

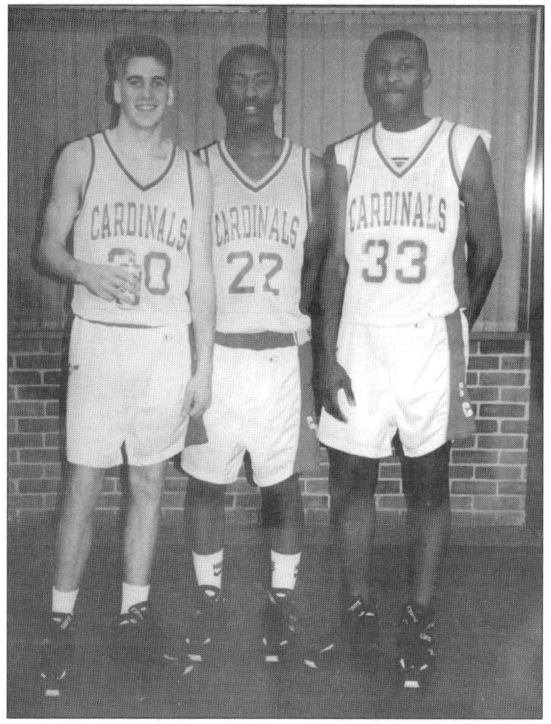

John McKay, Vince Williams and Tavar Witherspoon

"Play the game for more than you can afford to lose...
only then will you learn the game."

- WINSTON CHURCHILL

After another demanding and intense summer and preseason, Amatucci had the talent to make a run at championships in both the Baltimore Catholic League and Maryland Interscholastic Athletic Association in 1994-1995. The players change, but the ideals of the program stay the same.

Amatucci was aggressive with recruiting and remained determined to give players an opportunity at Calvert Hall. He brought in 6-foot-6 forward Sam Anyan, a transfer from Woodlawn High School, and Antoine Peoples, a 6-2 swingman from the Madison Buccaneers. Anyan gave the Cards immediate firepower inside the paint and on the perimeter with his short-range jumper. Once he realized the sacrifice required each day in practice, Anyan eventually became a starter and was a major contributor at both ends of the floor. Benefiting from a Calvert Hall education, Peoples would go on to graduate from Johns Hopkins University, and Anyan would graduate from Howard University School of Law.

Peoples fit the mold of a typical Buccaneers' player—great floor instincts, solid skills, and mental toughness. "Antoine had the talent to fit right into our transition and pressure D system," Amatucci said. The Cardinals also got a surprise transfer from Lake Clifton High School, a skinny, 6-foot-1 shooting guard named Juan Dixon, a young man who in the not-too-distant future would make his mark in the world of basketball.

Adding to the team's weapons was Greg Patchak, a tough player who also excelled in lacrosse. "He looked like a miniature sumo wrestler," Amatucci said. "Looks were deceiving. He could score, rebound and had cat like quickness. I loved his ability and attitude." Upon graduating from Calvert Hall, Patchak played lacrosse at Duke University.

Darrell "DJ" Walker made the team from the junior varsity squad and lived directly across the street from "The Dome," a basketball mecca in East Baltimore. Walker had a pivotal role within the program.

"Walker was a street-smart kid who loved Calvert Hall," Amatucci said. "You didn't want to mess with him. He was an intimidating force at the defensive end of the floor. He was your worst nightmare if you got him pissed off. He unselfishly bought into our hard-nosed, team-first philosophy. When you look at our makeup, we're strong inside and we're strong outside. Vince has made himself a premier point guard. With Tavar and McKay doing their thing, we're looking pretty damn good on paper."

The local media recognized the talent and Calvert Hall was ranked No. 7 in The Baltimore Sun preseason poll, the highest ranking since Amatucci returned to the school. The Cardinals flexed their muscle in the opener, running past Bishop Walsh, 83-41, and then beat McDonogh, 60-57, in overtime. Amatucci was not happy the Eagles were able to stay so close. Dixon had to a hit a 30-footer at the buzzer to earn the win. Calvert Hall followed up with a dominant 81-37 victory over John Carroll and an 88-22 blowout win over Nicholson Catholic of Canada. There were still issues with players' overall focus.

"We were winning, but I was concerned we were not being challenged," Amatucci said. "It's obvious we can put up points. The defensive effort and consistency is erratic. We have all this quickness and strength inside, but we are just not putting it all together. I don't see any fire in our eyes. They think they are very good, I think their heads are bigger than a beach ball."

Amatucci's doubts were further exposed at the Good Counsel Invitational just prior to Christmas break. Amatucci regretted that he had not made plans to stay overnight near the campus, which is close to Washington, D.C. Instead, the Cardinals had to travel back and forth for three games. Calvert Hall got stuck in traffic going to the opener and were late arriving to the game. Complicating things, Witherspoon forgot his shoes and an assistant coach had to scramble to find a sporting goods store tc buy a new pair. The distractions led to an 80-69 whooping by Archbishop Carroll.

"The guys are not realizing you can't just walk onto the floor and expect to win," Amatucci said. "I am surmising the basics of the four P's are non-existent. It was a long ride home after that loss."

The Cardinals knocked off Benjamin Franklin from Philadelphia in the next game. Utilizing the break and mixing up trapping defenses, Calvert Hall created double digit turnovers routing the boys from Philly. The Cards then dropped Walden in the final game, but Amatucci was convinced the team was still underachieving. Some of those concerns were realized the following week in the Bishop McCorristin tournament in Trenton, N.J.

During the tournament, the players begrudgingly participated in daily study hall. They did not follow Amatucci's scripted itinerary and angered some of the hotel guests by engaging in a pseudo-WWE wrestling tournament. Peoples' and Walker's rooms served as the main ring leaders.

Another big distraction for Amatucci was that New Jersey had a seatbelt rule, meaning coaches had to sit on the bench the entire game. He was able to get a waiver and was allowed to have his customary squat in front of the bench. Amatucci could also stand, but not pace the sideline. "I felt like a caged animal," Amatucci said. The coach did not like getting away from his standard routine, but he was learning to adapt.

The Cardinals beat Nazareth of New York in the first round, but then fell to host Bishop McCorristin, 68-60, in the semifinals as they struggled to score in transition. "We did not play consistently for 32 minutes," Amatucci said, "We got a little home cooking. Committing too many unforced turnovers and playing selfishly on offense did not help our cause." Calvert Hall shot thirty percent from the field.

After the players got settled in for the night at the hotel, the coaching staff went back into town to get some dinner and a few adult beverages. Some traditions are hard to break. This time, though, the locals were not as hospitable as previous stops.

"We certainly were not celebrating," Amatucci said. "It turned into a raucous coaches' meeting with bottle caps serving as players as each coach took his turn moving the players and vocalizing his opinion. These meetings usually revolved around the theme of what everybody thought I was doing wrong.

"Not surprisingly, the discussion lasted until the proprietor escorted us to the door," Amatucci recalled. "As we pulled out of the parking lot, Coach Capan, our designated driver, may have rolled a stop sign. The local constabulary was of the opinion he definitely rolled the stop sign. Observing flashing lights in his rear-view mirror, Coach Cap pulled the van over. There was some concern this incident might impact our future coaching careers. Initially, the officer was very officious."

Luckily, Coach Edwards, a native of the streets of Brooklyn, came to Coach Cap's rescue and applied his New York street-smart sensibility to the situation. Coach Edward's mediation techniques were totally effective, and eventually, the coaches were ready to head back to the hotel no worse for wear. Driving down the road, they were surprised to find Coach Healy walking down the road. He had decided to make a jail break during the traffic stop by slipping out the back door and heading for freedom. Despite Amatucci's protest, Coach Cap stopped to pick him up. All was well with the world.

It was the type of adventure Cap expected with Amatucci. They first met when Cap was assisting at a basketball camp hosted by Hereford High school. Amatucci visited as a guest speaker. This is also when Cap experienced Amatucci's work-hard attitude with his detailed instruction to the campers. The initial impression laid the groundwork for a long-term partnership.

Capan remembered, "Shortly after this, Tooch spoke to coach Mark Trotta about seeing if I had interest in joining the Calvert Hall staff as a junior varsity coach. Then came the interview, which was scheduled in the afternoon at Shakey's Pizza in Cockeysville. Other than I think he liked me as a person, I think he offered the job to me because I agreed to a pitcher of beer while we talked. It definitely wasn't because I knew how to put a practice plan together. I learned that after I later got to know him.

"I was hired in the summer and told to show up for practice that week at Calvert Hall. My idea, at the time, was that a workout involved some ball handling and shooting drills. I quickly found out that even though it was summer a workout involved high intensity in a steamy high school gym with lots of yelling."

Back in New Jersey, the Cardinals had an off day before playing Osbourne Park of Virginia in the consolation game. Amatucci had the players out of bed and performing conditioning drills at 8 a.m. in the parking lot. When that was completed, the players ate breakfast and attended a ninety-minute study hall. Amatucci was forced to hold a team practice on an outside court because there wasn't any gym time available. There were no limits with preparation.

As darkness and the temperature fell, the Cardinals practiced with the lights of the team van illuminating the court. Amatucci said, "We were not leaving until I was satisfied we were totally prepared for the next game." The extra work paid off. Calvert Hall rolled past Osbourne 80-42, in the final game before league play.

Going to extremes.

The balance of power in the MIAA that year leaned toward St. Frances, which was ranked No. 4 in the metro area. The Panthers bullied the Cardinals in the BCL league opener with a 65-53 victory at the University of Baltimore. St. Frances star Mark Karcher finished with 16 points. Amatucci was not happy with his team's lack of toughness, which had always been a staple of Calvert Hall basketball.

"If someone is mugging you or pushing you around, why don't you knock someone on their butt and maybe they'll think twice about doing it again," Amatucci later emphasized in the locker room. "We played like a bunch of scared rabbits. There was zero display of mental and physical toughness."

The players paid the price in practice, and Anyan caught the brunt of Amatucci's ire because he was knocked around by the Panthers the entire afternoon. The Cardinals got back in their coach's good graces with a 53-51 victory over Mount St. Joseph and an 86-49 win over Gilman. McKay averaged close to 20 points in the two games. Amatucci commented, "It's Gilman, don't get too excited."

This set up another showdown on the road against St. Maria Goretti and Coach Cokey Robertson, who was still keeping Amatucci up at night.

For its home games, Goretti employed local Hagerstown, Maryland, officials as opposed to the regular BCL refs. This proved to be an effective tactic. Even though the Cardinals arrived early for their game that afternoon, Goretti allowed only fifteen minutes for pregame warmup as opposed to the standard twenty under league rules. "That's how we do it up here," Amatucci was told by local officials. This distraction threw the players off their routine, and Goretti emerged with an 83-71 win.

"I let him get in my head," Amatucci remembered. "The kids were not focused, and they didn't handle Goretti's well-executed game plan. This was totally on me. I was fuming at myself for taking Cokey's bait. It's now Goretti three, Calvert Hall zero, and I'm not happy."

On Super Bowl Sunday, archrival Loyola ran through the host Cards pregame warm-up lines, perhaps to make a statement. Calvert Hall responded by dismantling the Dons, 68-52, before a standing-room-only crowd. The Cardinals outscored Loyola 20-8 in the decisive third quarter. Amatucci recalled, "The psychological warfare was not effective. It fired our guys up. " The perceived slight ignited McKay, who finished with 20 points.

Despite the success, Amatucci was constantly finding ways to challenge his players and make them better. Complacency was to be avoided at all costs. As a result, the Cardinals faced their toughest test to date in the Charm City Classic at Loyola College. In the opener, Calvert Hall played Oak Hill Academy, the top-ranked high school team in the United States and defending national champions. "I wanted to give the guys a taste of what it was like playing nationally ranked teams," Amatucci said.

The players got more than a taste with Oak Hill, which had a five-inch height advantage at each position in the front court and rolled to a 73-43 victory. Oak Hill was led by Kentucky bound Ronnie Mercer, who led all scorers with 20 points. "It was a game of two halves," Amatucci remembered, "Down nine at half, we did not put the same effort into the second half. We came down here to win two ball games. We did not come down here to just put time in."

Still licking their wounds, Calvert Hall played with more intensity and confidence the following night against Paterson Catholic (N.J), ranked 14th in the nation. The Cougars were led by Tim Thomas, who was drafted seventh overall by the New Jersey Nets in the 1997 NBA draft and played twelve seasons in the league. The Cardinals led 28-27 at the break before eventually wearing down in the second half on route to a 64-43 loss.

"They just turned it up to another level in the second half," Amatucci said. "We left Reitz Arena with our heads high; we felt we had earned some respect that night."

Witherspoon added: "No excuses. Height should not matter. We tried to take that bad game we had yesterday and turn it around."

The experience of playing those high-caliber teams almost immediately paid off. The host Cardinals got a measure of revenge against St. Frances with a dominant 86-63 victory the following week. Witherspoon led Calvert Hall with 21 points, McKay added 20, and Williams finished with 16. One of the keys to the game was holding Karcher to just eight points. All of the defensive work in practice had paid off. More importantly, the Cardinals showed determination, especially when they were underestimated.

"St. Frances was probably looking at those Oak Hill and Paterson scores, thinking the game would be a cake walk and that they would run us out of our gym," Amatucci said. "But St. Frances was not ready to play, and this was a turning point that would invigorate our motivation for the rest of the season. You win a game like that, holding them to 63 points and Karcher was not a factor. The message was clear: You better come prepared to play the Cards."

Goretti and Robertson heeded that advice and got the best of Amatucci again with a 71-62 win.

"He was just so prepared," Amatucci said about Robertson. "His offenses were geared toward penetrate, dribble, kick out or penetrate, dribble, drop off. They could just dissect you. If you're going to play man-to-man, you better stay with your fundamentals, and we didn't do that. I got wrapped up trying to figure out what defense he was in. It was a poor coaching job on my part. And him with that damn white towel, he got me again."

More drama occurred prior to the next game against Loyola the following Sunday afternoon. The life of a high school basketball coach is never short of crises. Witherspoon informed Amatucci before practice that he had injured his toe in 86-54 victory over Curley earlier that week.

"What do you mean you hurt your toe? What's the matter with it?" Amatucci asked him on the gym floor at Calvert Hall.

"It hurts," Witherspoon responded.

"Let me see the toe," Amatucci retorted.

Indeed, the toe was swollen. Amatucci, trying not to look overly concerned, told him to wrap the toe, and then ice it after practice. Witherspoon knew that if he couldn't practice, he couldn't play against the Dons, so he gutted out the injury. Amatucci knew that if Witherspoon did not play, he would be losing 15 points and ten rebounds.

Witherspoon was indeed back in the starting lineup against Loyola. He outdid himself by scoring 35 points and grabbing 15 rebounds in a dominant 83-67 victory. On Monday, Amatucci finally relented and had the team trainer look at the toe. Witherspoon did have a fracture.

The Cardinals kept the train rolling with a solid 74-57 victory over Towson Catholic. During warmups, McKay ran by a Towson Catholic player who was on his back stretching and stepped on his hand. McKay remembered, "I wasn't the cleanest player in the league. There was an incident with him the week prior where comments were made that I did not appreciate. You know, I was a pitcher, and in baseball I would have hit him with a fastball."

When Amatucci walked onto the court, he was met by an irate Towson Catholic coach Mike Daniel.

"Tooch, what the hell is McKay doing?" Daniel asked.

"What did he do now?" Amatucci responded before yanking McKay out of the layup line.

"You go down to Coach Daniel right now and apologize," Amatucci told McKay, who pleaded his innocence. "And then you go over and apologize to the player. Do you want to play?"

McKay agreed to shake the player's hand, but he was not going to apologize. Amatucci reluctantly accepted the compromise.

The Cardinals thoroughly beat Gibbons, 88-74, in the regular season finale. The Cards outscored the Crusaders 24-8 in first quarter. Five players were in double figures. Amatucci recalled," McKay got 22. He was in his zone, shooting the lights out like the gunslinger he was.

The 23-8 Cards drew Towson Catholic in the first round of the BCL tourney. Amatucci made sure there were no problems this time.

"Does everybody understand how to appropriately warm up for this game?" he asked his players while staring at McKay, who scored 18 points in the Cardinals 84-49 victory.

The win setup a semifinal game against the Cards' nemesis, Goretti. This time, the Cardinals finally broke the Goretti curse, running away with a 56-48 win, led by McKay's 21 points.

"We didn't get frustrated, and we were patient," Amatucci remembered. We didn't rush shots. We played a little zone. We made the decision to stay with the flex offense regardless of what they did. We took care of the ball and played a well-focused 32 minutes. It was a big win for me."

Calvert Hall faced St. Frances for the BCL championship. The Panthers learned their lesson from the previous blowout and played a box-and-one on McKay.

"St. Frances did a terrific job defensively," Amatucci said. "The last few games, everybody has played a box or a triangle against us, and we have played some of our best basketball all season. Today, we did not play our best and St. Frances had a lot to do with that."

McKay never got comfortable and was held to a single three-pointer. The Panthers came away with a convincing 45-34 win. Calvert Hall finished the season 26-9 and ranked fifth in the Baltimore-metro area and was crowned MIAA champions. Nonetheless, the Cards did not get invited to the Alhambra Tournament, which was a huge disappointment considering the success of the season and tradition of the program. The selection committee was now taking three teams from D.C. every year, and just the BCL champion, which meant St. Frances got the nod.

"Losing the BCL tournament was deflating, but when you look back, we had a great year," Amatucci said. "I was just tremendously proud of the guys."

In two seasons, the Cards had earned 52 wins, gaining respect from opponents and the media. Peoples, Gary Williams, Black, and Anyan had made strong contributions and improved greatly throughout the season. Dixon was emerging as a star of the future.

Vince Williams, McKay, and Witherspoon, also had a remarkable two-year run. The "three amigos" would be a tough act to follow. McKay remembered, "I think Tooch instilled some strong values in us. We may not have loved him at first, because of how hard he was, but by the time we finished he was beyond respected. All of us called him friend in addition to coach. That's a pretty special relationship."

Just one week after losing to St. Frances, Amatucci was back on the recruiting trail to keep the program climbing to new heights.

Patrick Ngongba, a highly recruited 6-foot-8 forward from Central Africa, decided to transfer to Calvert Hall from Mount Hebron High School for his senior year. As a result, the Cardinals were ranked No. 3 in the 1995 Baltimore Sun preseason poll. Ngongba, however, had an erratic tenure for the Cardinals, and his teammates played a bigger role with the success of that season. Amatucci had some doubts about Ngongba's potential impact from the beginning.

"I made a home visit with his host family and was floored by his size.

He's 6-foot-8, no doubt about it," Amatucci said. "Patrick is all muscle. He looks like a Greek god. He was polite, articulate, and a good student. My take was that Patrick was convinced Calvert Hall was a better opportunity for him to excel in the classroom and on the court. One drawback was that I had not seen him play. When he enrolled, I was able to put him through a workout at Calvert Hall. I wasn't overwhelmed. But, you cannot take away the fact he is 6-8. Knowing that taking a transfer always comes with a risk, I still believed it was going to work out."

More importantly, Amatucci picked up Aaron "AJ" Herbert, a transfer from Randallstown High that was ready to immediately step in and take the reins at the point guard position. Amatucci said, "I got a call from a rabid Randallstown supporter telling me, 'He's Vince Williams with a lot more offensive punch.'" AJ was unselfish and played his butt off on defense," Amatucci said. "He was going to make Juan Dixon a better player. Mentally, he understood his role and responsibilities as a leader on the floor."

Freddie Biggs, a quick guard, who would fit in well with the Card's defensive game plan, moved up from the junior varsity and fully understood Amatucci's expectations.

Jason Medinger, another JV addition was initially cut, but took the bold initiative to ask Amatucci to give him another shot. He made the team the second time around. Medinger, a gifted student, convinced Amatucci that he needed someone to push the starters.

"I can make this team better, and that's why you need me on this squad," Medinger remembered telling him.

Amatucci remembered making a wise decision to keep Medinger around.

"He made an argument with which I could not disagree. I give him a lot of credit for forcing my hand," Amatucci said. "He wound up being a solid contributor off the bench. He was scrappy, pushed Juan in practice every day, and would do anything asked of him to help the team."

Medinger said even though the players came from different backgrounds, they were "tight as a family" and were united by Amatucci's burning desire to win. Everyone was on board to take the program to a higher level.

After Calvert Hall, Medinger graduated from the University of Notre Dame and then received a law degree from Emory University. Today, he is a U.S. Attorney, using many of the ideals he learned as a player at Calvert Hall.

Medinger developed a list of what he called "Tooch's Life Lessons," which consist of:

1. Get your "stuff" together.
2. You have to earn your spot, every day, every inch.
3. When you think you have nothing left to give, that's when you reach down inside yourself and find that extra ounce of devotion.
4. Only the dedicated survive.
5. You play like you practice. If you don't practice well, you won't play well.
6. Trust Tooch was a model of tough love; he pushed and pushed and pushed because he cared about getting the very best out of each and every one of us.

"When you're a 16- or 17-year-old kid, you're like, why is this guy yelling at me and pushing me so hard," Medinger said. "As you get older, you realize he was trying to form you into someone that will push themselves. That's what I do. My respect for him just keeps growing. Folks will jump down a lion's mouth for him."

Chad Unitas, the son of former Baltimore Colts quarterback and NFL Hall-of-Famer Johnny Unitas was another talented addition from the junior varsity.

Patrick Venanzi played football and added toughness to the team. Amatucci said, "Pat had basketball sense, he had no fear banging with guys much taller and bigger than he was. He worked his way into the rotation with DJ."

As a result, the coach believed he had a special group capable of making a run at both tournament and league championships.

"Coming off the year before, I am thinking we can win the league, beat St. Frances and go to the Alhambra," Amatucci remembered. "AJ and Juan are a formidable duo, and up front we are big. The Baltimore Sun preseason preview noted, "The Cards should pose the biggest threat to St. Frances in the BCL, but developing a winning chemistry and leadership will be crucial."

One of the distractions to putting it all together was that a number of players were also part of AAU teams. AAU games and workouts sometimes conflicted with Calvert Hall practices. Amatucci allowed the players to compete with AAU teams, but Calvert Hall had to be the priority. If they were late or didn't show up for practice, there was going to be major consequences. Sure enough, Amatucci had scheduled a summer preseason practice on a Sunday that began in the weight room. Dixon and Herbert showed up late. After the practice ended, Herbert and Dixon completed a grueling workout, sending a clear message on priorities to the team. Going forward, the players had no misunderstanding of their priorities.

"Looking back, it is always hard to compare teams," Amatucci said. "This 95-96 team may not have been at the same level as the teams in the early 1980s, but these guys were pretty damn good. When we got going defensively, it was a blitzkrieg. People could not score against us. It was more captivating to watch us defensively than offensively, and we were scoring 70 to 80 points."

The Cardinals opened the season with solid wins over Good Counsel and City College. The game against City's Knights had concerned Amatucci because Ngongba noticeably did not get back on defense, a disturbing trend that would haunt him the rest of the season. A player that was not dedicated to defense was going to struggle under Amatucci's system at any level.

Soon after, Ngongba planned to travel back to Africa for an unspecified reason. Amatucci did not approve the trip. Ultimately, Unitas and Gary Williams talked him out of flying home. "He was becoming a major distraction," Amatucci said. Because of his lack of focus, Amatucci held Ngongba out of the lineup for two games. Even though the media asked questions about Ngongba's status, Amatucci made sure to protect his player, deflecting the reasons for his absence.

Calvert Hall beat Arundel, 65-59, the following game, which was significant because Maryland assistant coach Billy Hahn saw Dixon play for the first time. Dixon, who scored 23 points that night, became a main target for the Terps and coach Gary Williams. Bill Free of the Baltimore Sun wrote, "Dixon was superb at both ends of the court and was too quick and smooth for the Wildcats at crucial parts of the game."

Amatucci remembered, "Billy Hahn grabbed me after the game and said that Coach Williams is going to love this kid."

Still, Dixon could be exasperating and had missed practice the day before a game against Atholton—a violation that would normally have kept him from playing. This time, the circumstances took a dramatic turn.

"The morning of the Atholton game, Juan came to see me before homeroom and stoically told me, 'Tooch, the reason I missed practice yesterday, is that my Dad died.' It hit me hard," Amatucci said. "Here's a kid who has lost both of his parents within a year. I told him I was here to support him, and it was okay if he did not want to play. Juan looked me in the eye and said, 'I want to play.'"

Dixon led all scorers with 23 points in the 74-71 win. He did not shed a tear. Amatucci recalled, "Juan's play that night was a powerful display of courage."

As the victories piled up, Amatucci was perplexed by Ngongba's inconsistent performance. College coaches, focusing more on his potential, considered him a five-star recruit. One college head coach was bypassing Amatucci in the recruiting process, calling Ngongba directly during a dead period. This ended when Amatucci threatened to inform the NCAA about his actions.

"I have a little bit of a history with the NCAA, so I'll be able to get right through to them," Amatucci emphatically proclaimed, "You get where I coming from?"

On another occasion when Amatucci was sitting down to dinner with his family, his daughter Stephanie rose from the table to answer the phone, thinking it was one of her friends.

"Yes, sir … yes, sir … okay … I'll get my dad right now," Amatucci heard her say from the other room.

"Dad, dad, it's Coach K on the phone," she told him.

Amatucci didn't think Ngongba would be a good fit for the Duke basketball program under Mike Krzyzewski. Nogongba ended up at George Washington University where he averaged 4.9 points per game.

Calvert Hall learned more valuable lessons and strengthened its national brand at the King Cotton Classic in Pine Bluff, Arkansas, which included #1 ranked Oak Hill Academy. The tournament started disappointingly with the Cardinals losing to Jefferson Davis, of Alabama, 67-61, in double overtime.

"Physically, they outplayed us. We didn't have the intensity to finish the game in regulation," Amatucci said. "We got pushed around."

Calvert Hall rebounded the next night with a 64-58 victory over J.A. Fair of Little Rock, Arkansas. The Cardinals came out flat and were never in sync in a 69-52 loss to Holy Cross of New York. "It was a bad outing," Amatucci said about the loss. "What really upset me the most was that I thought we should have been pumped up for a team of Holy Cross' caliber."

The Cardinals returned home and beat Cardinal Gibbons (69-64) and Curley (72-44) to improve to 12-2. Goretti halted the momentum and handed the Cardinals their first loss in the state of Maryland, 50-46. Calvert Hall shot just 29 percent from the field. "We stunk," Amatucci said after the game. "As good as we've been against Gibbons and some other teams, we were horrible tonight."

The Cards returned to form and earned the biggest win of that season, taking down No. 3 St. Frances, 60-54. The Cardinals outscored the Panthers 20-10 in the final quarter. The Panthers' box-and-one defense was ineffective. Dixon finished with 20 points. "Defensively, we were getting after them," Amatucci said. "They did not push us around." St. Frances coach William Wells commented, "They weren't going to let us come in here and go home with a win."

After beating Gilman, 59-45, the Cardinals had a lackluster performance against the Mount St. Joseph Gaels and their new coach, Pat Clatchey, who eventually built a dynasty of his own in Irvington. Dixon was late for practice and sat out the first quarter. Calvert Hall managed to overcome the slow start and was in position to win the game in the final seconds. However, unable to shake free for a three-pointer, Herbert drove to the basket and made a layup with four seconds left and watched as the clock ran out, giving the Gaels a 60-59 victory.

"Somebody forgot to tell AJ that a two-point layup was worthless when you are down three," Amatucci said. "The message to the team was, 'There are consequences for being late' and losing to Saint Joe cost us severely in the standings."

Next up was the Charm City Classic at Towson University. Calvert Hall lost to Strake Jesuit of Houston, 75-66. The Cardinals had pulled to within three with 2:56 remaining before Strake pulled away. "We got close, and then they forced two consecutive turnovers to shut the door on our comeback," Amatucci said. "They were strong, quick and had legitimate Division I players. We couldn't match up with them." Michael LeBlanc led Strake with 31 points and 14 rebounds.

That loss set up an intriguing game with Dunbar of Baltimore. An Amatucci-led team had not played the Poets since the triple-overtime thriller in 1982. It was a game Amatucci desperately wanted to win.

"This was not a typical Dunbar team. They were beatable," Amatucci said. "We talked about the history and the opportunity to beat them for bragging rights in town."

The Cardinals took a 48-46 lead with 3:37 remaining in the game before the Poets scored seven straight points to escape with a 53-50 win. Tommy Polley, who later played football at Florida State and was selected by the St. Louis Rams in the second round of the 2001 NFL Draft, had 19 points for Dunbar. Dixon led Calvert Hall with 22 points.

Amatucci was not happy with the loss and decided to practice the following day, which also happened to be the day of Super Bowl XXX between the Pittsburgh Steelers and Dallas Cowboys.

"I was really pissed off," Amatucci said. "It was Dunbar. The loss left a real sour taste in my mouth."

Amatucci scheduled practice the following night for 7 p.m. Several players groaned about cancelling their plans to watch the Super Bowl.

"You can imagine how that went over," Amatucci said with a laugh. "If they didn't show up for practice, they could turn in their uniform."

He eventually received a call from the mother of Freddie Biggs who pleaded with him to reconsider the practice. For the first time in his coaching career, Amatucci backed off. The following day, the players paid a heavy price. As the players walked onto the practice floor, they soon realized there were no balls.

Those no-ball practices were just part of life with Tooch. Medinger remembered the always tough Venanzi getting light-headed from the running. After the players realized Venanzi was okay, they thanked him because they knew the running was finally over; someone had virtually passed out.

Calvert Hall took down McDonogh, 61-60, in double overtime the following game. Dixon led the team again with 23 points. It was becoming a habit for Juan to be The Hall's leading scorer. Playing with confidence, the Cardinals then took down Goretti in a key BCL showdown, 74-64. Tied after three quarters, the Cardinals, led by Dixon's 31, pulled away for the win. Amatucci remembered, "Our team defense in the fourth quarter turned the game around."

On the horizon was a rematch against No. 2 St. Frances, which was rolling through opponents and had won the Charm City Classic. This time, the Panthers got their revenge with a 91-61 victory before a capacity crowd at the University of Baltimore.

"We were ready to play, but we got into foul trouble early," Amatucci remembered. "They beat our butt. That's really the only thing I can say."

Karcher finished with 30 points, and St. Frances improved to 21-4 on the year. "When I got things started, everybody got into it," Karcher said after the game. "We got after it tonight, diving for loose balls and doing whatever it takes."

Calvert Hall closed out the regular season by beating Loyola Blakefield twice and Cardinal Gibbons. In the second victory over Loyola, the Cardinals held the Dons scoreless for thirteen minutes. With the victory, the Cardinals clinched the MIAA A conference championship for the second straight year.

Calvert Hall also earned the second seed in the Baltimore Catholic League Tournament. The Cardinals took down Towson Catholic, 64-57, in the first round with Dixon scoring 12 of his 21 points in a three-minute and 30-second span in the third quarter.

"Dixon is playing as well as any guard that I ever had, including Marc Wilson and McKay," Amatucci said. "He's doing it at both ends, too."

Calvert Hall beat Mount St. Joseph 75-63 in the semifinals. In the Baltimore Sun, Bob Clark wrote, "Leading 45-38 with 1:50 left in the third quarter, the Cardinals put on a defensive stand that shut out the Gaels for the next 3:46 while the lead increased to 57-38."

All five of Calvert Hall's starters—Dixon (24), Herbert (10), Peoples (12), Ngongba (13) and Anyan (12)— scored in double figures. That set up a rubber match in the championship against St. Frances, which beat Gibbons, 83-73, in the other semifinal.

Karcher was the difference for the Panthers in the title game. He broke a 60-60 deadlock in the fourth quarter with six points in 14 seconds, and St. Frances emerged with a 71-67 victory before more than 2,000 fans at Goucher College. Karcher finished with 26 points. Dixon led Calvert Hall with 23.

The most disappointing element of that game was Ngongba, who unexpectedly pulled himself out of the contest late in the fourth quarter with an apparent injury. "He never went back in the game, and I didn't think there was anything really wrong with him," Amatucci said. "That's how Patrick Ngongba's career ended at Calvert Hall. He quit on us."

Calvert Hall finished the season 25-8 and St. Frances won the Alhambra Tournament by taking down DeMatha (54-47) in the semifinals and Gonzaga (61-46) in the title game. Amatucci was disappointed the Cardinals did not even get an invite.

"You would think with the team and tradition we had, we would have gotten an invite," Amatucci said, "We would have competed with any of those teams in that tournament. That was a shame. Invite or not, 25-8 was a great season, or was it? We have a lot of parts back for the next season, but I'm looking for more growth – P's and absolutes."

Up next – Juan more year!

16

NEVER A DOUBT

Juan Dixon returns to The Hall for a visit.

"Reach for the light, you might touch the sky.
Stand on the mountain top and see yourself fly.
Reach for the light to capture a star.
Come out of the darkness and find out who you are."

- STEVE WINWOOD

On April 27, 2017, Juan Dixon was formally introduced as the new head coach at Coppin State University. For the first time in maybe his life, tears flowed as he thanked his family and the Coppin State administration for their support. His life had truly come full circle. Dixon even gave a shout out to his former high school coach.

"I didn't read my first book until I got to Calvert Hall, "The Catcher in the Rye." Thank you, Coach Amatucci," Dixon said.

Amatucci said, "Juan's comment is a great example of what I have always stressed. We encouraged our guys to broaden themselves intellectually. It's always been about more than hoops."

Indeed, it was a long road to Coppin State. Throughout his life, Dixon constantly had to deal with detractors and each time he proved them wrong. Amatucci had seen that tenacity from Dixon's days at Calvert Hall.

"I get attached to the kids I coach, but this one's kind of special," Amatucci said. "Anyone who gets to know Juan Dixon has to respect what he's been through and the decisions he's managed to make, in spite of those experiences."

By his senior year at Calvert Hall, Dixon was being touted as one of the most talented high school basketball players in the nation. He was named First-Team All-Metro by The Baltimore Sun his junior year, so expectations were high. Dixon was a natural scorer who was also cunning defensively. University of Maryland coach Gary Williams had him in his sights as a prized recruit.

His rise to basketball prominence was the culmination of hard work, passion and persistence in the face of adversity. Amatucci vividly remembers the early days of his prized pupil.

In the summer of 1994, Amatucci was conducting the annual grueling summer workouts with the Cardinals' returners and hopeful prospects. One evening, he received a call from Phil Dixon, who had played against Amatucci's teams with St. Frances and was a key contributor for Shenandoah University, a Division III program in Virginia.

"I want you to take a look at my brother, Juan, who will be a sophomore at Lake Clifton High School," he said. "Believe me, you are really going to like this kid. He's your kind of player."

They set up a time to have Juan work out with the team. The Dixon brothers showed up later that week.

"My first impression of Juan was that when he turned sideways, you could barely see him because he was so skinny," Amatucci remembered. "He was 6-foot-1, 130 pounds, maybe. He always looked me in the eye when I was speaking to him. Not knowing our players, it had to be uncomfortable for him walking into Calvert Hall's gym. He had heard about me, but didn't know anything about me."

Dixon recalled: "I didn't know what to expect from Mark Amatucci. I really didn't get the opportunity to watch him coach. People had told me he was a very intense coach. He was passionate, and he talked about how much he cared for his kids."

Immediately, Dixon impressed Amatucci with his effort and ability to blend in with the other Cardinals players. Defensively, Dixon quickly picked up concepts in terms of denying the ball, getting into passing lanes and putting pressure on opposing players. Amatucci realized that he had great potential.

"Remarkably, he was outworking everybody on the floor," Amatucci said. "He knew what he was doing and had the skills to back it up. It was surprising for a kid at his age to have that type of defensive skill. Phil was wrong; I just didn't like this kid. I fell in love with his game."

After the session, Amatucci sat down with Dixon and explored the reasons he was considering coming to Calvert Hall. The maturity expressed in his answers caught Amatucci's attention. "Academically, this is a better challenge for me," Dixon told him. "I want to have the opportunity to play in the Catholic League. I also want to get out of the city."

Amatucci said, "I did not think he was just saying what he thought I wanted to here. I found him very sincere and straightforward."

Dixon had to go through the application process and take the entrance exam. Amatucci found out that Dixon, prior to his freshman year, had applied and was accepted into Calvert Hall. Dixon had been recruited to play football based on his potential to be a big-time quarterback. The financial aid package offered was not substantial enough, and Dixon enrolled at Lake Clifton. Amatucci expected the admission process for Dixon's transfer from Lake Clifton to be a formality.

Believing there were no issues with Dixon's acceptance, Amatucci scheduled an appointment with assistant principal for academic affairs, Lou Heidrick, to finalize Juan's transition to The Hall. Unexpectedly, Heidrick informed Amatucci that Dixon would not be accepted because of his poor performance on standardized testing.

"Lou, he got accepted last year," said Amatucci, his voice rising. "His grades are good. What are you talking about?"

Tempers rose as they debated Dixon's status.

"Whatever you need me to do academically, I am going to make sure we're covered here," Amatucci told Heidrick. "He will be assigned to the Learning Resource Center, and I will schedule regular tutoring sessions with his teachers. You know the success our players have had academically. It's a priority for me—academics come before basketball."

By this time, their voices could be heard outside the office as they went back and forth. Finally, Heidrick relented.

"You better make sure he doesn't screw up. Make sure he is seeing Jane Baker," Heidrick said while pointing at Amatucci. Mrs. Baker had been the founding director of the Learning Resource Center at The Hall in 1983. She created a very effective program to provide academic support for students. Amatucci said, "Mrs. B worked tirelessly with our players. She knew students individually. She would meet with them before and after school."

Amatucci travelled to Dixon's grandmother's home in the Edison community of Northeast Baltimore. When Amatucci arrived, Dixon was waiting for him on the front steps. Amatucci said, "It was obvious to me that Juan wasn't comfortable taking me into the house. What I learned during our conversation was that his mom was staying there and was gravely ill. Knowing his mom's situation had to be tearing him up inside, Juan's outward affect was stoic."

Trying to make Juan more at ease, Amatucci shifted the conversation to the expectations that came with being a student-athlete at Calvert Hall. Dixon was totally on board right away. Amatucci was impressed by

Dixon's clear vision of what he wanted to accomplish.

Amatucci said, "I felt like we were making a connection. At the end of our conversation, I saw the famous Dixon smile for the first time. When we finished, Juan invited me in to meet his grandmother."

The home visit left a lasting impression on Dixon, who immediately knew he could trust Amatucci.

"I knew how much he cared from the very beginning," Dixon recalled. "He also came to my home a few more times in Northeast Baltimore, which I thought was a great gesture on his part. It showed his sincerity."

From there, Amatucci went to work on the financial aid package. He was finally getting close to securing enough money for Dixon to enroll. Amatucci, said, "I had to fence with Calvert Hall's long-time treasurer, Frank Clary, several times to get enough aid. Mr. Frank was a tough negotiator, who good naturedly enjoyed seeing me grovel for help. In the end, he always came through. He had a long record of helping guys attend The Hall. Over the years, some of his favorite students were our hoops guys."

Phil Dixon directed Amatucci to talk to Juan's Aunt Janet about helping out financially. Amatucci was getting a clearer picture of the support Dixon was getting from his family, who were determined to keep him on the right path.

Aunt Janet would be the point person to help with tuition for the next three years. When Dixon's mother died in August 1994, he moved in with his cousin Shareece, who lived near Calvert Hall off Loch Raven Boulevard. "She was just a wonderful person to be around and was heavily involved," Amatucci said. "We clicked right away."

Amatucci was confident he had the foundation in place for Dixon to succeed at The Hall. Still, it was a big adjustment for Dixon when he walked through those doors of Calvert Hall for the first day of school as a sophomore transfer.

"To be honest, I didn't know what to expect. Being a kid from East Baltimore, I always attended public school," Dixon remembered. "The initial experience at Calvert Hall was culture shock. I was grateful to have the opportunity to go to Calvert Hall, but I didn't know what to expect from the school and Mark Amatucci."

Dixon was naturally inquisitive and blended in well with the student body. The academics were a challenge, but he was committed to taking advantage of study hall and utilizing support from his teachers. Dixon said, "I quickly learned the importance of time management and developing a solid work ethic."

Amatucci added: "The curiosity was really something that shined with him. He wanted to be educated. He wanted to learn. You just had to be encouraged by his personality and how he lit up a room."

Amatucci remembered driving up Route 70 on the way to a game at Bishop Walsh. Dixon, noticing a sign for Antietam National Battlefield, eagerly asked questions about its place in American history. Amatucci said, "Juan was amazed that such an important location in American history was so close to home."

However, it did take some time for Dixon to fully embrace Amatucci's expectations. Practice on Saturdays began at 11 a.m. This meant the players were expected to arrive by 10:30 and be on the floor by 10:45 or they were considered late. One day, Amatucci was about to leave his house around 9:30 when the phone rang.

"I can't come to practice," Dixon said on the other end of the line.

"What do you mean you can't come to practice?" Amatucci responded.

"I don't have a ride," Dixon retorted.

"I'll tell you what, you better find a ride or there will be consequences. Do you understand that? If you're late or don't make it to practice, you're in big trouble." Amatucci then hung up the phone.

About an hour later, a taxicab pulled up to the back of the Calvert Hall gym and Dixon emerged. To avoid future issues on Saturdays, Coach Healy agreed to pick him up on the way to practice.

Amatucci and Dixon didn't always see eye-to-eye, but there was always mutual respect. Amatucci also made sure he kept Dixon on the right path, and sometimes that meant tough love. During his junior year, Dixon had his entire family in the stands for a game against Curley. Early on, Amatucci immediately recognized that Dixon was not getting back on defense. Dixon and Amatucci had been butting heads over the finer details of his game—footwork, support off the ball, etc. Dixon had natural instincts that were superior to most players. Amatucci believed improving his technique combined with his instincts would make him a complete defensive player.

"We were having our little battles," Amatucci said. "Not getting back on defense was a battle Juan was never going to win."

Late in the second quarter, things boiled over against the Friars. Dixon was making no effort on defense. He was allowing his man to easily penetrate to the basket, was not sprinting back, and his body language said — "I'll do what I want to do." Amatucci subbed him out of the game and erupted within earshot of Dixon's family. The rule for every player coming out of the game was to sit directly between Amatucci and Coach Healy to get feedback on his performance. Dixon then abruptly stood up and walked to the end of the bench to pout. Amatucci not appreciating his antics kept him on the bench for the remainder of the first half and ripped him at halftime in front of his teammates. Dixon sat out the entire second half. Lesson learned. Point made.

Dixon admitted it was a challenge dealing Amatucci's coaching style.

"It took some time getting used to his intensity with the yelling, screaming and stomping on the floor," Dixon said. "Those were the things I had to get accustomed to. For a while, I was against it. We would butt heads about how much he yelled. Growing up, my parents didn't yell at me in that manner. For him, it was just what he did. All of the yelling I endured in those three years at Calvert Hall definitely prepared me for Coach Gary Williams at the University of Maryland."

There were ups and downs, but Amatucci never questioned Dixon's commitment, enthusiasm and potential. Coach Edwards remembered Dixon picking up a loose ball in the Bishop McCorristin Tournament his first year with the team. He stepped over a few players on the floor and made a jumper. "I just looked at Tooch and said, 'Wow, this kid can play.' He was just a good all-around basketball player," Edwards said. "I think what made him a great player was that his heart was as big as any player I've ever seen. I'm sure Tooch helped make him the player that he was."

Two years after that fateful workout at the Calvert Hall gymnasium, the highly recruited Dixon was the most talked about player in the Baltimore area. He was the topic of newspaper articles and sports radio discussions. Where is Juan Dixon headed? The 1996-1997 preseason was on the horizon and all was well in the house of Amatucci. Well, maybe not.

Amatucci is on the edge. He is not sure he likes the way things are going. "Juan was getting full of himself a little bit," Amatucci remembered. "He was already a big-name in town because of how well he was playing."

Amatucci thought Dixon was not giving the maximum effort on the court or in the classroom and inevitably things were going to boil over again. One day after practice, Amatucci calmly explained that he was disappointed with Dixon's performance. As a result, Amatucci told him to take three days off, which was ostensibly a suspension. He also told Dixon's teammate and partner in crime, Gary Williams, to take a day off as well.

"When you guys come back, we'll do something aerobic to make sure you got the message," Amatucci told them.

Amatucci met privately with Dixon the following day. "Juan, what are you doing?" Amatucci said, expressing his displeasure. "How do you expect to transition to play at a major Division I college when you're making absolutely no effort. You're being totally selfish."

Dixon got the message and came back even stronger. Dixon was not averse to the tough love. He understood the opportunity in front of him and had the instincts to thrive. Sometimes, he just needed to be pointed in the right direction.

Dixon quickly dismissed any questions about his commitment to the program as soon as his senior season began. The Cardinals took down

Central, 53-38, and Good Counsel, 56-49, in the Towson Catholic Tip-Off Mixer at Goucher College. Dixon had 21 and 26 points, respectively. Amatucci was upbeat about the defensive effort in both of those games.

The Cardinals suffered their first setback in the Gonzaga Classic with a 64-53 loss to Rice of Harlem, New York. Rice was coached by Maurice Hicks, who played for Amatucci at Loyola. Contemplating the loss, Amatucci began to have concerns about his team's offense. Besides Dixon, he was not getting much production out of the other starters. Dixon had 28 against Rice, but only three other players—Herbert, Bryant and Williams—scored.

Antoine Peoples had come down with the flu prior to the game, which put a significant hole in the lineup. Before the game, Amatucci tried to will Peoples to health and encouraged him to suit up and try a short stint. Moments later, finding Peoples throwing up in the bathroom, Amatucci realized his healing powers were ineffective. Without Peoples available, Rice was able to dominate inside and come away with the victory.

"I was disappointed no one stepped up to fill the hole created by Antoine's illness," Amatucci said. "We were still not getting any production offensively. Fifty-three points, especially against a team like Rice, is not going to win you many games. We got beat up physically. There was no consistency. It wasn't a good night. I was a little ticked off. Pupil beats teacher, did not help."

The Cardinals bounced back in a big way against Anacostia, which was the No. 1 ranked team in Washington, D.C. Dixon was pumped up because he was facing his future Maryland teammate, Lonnie Baxter.

Amatucci's pregame message to the team was brief, "We're going to be aggressive. We are going to press full court. We are going to take the game to them."

Calvert Hall stormed the court and played man-to-man defense and trapped the entire game. "Until we either break down or they give up, we're going to trap for 32 minutes," Amatucci said. In the second half, Anacostia folded under the pressure and the Cardinals emerged with a

78-67 signature victory. Dixon scored 47 points, breaking the tournament record for points in a game. After the game, Amatucci told the press, "Juan makes threes like everyone else makes layups." Baxter finished with 20 points.

"We needed that win to get our confidence," Amatucci remembered. "Back in the day, I had Wilson, Tubman and Kauffman, now I had Bryant, Herbert and Dixon. It was the same kind of defensive mentality. I was comfortable letting them trap on their own."

Calvert Hall took down Goretti, 57-40, in the third game of the tournament. The Cards totally dominated the game start to finish. The team created double digit turnovers. The Gaels in-game adjustments were ineffective. The Cardinals were rolling at both ends of the floor.

Calvert Hall then got a measure of revenge in the Bishop McCorristin Tournament in New Jersey. "We had a much more disciplined squad going into the tournament than the previous year," Amatucci remembered. Calvert Hall took down Bishop McDevitt (PA), 52-45, in the opener. Dixon led the way with 15 points. The Cardinals then breezed past St. Peter's (NY), 66-52, in the semifinals. Dixon led all scorers with 32 points. Calvert Hall then pulled out a hard-fought 60-55 victory over Bishop McCorristin in the championship game. The Cardinals had come out flat and were getting pushed around before Amatucci made the proper adjustments.

"It was déjà vu of the year before with the boys in stripes. We were getting jammed," said Amatucci, whose team trailed 26-18 at the half. "We couldn't get across half-court without a hand-check being called. When we were running the break, they were knocking us on our butts and there was no whistle. It was blatant."

Amatucci was hit with a technical for breaking the seatbelt rule when he stormed down the side of the court.

"Look, I don't bitch a whole lot, but this is either going to be a physical game or a ticky-tack game. Pick one or the other because I am having trouble understanding what's going on." Amatucci told the lead official.

The Cardinals matched McCorristin's physicality in the second half and picked up their intensity. Calvert Hall took control in the fourth quarter and held on for the win. Dixon led the Cardinals again with 27 points. Reggie Bryant was the unsung hero of the championship game. "Reggie loved a physical, fast moving game," Amatucci said. "He ignited our fourth quarter surge."

However, Dixon disappointed his coach prior to the BCL opener against Mount St. Joseph because he was late for the pre-game meeting. Bryant missed the bus and his mother drove him to St. Joe. Amatucci benched both of the players for the entire first half. "I don't know many league coaches that would sit impact players for a half," Amatucci said. As a result, the Cardinals trailed 35-18 at the break. With Dixon and Bryant back in the lineup, Calvert Hall made a run but fell short 60-59. Dixon scored 17 of his game-high 21 points in the fourth quarter, but it was not enough. "That loss wound up costing us the regular-season championship," Amatucci said. "I made life miserable for the both of them in practice the next day."

Amatucci realized there was more to Bryant's tardiness to the game than an issue of punctuality. Bryant was struggling with his role on the team. The coaches felt he was making a significant contribution and was a key ingredient to the team's positive chemistry. Bryant felt, however, he was under appreciated. A tension was building between coach and player.

Amatucci said, "Reggie was an important part of our team, but I was not going to turn my head to his sulking and sullen attitude. I told Coach Baker to call his mom and find out what we needed to do to straighten Reggie out."

Coach Baker remembered, "I talked to Mrs. Bryant. She recognized that Reggie was not happy. She told me, 'Mr. Baker, ever since Reggie was little he went around the house bouncing a ball and making up songs about basketball. He's not singing any songs these day."

Coach Baker gave the message to Tooch, who immediately met with Reggie and mom. Amatucci said, "This situation was a learning experience for me and Reggie. Don't assume. Reggie's negative behavior was not about selfishness, it was about misunderstanding feelings." Fast forward, Reggie would become one of the most enthusiastic and leading scorers in Calvert Hall's basketball history.

Ever since, Coach Baker has regularly spoken to basketball campers about developing their game through hard work and enjoying playing the game. He encourages them to make up songs about basketball.

After beating Goretti, 76-60 ("I haven't seen Cokey throw that towel in a long time," Amatucci said), next up was a showdown with No. 1 St. Frances at the University of Baltimore. The Cardinals were forced to practice at Goucher College leading up to the game. Gary Williams and Dixon were late again. To further annoy Amatucci, there was no energy on the practice floor.

Amatucci made the players go forty minutes without a ball to wake them up. "Do you want to continue with this or do you want to get ready for St. Frances," Amatucci asked them. Once he got their attention, the players displayed the effort and intensity Amatucci expected.

The next day, the Cardinals arrived to a packed house at the University of Baltimore's gymnasium, located on the top floor of an academic building. Amatucci said, "It's a real band box. The team benches are jammed against a wall. The players and coaches feet are literally on the court. There are stands behind both baskets. The same light every year is out over the south basket."

The Cardinals were well prepared for the Panthers' box-and-one defense and came away with a huge 61-59 victory. Amatucci placed Peoples in the middle of the box. He was open the entire game. He was able to effectively score and distribute the ball. It was a tight and hotly contested game the entire way. The final minute went back and forth. With 37 seconds to go, Dixon hit two free throws to put the Cards up, 61-57. St. Frances closed the gap to two points with a Darran Byrd layup with 14 seconds left. The Hall's AJ Herbert missed the front end of a one and one with 11 seconds on the clock. After a mad scramble for the rebound,

Byrd recovered the ball for the Panthers and called a timeout with five seconds showing on the scoreboard.

Amatucci remembered, "In the timeout, I told the guys we weren't going to let Karcher beat us. If he touches the ball we will trap him right away and put the pressure on somebody else to beat us."

After the timeout with the sell-out crowd collectively holding their breath, the Panthers inbounded the ball to Karcher who was aggressively double teamed by Cardinal defenders. He was able to pass the ball to Byrd who made a layup as time expired. The referees waived off the basket as Byrd's shot did not beat the final buzzer.

Dixon led all scorers with 26 points, and Peoples added 12. Karcher led St. Frances, ranked 24th nationally by USA Today, with 23. Dixon commented after the game, "We came into this game with confidence. Coach Amatucci put us through some hard practices and got us believing we could win." Amatucci added, "Juan did not get into detail about the background history of those practices."

"We played exceptionally well," Amatucci remembered. "It was one of our most complete games. The referees did a great job letting both teams play. The fans got their money's worth. With a win like this you know you have your team believing they can take down the best."

By this time, Dixon was averaging 23 points per game and playing shutdown defense. Games were selling out as fans wanted to get a glimpse of the future Terps star, and Dixon did not disappoint. Before a packed gym at Arundel high school, Dixon scored 29 points and Calvert Hall was dominant in an 85-58 victory, improving to 15-2 on the season. The Cardinals continued to roll, entering the Charm City Classic at the Towson Center. Calvert Hall matched up against Thomas Johnson High School, led by another Maryland recruit, Terence Morris, in the opener. The Patriots were coached by famed coach and Amatucci's good friend, Tom Dickman.

Dixon once again got the best of a future Maryland teammate with 25 points, while Morris scored 23. Calvert Hall emerged with a 60-58 victory. "They were one of the top public school teams in the state," Amatucci said. "They were scrappy and disciplined and we matched up well with them." That set up a game with St. Benedict's of New Jersey. The Cardinals did not make crucial plays down the stretch and lost, 66-55. Even though he missed a couple of free throw late in the fourth quarter, Dixon led all scorers with 36 points.

"We played good enough to beat most teams tonight, but not St. Benedict's," Amatucci said. "The effort in the first half was outstanding but something we could not sustain for the final two quarters. Unfortunately we turned the ball over late in the game, which was unusual for us." A win likely would have catapulted Calvert Hall into the national rankings.

Calvert Hall took down Goretti again, 56-45, on the road. Amatucci was agitated because there were problems with the game-clock throughout the contest. After the game, Amatucci lit up a cigar in the locker room just to add an exclamation point.

"Don't you know you're not supposed to smoke in here," Goretti's principal told Amatucci.

"I didn't know that," Amatucci responded, while continuing to blow smoke.

The season took a disappointing turn in the rematch with St. Frances. This time, the Panthers were focused and ready the play. They abandoned the box-and-one and played strong man to man defense in a 63-50 victory before a standing-room only crowd at Calvert Hall. Despite foul trouble, Karcher led all scorers with 20 points, while Dixon finished with 15. "I can honestly say we never threatened," Amatucci said. The loss dropped Calvert Hall to 20-4.

After winning the next four games, Calvert Hall suffered what Amatucci calls, "one of the worst defeats in all my years of coaching." The Cardinals led Loyola, 50-45, with just 17 seconds left in the game. The Dons pulled to within one point on free throws by Ryan Heacock and Chris Malone with 12 seconds left. Calvert Hall later missed the front end of a one-and-one and allowed Loyola's Brian Cosgrove to grab the rebound with 7.6 seconds remaining. Amatucci's long-time nemesis Jerry Savage called a timeout.

"Listen, stay with your man. There are only seven seconds to go," Amatucci told his players. "It's all fundamentals. If your man has the ball, get good spacing on the ball. Stop penetration. Off the ball, stay with your man."

On the inbound, the Dons worked their way up the court. Dixon, who had a game-high 16 points, backed off Heacock, who took advantage of an open look and nailed a 3-pointer for a 52-50 victory at the buzzer. With the win, Loyola (20-9) captured the MIAA A conference crown and gave Savage his 13th 20-win season. It was also the first time Loyola beat Amatucci since he returned to Calvert Hall, snapping an eight-game skid.

The Cardinals got their revenge in the Catholic League Tournament by breezing past Loyola, 71-47, in the semifinals. "We were not taking any prisoners," Amatucci said. "I reminded them what the previous loss cost us, not to mention the embarrassment. We destroyed them."

This set up the title game with St. Frances. It was the third straight year that the tournament final pitted the Cardinals versus the Panthers. Once again, the Panthers found a way to win, emerging with a 61-57 victory before a Goucher College crowd of more than 2,000, including Maryland coach Gary Williams. Dixon scored 23, but the Panthers 6-foot-8 center Shawn Hampton was the difference, scoring 18 points with eight rebounds. Hampton was also eight-for-eight from the foul line. The Cards big man, Gary Williams, fouled out with seven minutes to play. "Shawn manhandled us," Amatucci said. "We didn't play our best game, and they wanted it more. We didn't answer. In crunch time, we failed to capitalize on opportunities to get control of the game."

After the game, Amatucci shook the hand of BCL Hall of Fame St. Frances coach William Wells, but declined the runner-up trophy, telling the seniors to grab the consolation prize. Amatucci said, "William is an excellent coach, and his kids deserved to win. But after losing three championship games in a row, I was an angry man." In the locker room after the game, Amatucci, a man who is known to speak his mind, spoke volumes with his silence. The Cards packed up and went home.

Calvert Hall, which was 26-6, was invited back to the Alhambra Tournament. It was the Cardinals' first return to the tourney since Coach Baker's 1989 BCL championship team participated. The BCL tournament loss had zapped the energy from the team. That did not bode well for the Cards heading into a tournament that featured some of the region's top programs.

"If I'm feeling this down, you can imagine what the players are feeling," Amatucci said. "We've always made winning the Alhambra a team priority. The St. Frances loss completely drained us. We didn't rebound."

The Cardinals were run off the court by Washington's Archbishop Carroll, 84-55, in the opening round. Ruben Boumtje Boumtje, who later played at Georgetown and was a second-round pick by the Portland Trail Blazers in the 2001 NBA Draft, led Carroll with 23 points.

The Cardinals then lost to Archbishop Carroll, of Pennsylvania, 68-51, in the second round. In the final game the Cards defeated Bishop Walsh, 78-49.

Amatucci's wife, Pat, was expecting the couple's son, Mike, in June. At the Alhambra Tournament, the players' parents planned a baby shower for Amatucci. He was not in a festive mood, but he greatly appreciated the gesture.

"The shower helped to lift me out of the darkness" Amatucci said. "For the coaches, the team's play had not been to our standard when playing in celebrated tournaments like the Alhambra. It was a letdown. The three-hour trip home felt like a week-long trek."

After the season, Dixon was named to the First-Team All-Metro squad by The Baltimore Sun after averaging 23.4 points and 4.5 rebounds over that 1996-97 season. Dixon was described as the "one of the best pure shooters in the country," by recruiting expert Bob Gibbons.

For Dixon and Amatucci it was the end of three years of battling and embracing. Amatucci remembered, "His growth and our interactions were tedious and exhausting. Three steps forward, one step back. Sometimes working together, sometimes butting heads. What always kept me grounded was being aware of the difficult circumstances in which Juan grew up."

"Juan had a great year," Amatucci continued. "I don't want to throw cold water on his success that year because of the outcome of the Alhambra. Juan put up big numbers, and he wasn't a ball hog. He was under a lot of pressure. He was so mature in some areas, and so immature in others, like often being late. In the end, though, what kind of year did Juan Dixon have? Phenomenal."

Dixon admitted there were some challenges attending Calvert Hall.

"It was difficult," Dixon said. "When I was at public school, things came a little bit easier. Calvert Hall was different than anything I had experienced before. The support that I received from the faculty and staff showed they believed that I could become a better student even though the curriculum was on a completely different level than I ever experienced. I owe a great deal to Coach Mark Amatucci. He taught me discipline and showed me I could accomplish anything I wanted through hard work."

The 1996-1997 season was really two seasons. One for the Cardinals on the court, and the other one for Amatucci and Dixon managing the college recruiting process.

From the end of Dixon's junior season, Amatucci was barraged by calls and letters from top-twenty basketball programs hot on the recruiting trail for Juan Dixon. Amatucci said, "By the fall of 1996, Juan had Maryland as his number one choice. I encouraged him to take the time to look at a couple of other schools. In the end in addition to Maryland, he considered LSU, George Washington and Providence."

Dixon felt a positive connection with Maryland's coach, Gary Williams. Amatucci remembered, "Coach Williams' home visit solidified Juan's decision. He put as much emphasis on academics as he did on basketball. Personally, Gary impressed me with his sincerity and intensity."

Dixon made the decision to attend Maryland. He had earned the NCAA qualifying grade point average. The challenge was meeting the required scores on the SAT exam. Dixon worked hard to prepare, but did not make the necessary score in his junior year. He took the test again in October of his senior year, but once again fell short of the minimum score of 930. Dixon became discouraged and angry. It was a frustrating experience. Amatucci said, "I had never really seen him get that discouraged. I scheduled him to take the test again in February."

This led to another battle between the player and coach.

"Are you all set to take the test?" Amatucci asked after practice the Friday evening before the test.

"I'm not taking it," Dixon responded. Continuing the conversation in the coaches' office, Amatucci asked incredulously, "What do you mean you're not taking it?"

"I don't want to do it," Dixon sharply replied.

What started out as a calm conversation, turned into a heated argument. Amatucci had to physically grab Dixon to keep him from walking out of the office.

"First of all, don't do you dare walk out on me," Amatucci yelled. "Second of all, you're taking that damn test. Do you understand?"

The next morning, Dixon reported on time to take the test. He took the test several more times. He eventually scored a 1,060, easily meeting the requirements.

However, the improvement raised flags with SAT administrators. Dixon was forced to take the test again. This time, he scored 1,010, meeting the requirements once more. Dixon 2 College Board 0. The path to Maryland was officially cleared. Amatucci said, "Juan fought to make the SAT score with his usual tenacity. Making the score was personal for him. That's Juan Dixon. He could have folded but didn't. Never a doubt!"

Dixon didn't enroll in Maryland until after the first semester of 1997. He could practice with the team December 21, the day after first semester exams ended. Williams planned to redshirt Dixon because of the late start and to give him more time to develop. Dixon admittedly needed to get stronger.

While there were still some doubters about his ability to play in the ACC, Dixon seemed to thrive under those circumstances. Amatucci often used Dixon as a model of perseverance to younger players. "Juan just knocked down whatever walls got in his way," Amatucci said.

While at Maryland, Dixon became close with Terrapins guard Steve Francis, who helped him improve his offensive game. Francis encouraged Dixon to focus on aggressively attacking the basket and finishing with either hand. Francis was on the fast track to the NBA and was later the second overall pick of the 1999 NBA draft by the Vancouver Grizzlies. Moments before Dixon's first official practice, Francis approached him in the tunnel leading to the court. Francis wanted to give Dixon a warning about how intense Williams could be on players.

"Man, don't you know who I played for in high school?" Dixon responded.

Dixon returned to Calvert Hall several times in the summer after his redshirt season. He spent time talking to young players at Amatucci's basketball camp. On a sweltering day in late August, Amatucci received an excited voicemail from Dixon.

"Tooch, you have to call me right away," he said.

Amatucci worried that something was seriously wrong and called him back.

"What's wrong?" Amatucci nervously barked.

"Tooch, you have to get me in the gym," Dixon told him.

Amatucci agreed and opened the gym, which was oppressively hot. Dixon then commenced to take jumpers for more than 90 minutes. It was part of his daily routine where he would shoot three times per day, taking 500 jumpers in each session. He would then set up chairs to practice ball handling and concentrating on strengthening his left hand. It became a habit that whenever he was in the area with his entourage, Dixon would ask Amatucci to open the Calvert Hall gym so he could grab a workout.

"The hard work was a daily routine, even in the summers," Dixon remembered. "During the school year, I worked even harder on and off the court. I was trying to become a better person. It made me the man I am today."

Dixon didn't waste much time putting his stamp on the Terrapins program. He appeared in 34 games as a freshman, averaging 7.4 points and 2.6 rebounds. Dixon was named to the honorable mention ACC All-Freshman team He led all ACC freshmen in steals (50) and steals per game (1.5). The 50 steals ranked as the second-best single-season by a Maryland freshman since Johnny Rhodes had 71 in the 1993 season. Maryland finished the year 28-6 and made the Sweet 16 of the NCAA Tournament.

Dixon credited his time at Calvert Hall in making a smooth transition to Maryland and the ACC, widely regarded as the best college basketball league in the nation.

"I learned the value of time management and having a solid work effort. These ideals helped me at the University of Maryland," Dixon said. "When I got with Tooch, I really gained an appreciation for the importance of fundamentals in dribbling, passing, shooting, and defense. I really discovered how to become a sound, all-around basketball player. That's what I try to teach my guys today. Just be fundamentally sound and disciplined. On defense, make sure you communicate. I learned a lot from Tooch, for sure."

Amatucci made sure to watch Dixon's games at Maryland and attended several games in College Park. He was especially impressed the way Dixon was becoming a marquee player. Looking ahead, Amatucci envisioned Dixon becoming a legitimate NBA prospect.

"Gary Williams was so essential to his game, in terms of teaching him its finer points," Amatucci said. "Gary was able to get into the things that I never had the opportunity to work on in high school because I was starting from scratch. I don't think there was any doubt in Gary's mind that Juan was going to be in the NBA."

There was no sophomore slump for Dixon, who started all 35 games and led the ACC in steals (2.7) and finished second in scoring with 18 points per game. He averaged a team-high 34 minutes per game and was named first-team All-ACC and honorable mention All-American. His 630 points that season were the ninth highest in Maryland history at the time. The Terrapins went 25-10 and advanced to the second round of the NCAA Tournament.

"Juan is the kind of player that just wants the ball in key situations against good teams," Gary Williams said. "He has dramatically improved his ball handling, and he has become a very good outside shooter to complement his scoring ability as he drives to the basket. The thing I like most about Juan is that he has no fear of anybody that plays against him. He is not afraid to place himself in pressure situations. He's one of the most positive players I've coached in terms of staying with his shot and not letting slumps or setbacks get in his way. He's very resilient."

Expectations were now soaring for Dixon as the Terrapins entered the 2000-01 season. Maryland had the talent and depth to make a run at the national title. Once again, Dixon started all 36 games and was named to the first team All-ACC and to the ACC All-Defensive Team. Dixon was also named third team All-America by Basketball Times and the NABC and was an honorable mention All-American by the Associated Press.

Maryland advanced to the NCAA Final Four against Duke. The Terrapins led by 22 points in the first half before the Blue Devils rallied and emerged with a 95-84 victory. Dixon finished with a team-high 19 points. Maryland ended the year 25-11 and had its sights firmly on a national title run the following season.

"He carried the Terps," Amatucci said about Dixon playing against Duke. "Every time he played against Duke he came up with a big game."

Indeed, the Terrapins did not shy away from the fans and media's high expectations in Dixon's senior year. Maryland entered the season ranked No. 2 in the nation in the ESPN/USA Today Coaches' Poll. The Terrapins rolled past teams behind Dixon, who started all 36 games, averaging

20.4 points, 4.6 rebounds, 2.6 assists and 2.4 steals. He was named ACC Player of the Year, First-Team All-American, and most importantly led Maryland to its first national championship in men's basketball. Dixon was a finalist for the John Wooden and James Naismith national awards.

He had one of his finest performances in the Final Four semi-final in a 97-88 victory over Kansas. Dixon scored a game-high 33 points and was stellar defensively. Amatucci remembered watching the game at a local restaurant and marveled at Dixon's performance.

"I still watch it whenever it shows up on ESPN," Amatucci said. "I get worked up seeing him getting into the passing lanes, getting touches and diving on the floor. He did everything. Juan was unequivocally the leader of the team."

Juan Dixon leads Maryland to a national championship.

In the championship game against Indiana, the Terrapins stayed in control throughout both halves and came away with a comfortable 64-52 victory. Dixon had a game-high 18 points, and Maryland finished the season 32-4. Dixon received the NCAA Final Four MVP honors.

"It's like I'm dreaming right now because I'm part of a national championship team," Dixon said after the game. "A lot of people at home counted me out. But, I got better each year."

Dixon finished his career as Maryland's all-time leading scorer with 2,269 points. He also became the only player in NCAA history to amass 2,000 points, 300 steals and 200 three-point field goals. Dixon was named to the ACC 50th Anniversary men's basketball team. His No. 3 jersey hangs from the rafters at Maryland's Xfinity Center.

"His play in big games is great because there are some guys who can score a lot of points, but when it comes to the big games they may not want to take the big shot," coach Gary Williams said.

Reflecting on Juan's career at Maryland, Amatucci said, "When you look at all of his accomplishments, there is no doubt in my mind the Juan is Maryland's GOAT. That's an absolute."

After the storybook career at Maryland, Dixon was selected 17th overall by the Washington Wizards in the 2002 NBA draft. Life was a challenge at the pro level and Dixon averaged eight points per game over three seasons in Washington. However, Dixon still had presence on the big stage and scored a career-high 35 points in a 106-99 victory over the Chicago Bulls in game four of the Eastern Conference Quarterfinals in 2005.

Dixon signed with the Portland Trail Blazers as a free agent in 2005 and averaged a career-best 12.3 points per game. He was traded to the Toronto Raptors in 2007 and averaged 11.1 points off the bench. In 2008, Dixon was traded again from the Raptors to the Detroit Pistons, where he averaged 6.5 points over 17 games. He spent his last full season in the NBA with the Wizards, appearing in 50 games, including six starts.

Dixon admitted the NBA was a challenge for him.

"I wasn't as prepared for the NBA," he said. "That's part of my purpose and what I'm doing today. I was blessed to spend eight years in the NBA. I learned a lot of life skills and what it meant to be a professional. I really enjoyed playing at that level. But coming out of college, I wasn't prepared mentally or physically. That's part of why I wanted to become a coach. I want to help young men be prepared for the highest level."

Dixon played in Europe from 2009-2011 in Greece, Spain and Turkey. However, he also had mixed emotions about the overall experience. Persistent knee injuries hampered any comeback attempts in the NBA.

"I spent a year and a half overseas. It was just something I could not get used to," Dixon said. "But I did enjoy the opportunity and did see places I would have never had seen if I didn't play basketball."

Years earlier, Amatucci had travelled to College Park as a guest of Dixon to celebrate the national championship at Maryland. It would be one of the few times they would see each other for the next several years. Amatucci said, "Now that Juan was moving to the pros the doubters were back. I once again found myself having to defend his ability to have a successful career in the NBA."

"I was very proud and excited about him getting the opportunity," Amatucci said. "He didn't lose his composure or get a big head. I think he had the same attitude about having to prove himself. He was not going to have a problem mixing with the veterans because he wasn't intimidated and he was easy to get along with. He played with a lot of those guys in the summer. For Juan, he wasn't losing any sleep over it. It was another day at the office."

Several years into Dixon's career, Amatucci was becoming concerned by the increasing lack of communication with his star pupil. Amatucci said, "He was moving from team to team and his stats were not showing much improvement from year to year. I wanted to find out what was going on."

Juan didn't return several voice messages left by Amatucci. His next message included some sarcasm, "I know you're busy, but I thought by now that you would get back to me. I guess I'm at the bottom of the totem pole now."

Dixon returned the call, upset about the message. "Tooch, why are you saying that?" Amatucci said, "It was like old times. We were butting heads and pushing each other's buttons. After the tension subsided, we had a good conversation about his situation and plan for the future. I reminded him, if things are not going well you can always call me. It was a good call, but our conversations remained infrequent."

"He got trapped in that vacuum of not doing what he was supposed to be doing," Amatucci said. "I don't think he was prepared mentally for the NBA world. He should have called me more often."

After another break in the connection closing in on two years, the prodigal son returned one afternoon during basketball camp. After catching up, Juan told Amatucci he felt his days in the NBA were numbered and was considering playing overseas. Amatucci invited Dixon to speak to the campers. The following day, Dixon gave the campers a great presentation—part hoops, part life lessons.

After his presentation, Amatucci and Juan sat down in the Calvert Hall dining hall to discuss his next steps. Dixon described the challenges of playing in the NBA and the politics that often surrounded playing time. If the team wasn't heavily invested in him, he often found himself on the bench. Looking back on his career, Dixon realized that there were things he could have done differently that would have taken his career on a different path. In terms of his relationship with Amatucci, he apologized for not giving Amatucci a maximum effort in the Alhambra Tournament his senior year. He understood that the significance of his lack of effort had a greater implication then basketball. Amatucci said, "He was very emotional about it. I believed him. He wanted to make amends for his regrettable behavior which he knew had hurt me. It was a tough conversation. Healing is hard."

Dixon was ready for the next challenge in life, and he wanted it to include basketball. After finishing up his degree and graduation from Maryland, Dixon joined the coaching staff at the University of Maryland as a special assistant to coach Mark Turgeon in November 2013. Dixon spent three years in College Park, and then began looking for head coaching opportunities.

Juan landed his first head coaching job in 2016 with the women's team at the University of the District of Columbia, a Division II program. He spent one season in D.C., where he went 3-25.

"He only had about four girls returning to the team because so many players had graduated," Amatucci said. "I was really concerned about how he was going to handle it. He was amazing. He was patient with them and did a good job controlling his temper. It was obvious they were not going to win a lot of games. When your team is putting up losses and dealing with a lot of adversity, it really tests your commitment to coaching. Juan passed the test with this team. He understood success was not all about Ws and Ls. The players loved him, and he earned their respect. By the end of the year, they got better even though it did not show up in the win/loss column. The season made him a better coach." Handling the tough situation he was given to work with at UDC was an excellent addition to Dixon's resume for being an effective DI head coach.

Dixon's life took a dramatic turn in 2016 when he met his biological father, Bruce Flanigan. In the summer of 2016, family members had told Juan that Phil Dixon was not his real father. Dixon discovered through the help of relatives that Flanigan was his father and still alive. Flanigan had a relationship with Juanita Dixon while she was separated from Phil Dixon. Flanigan and Juanita Dixon stopped dating before Juan was born. Juan and Flanigan, a retired Baltimore County correctional officer, eventually agreed to meet at Arundel Mills Mall. The two of them knew almost immediately that they had a connection. "I saw his demeanor. I looked at my wife Robyn and said, 'That's my dad,'" Dixon recalled. "It's crazy. I appreciated everything my father did for me"—he meant Phil—"but this is my real dad." A DNA sample later confirmed that Bruce was Dixon's true father.

Amatucci had just returned from Ocean City, Maryland, when he received a harried call from Dixon, who was already at Calvert Hall waiting to talk to him. Amatucci told Dixon he was about 10 minutes away. Five minutes later, Juan called again asking where he was. "I'm on my way," Amatucci told him. The two sat down in Amatucci's office and Dixon told him about Bruce.

"With Robyn's help, Juan went out on his own and reached out to Bruce" Amatucci said. "It was a neat moment for me because I knew how much it meant to him. I knew it hurt him not having a dad in his life. He missed out on his dad seeing him and all of the accomplishments he piled up. It was emotional. Juan was very fortunate to have supportive family members throughout his life, but it wasn't the same as connecting with his dad. It was a genuine family moment for Juan and I."

Dixon finally had closure and put to rest many questions surrounding his past. Amatucci remembered a time when Dixon was attending a press conference prior to the Final Four his senior year. A flippant journalist from the Midwest kept harping on the death of Dixon's parents. Dixon finally had enough and erupted at the writer for being disrespectful. Now, Dixon was getting positive press about reuniting with Flanigan.

Being the head coach at Coppin State is rewarding to Dixon on a number of levels. It's a chance to make his mark as a Division I head coach, an opportunity to showcase his talents as a teacher and a mentor, and it's an experience he will be able to share with his dad. Amatucci said," Coppin is a great fit for Juan, and Juan is a great fit for Coppin and the City of Baltimore. He brings instant credibility and personality to the program." Ironically, Dixon was not even on the original list of candidates for the coaching position. Amatucci made a number of phone calls to help Dixon at least be considered for the job. Dixon eventually travelled to the Coppin State campus and asked athletic director Derek Carter for a few minutes to talk. Several weeks later, Dixon was named the head coach.

The Eagles went 5-27 in Dixon's first season. Amatucci was impressed with the way Dixon carried himself and with his ability to keep his team in games against superior opponents. "I sat right behind Juan's bench for a game at Coppin and Juan did an excellent job during time outs," Amatucci said, "The players were focused on him. He did not waste any time and made the important adjustments needed at that point of the game." Amatucci also attended a 6 a.m. practice and liked what he saw as far as Dixon's demeanor at practice. "Juan has made a good start at Coppin and has them moving in a positive direction," Amatucci reflected. "There is no question he'll need to recruit more talented players to challenge top teams in the league. There's no doubt he will hustle and work hard on the recruiting trail."

After that session, Dixon introduced Amatucci to one of his players who had potential but needed to improve his overall attitude. Dixon asked Amatucci to give the player some advice.

"Listen to your coach, Amatucci told the player. "He knows what he's doing. He's earned the right for you to respect him."

"It was a good experience. I learned a lot," Dixon said about his first year at Coppin State. "We progressed throughout the year. I think I helped some men prepare for life, which is the main reason I am coaching. Basketball is the easy part. It's just getting the right men into the program that can allow us to have success. The key is helping them develop the skills for life after basketball."

"Juan is the epitome of what I believe in when I talk about no limits," Amatucci explained. "He's not going to be defeated by adversity. He is relentless. He is not going to let public opinion or the media define who he is and where he is going. Juan has his faults. He can be hard-headed and stubborn which can cloud his perspective."

"At the end of the day, anybody who engages with Juan will become a Dixon believer," he asserted. "While I like to highlight the 'Dixon smile,' people who believe in Juan realize there is much more behind the smile. Juan is ready to knock down some more walls."

PARTS & LABOR

Steve Morton versus BCL's Archbishop Spalding.

"Let's get this straight— I provide the parts and you perform the labor and that's how it works."

-MARK AMATUCCI

Juan Dixon's Calvert Hall career ended in 1997, while Mark Amatucci's career would continue for another ten seasons. During that time, the Cardinals' team would be competitive, always in the mix for the BCL and

MIAA championships. The Cards stayed true to their tradition, playing transition offense and pressure defense. Individual players represented the ideals of Calvert Hall basketball with distinction

There were players with star power who played unselfishly with passion and had the ability to take over games.

• • •

REGGIE BRYANT

Reggie Bryant was a highly recruited player from the Madison Buccaneers. His coach, Derrick "Baseline" Oliver, was a big influence in his life and told Amatucci he needed to get down to the Dome and watch Bryant compete. "Baseline was a big influence in my development," Bryant said. "I remember Baseline working me out in the summertime. I saw my game getting better on a daily basis. Baseline introduced me to Calvert Hall."

The first time Amatucci caught Reggie's game he quickly realized he was the best player on the floor. Bryant was the perfect combo two-three guard. Reggie had long arms, was able to get to the basket with ease, and was a consistent mid-range shooter. His game resembled that of Marc Wilson: scorer, finisher, wants to take the last shot, and gets it done. Wasting no time, Amatucci scheduled a meeting with Reggie's mom and dad at their West 32nd Street home. The home visit was a success. Reggie's mom and dad were very comfortable with Amatucci. They agreed with his academics first philosophy. They saw Calvert Hall as a great opportunity educationally and athletically.

Reggie Bryant with the assist versus Loyola.

"One of the hallmarks of a great player is that he feels the game," Amatucci said. "He understands time and score, sees the entire floor, anticipates play, and his motor is always in gear. That's Reggie. Adding to the mix was that I believed he would be a defensive stopper. He was really quick and he had great instincts like Juan (Dixon) and Aaron Herbert."

Bryant worked hard to meet Calvert Hall's rigorous academic requirements. Amatucci said, "From day one, Reggie voluntarily took advantage of the many academic resources we have here at Calvert Hall. He regularly worked with his teachers outside of the classroom. When Reggie was having any academic difficulty, he didn't hide it; he would come tell me about it and we would put a plan together to get him squared away."

For Bryant, there was a learning curve in meeting Amatucci's basketball demands.

"Playing for Tooch was challenging," Bryant said. "He is a coach that demands maximum effort on defense and offense."

At one point during his career at Calvert Hall, Bryant grew frustrated with his role and playing time. He became depressed and Amatucci provided an ultimatum: Get it straightened out or you can play somewhere else. He got it straightened out. Bryant eventually became the go-to guy on offense during his junior and senior seasons. He also thrived defensively and matched up against the opposing team's top guard.

"In games, he never lost his confidence," Amatucci said. "Reggie, like all great players, did not worry if he missed his first five shots. Next time down the floor, if he got a good look, the shot was going up."

Bryant averaged 23.3 points, 4.5 rebounds and 2.2 assists his senior year. He was named the Catholic League Player of the Year and was recruited by several Division I programs. After Calvert Hall, Bryant attended prep school at St. Thomas More Prep School in Connecticut where he averaged 20 points in the 1999-2000 season. He was then recruited to Villanova by coach Steve Lappas.

Bryant thrived under Lappas and averaged 5.7 and 9.1 points in his freshman and sophomore years. In 2001, Lappas left Villanova for the

University of Massachusetts. The Wildcats hired Jay Wright and Bryant began to struggle.

Wright eventually called Amatucci and told him about the issues. They decided the best decision was for Bryant to transfer to St. Louis University where he thrived again as a player.

In 2004, Bryant shared the Billikens' Most Valuable Player award with fellow guard Josh Fisher. Bryant was Conference USA's third-leading scorer with 16.9 points per game and led the team with fifty-nine three-pointers.

"Calvert Hall prepared me for college educationally and basketball wise," Bryant said. "I started off strong as a freshman, being one of Dick Vitale's 'Diaper Dandies.' I was well prepared for college because Tooch is known for his conditioning. I was always one of the most fit players on the team."

Building on his strong college career, Bryant looked to play professionally overseas before injuries derailed that plan. His challenges did not end there as Bryant developed prostate cancer several years later. He was able to beat the cancer, but then developed cardiac issues requiring surgery. Amatucci said, "With his serious physical hardships, I marvel at Reggie's ability to stay positive and always have a smile on his face." Today, Reggie is optimistic about the future. "I'm feeling good physically," Bryant said. "I am blessed to have the family I have. God has blessed me."

Bryant enjoyed his experience at The Hall. He commented, "Not only is Tooch a great coach, but he is a father figure. I feel like I am a part of his family."

RICKY HARRIS

Unlike many of the Hall's impact players, Ricky's star was not shining when he started at Calvert Hall. He played freshman basketball in ninth grade. In the preseason of his sophomore year, an inauspicious tryout left him on the verge of being cut from the squad. Amatucci recalled, "I had to put the brakes on the JV coach letting Ricky go. I saw his offensive potential, but there were a lot of holes in his game. He was a little pudgy, didn't play D, and he tended to pout. All that being said, I thought it was worth giving him a chance to prove himself."

Harris said, "My first two years at Calvert Hall were tough. I was immature and kind of afraid of Coach Tooch. But those years were good because they helped to shape me into who I am today. Coach Tooch taught me how to become a man and accept responsibility. My last two years, he was on me hard because he could see my potential. Off the court, I loved talking to him. I would go in his office on breaks and watch film of Juan Dixon and Reggie Bryant just to become a better player."

Entering his junior year, Harris showed potential as a dangerous scorer. However, Amatucci was still not impressed with his defense or work habits. One practice, Amatucci made the entire team run because Harris was not providing the maximum effort. The players were getting increasingly angry at Harris, who was pouting on the baseline.

Amatucci erupted.

"Enough with the pouting," Amatucci yelled at him. "Get your game together or leave."

Ricky Harris scores his 1500th point.

That proved to be the turning point as Harris got tougher and better. Harris averaged 19 points, four rebounds and three steals per game in his junior year. In 2005, Harris dominated and was named Baltimore Catholic League Co-Player of the Year, averaging 23 points, six rebounds and two steals.

"Over those last two years, Ricky really stepped up his game," Amatucci said. "He scored over 1200 points in two seasons. We were running our sets through Ricky. He had incredible games where he single-handedly took over. By the end of his senior year, he was in the same league as the Hall's gunslingers of the past."

Harris remembered, "Coach Amatucci taught me the fundamentals of the game. He instilled in me the importance of hard work, being humble, staying focused on your dreams, and listening to your coach."

Harris was being heavily recruited by Loyola University Maryland. Amatucci thought that was a good fit, but Harris wanted to play in a bigger conference. As a result, he enrolled in prep school at The Winchendon School (MA) where he averaged 17 points in the 2005-06 season. He also shot 43 percent from three-point range and made 81 percent from the foul line. Harris was a standout at the National Prep School Invitational and was ranked as the 27th-best fifth-year player in the nation. After the season, he signed with the University of Massachusetts of the Atlantic 10 Conference. On signing Harris, UMass head coach Travis Ford said, "Right away he will be a spark plug. He plays with a lot of energy on both ends of the court. I think he will develop into a go-to type player."

At UMass, Harris averaged more than 18 points per game in three straight seasons (2006-10). Harris and the Minutemen played twice in the NIT, reaching the finals in 2008. Harris' 1,960 career points place him third on UMass' all-time scoring list, above Marcus Camby and Julius Erving.

Harris has played professionally overseas in Italy, Germany, Lithuania, Philippines and Ukraine. In 2017-2018 he played in Argentina. He also played in the 2013 NBA Summer League with the Toronto Raptors.

Coach Baker said, "Ricky is an outstanding role model for our players. He is not complacent. He is constantly working to improve his game."

Despite the travels, Harris never lost his Calvert Hall ties

"Ricky comes back and talks to the guys. He's great with them sending the right message about the 4 P's. He talks about his journey," Amatucci said. "He worked twelve months a year to make himself into a player. Summer, fall, winter and spring—morning and night. He would call me at all hours to ask me to let him in the gym. One August, it had to be 120 degrees in the gym. There was no air. He was in there for at least an hour and a half. He was working on his shooting, his handle, and his moves to the basket. Like all of our guys, folding chairs were all over the floor as part of the workout. That's what it takes . . . that's what it takes. That's Ricky Harris."

Harris remains close with Amatucci. "I talk to Tooch about everything still 'til this day," Harris said. "He's a father figure to me. I wouldn't be the player that I am today without him."

• • •

Amatucci's teams always included a couple of blue collar players who brought their lunch box and came ready to work every day. In his last ten seasons there were a corps of players who followed in the footsteps of Sikorsky, Venanzi and Medinger, players who weren't in the highlight reels and whose game time was limited, but were always ready to play. In practice, they made the Ferrells, Dixons and Bryants better. Although often playing in obscurity, there were many times when they stepped in to pull the Cards out of the fire.

Amatucci said, "At the end of the day, these are the guys I respected and appreciated the most. They were selfless, committed to the team. They weren't afraid to get their hands dirty: dive on the floor, take a charge, match up against opponents that physically overshadowed them. No fear."

STEVE MORTON

Steve Morton was a two-sport athlete: baseball and basketball. He was the co-captain of Amatucci's 2004-05 team. "He was a real handyman, Amatucci said. "He could do a little bit of everything—work inside, handle the ball, play on the perimeter, and most significantly stick guys on D." In one memorable game, Morton at 6-2 and 180 pounds, battled Archbishop Spalding's University of Maryland bound Will Bowers, 7-0, 250 pounds. Amatucci recalled, "Steve effectively took Bowers out of his game."

Morton recalled, "Tooch taught me what it meant to play hard as hell, to do your job, to be accountable, and to play and live without fear. I spent my last two seasons at The Hall setting hard screens, diving on the floor for loose balls, and taking charges. I was a pest. I would guard guys twice my size, but I would outwork them. Sure, I'd get dunked on, but who cares? Sometimes in life you get dunked on. It's about what you do after being dunked on that matters."

EDDIE HEALY

"Eddie was always upbeat," Amatucci said, "He took it literally when I told him, 'Your job in practice every day is to beat somebody's ass.' His effort and attitude in practice made the starters better. He gave 100 percent whether he was running with the first team or replicating our opponent's offense or defense to get us ready for the game. When given the opportunity, his ability to shoot the three, especially against zone defense, contributed to a number of well-earned wins."

Healy commented, "Tooch is one of the few people that can come into your life and legitimately push you to work harder than you thought you could. You always knew you had to be ready for practice. It was never easy, but I can look back on it and be thankful for the work ethic ingrained in me during my athletic career, a work ethic that can be translated into my professional and personal lives."

CALVIN WISE

Wise's hoop career at The Hall, almost never happened. He was cut from the freshman team his first year and barely made the junior varsity as a sophomore.

Amatucci said, "Calvin's a guy who always finds a way. He has a 'never quit' attitude. As a basketball player, he never let the odds affect his self-confidence. By his senior year, 2004-05, Calvin was a co-captain and had earned a spot in the starting line-up. Calvin was a quiet leader on the court. He was a defensive stopper in the paint, rebounding at both ends of the floor. He had a soft touch around the hoop."

Wise said, "The lessons I learned from Tooch went beyond those I learned on the court. After seeing Tooch go after an opposing coach for giving him a dead fish handshake, to this day, my handshakes are firm. Water breaks and hands on the knees were a sign of weakness. No matter how bad your man beat you off the dribble for a bucket, you better get the ball out of the net and inbound it without it hitting the floor."

Midway through his senior season, Wise suffered a severe knee injury. The initial report was that he would be finished for the season. Showing real determination during rehab, Calvin was able to get back on the practice floor just prior to the BCL Tournament. In the Card's semi-final contest against Towson Catholic, early in the second half, with the team down double digits, Calvin talked Amatucci into putting him into the game, on essentially one leg. "To my amazement, Calvin not only gave his teammates an emotional lift, but he also rebounded and scored as if he was 100 percent," Amatucci recalled. It was one of the most heroic displays of perseverance that I have ever seen."

After graduating from The Hall, Wise had a stellar career at Division III St. Mary's (MD). He is currently a member of Calvert Hall's Board of Trustees. Wise noted, "I was not a blue chip basketball recruit. I worked hard simply to make the starting lineup by my senior year. That did not matter to Tooch. He invested and still invests in my success. His dedication and support to his players has no limits."

WOODY STEVENSON

"The first time I saw Woody play he took a charge in a rec league game. I knew right away he was our kind of guy," Amatucci said, "He could score in transition and was aggressive mixing it up on the offensive and defensive boards. He had solid man-to-man skills. Woody brought a physical presence with his game. He never got pushed around."

Stevenson came to The Hall as a sophomore and played two years on the varsity. Amatucci recalled, "Woody was primarily working the three and four spots for us. One game, we were in deep foul trouble at the two position and I made a spontaneous decision to sub Woody into the game at the two. Playing with confidence he gave us a great run that kept us in a close game that we eventually won. His effort in that game was a great example of his versatility. Woody would charm you with his big smile, but was all business once it was game time."

TIM TAYLOR

As a senior, Taylor was captain of both the football and basketball teams.

Amatucci recalled, "Our team was struggling early in the season, especially with our attitude. I decided to shake the lineup and told Timmy after warmups before our game with Mount St. Joe that he was starting. He took a charge in the first quarter and banged his head on the gym floor. I thought he was done for the night. At the start of the second quarter, he told me, 'I am ready to go." I got him right back in there, and he played his butt off. That's Tim Taylor: team first, leader by example, fearless, played hard whistle to whistle." Tim went on to play football at Washington University in St. Louis. Today, Tim Taylor works as a software engineer in New York City.

• • •

A dynamic floor general at the point guard position has always been vital to the success of Amatucci's teams. He is the coach on the floor at all times and totally entrusted with making sure all of the parts are working in sync. His leadership both vocally and by example will determine the outcome of the game.

RUSSELL FREDERICK

The 5-11, three-year starter was a prized recruit. He was mentally tough and physically strong. Frederick rarely had a change in his demeanor whether the Cards were winning or losing.

"Russ had cat-like quickness," Amatucci said. "He took opposing point guards out of their game. He was never afraid to question my decision-making because he had a great basketball I.Q."

Frederick embraced the big stage and had the respect of his teammates. "He was unselfish and kept everyone happy on the floor," Amatucci said. "I could always depend on thirty-two minutes from him." Frederick scored over 1,000 points in his career, led the team in assists all three years, and wreaked constant havoc with his pressure defense. "He was a man of a few words, but when he spoke, people listened," Amatucci said. Frederick served as captain both as a junior and senior. He was Second-Team All-BCL his junior year and First-Team as a senior. Frederick played collegiately at Philadelphia Textile and started all four years under revered coach Herb Magee. Frederick also played professionally in Poland. He now has a successful career in finance.

Russell Frederick pulling up for the J versus Towson Catholic.

Amatucci added: "I first saw Russell play in the Kinney Classic as an eighth-grader. It took me about two quarters of basketball to realize Russell would be my leader for the future in the mold of Tubman and

Vince Williams. Russell never gave less than 100 percent in practice or games. I gave him the ball as a sophomore and never looked back."

Frederick commented, "The biggest trait coach conveyed was accountability. It was tough to understand as a teenager why he was so tough on me and why he didn't let me get by at times. But as you grow up you learn it was all for a reason and he wanted to see you grow as a player and as a man. Which is why we have a great relationship til this day."

KYLE WISE

"Shorty" was part of Amatucci's last recruiting class. Wise, 5-8, made varsity as a freshman and started all four years. He was the first freshman starting point guard under Amatucci. "He was smooth and cool under pressure," Amatucci said. "Kyle was way beyond his years maturity wise in understanding the game. He accepted my demands without question. Kyle was exceptional with both hands and had lightning quickness."

Wise loved to play up-tempo and was disciplined and played under control. In his first game as a freshman, he had double-digit points and assists. Wise is just behind Tubman as Calvert Hall's all-time assist leader. He led the Cardinals to the BCL tournament championship in 2010. He later starred at St. Mary's College. Wise currently serves as an admissions counselor at St. Mary's.

"I was really hard on Kyle, and he turned out to be an exceptional point guard," Amatucci said. "Years later, my son Mike and I were visiting St. Mary's where Kyle was working in the admissions office. Kyle gave us a tour of the campus, and we had an opportunity to talk by ourselves about his Calvert Hall experience. I was his guidance counselor, and we had discussed three other schools besides St.Mary's. During that conversation, I asked him why he decided to attend St. Mary's. He said, 'I came here because of you, Tooch.' I had only coached him one year, but it gave me great satisfaction as his guidance counselor that he took my advice. That decision turned out to be the right choice, and he had an outstanding experience as a student-athlete. His comment really hit me."

• • •

In the world of Amatucci's NASCAR offense and blitzkrieg pressure defense, the final part and a determining factor in achieving the fruits of labor fell in the lap of the big guy. He needed to rebound at both ends of the floor, start the train moving in transition, stop penetration, intimidate the opposition from getting to the basket, and be nimble and quick enough in the back-end of the trapping defenses to finish the job and create the Hall's signature "controlled madness." He is the anchor on both sides of the ball.

JONATHAN GRAHAM

The son of former Maryland great Ernie Graham had a stellar career and was another prized recruit. Graham was a four-year varsity player. He immediately showed tremendous potential at both ends of the floor the first time he stepped on the court as a freshman. Graham was willing to listen to his coaches and take instruction on how to become a better player. He was exceptional at blocking shots and was quick around the basket with both hands.

"He had great quickness and anticipation in our trapping defense," Amatucci said. "He was intimidating in the paint defensively. The opposition would think twice about going to the hole. Jonathan made himself a good, mid-range jump shooter."

Graham had solid hands, great vision, and was unselfish. Jonathan never backed away from a battle inside the paint and exuded confidence. During both his junior and senior years, he became a game-changer and was a force in leading the team to the BCL tournament championship. He finished just behind Duane Ferrell as the all-time rebound leader and is in the top five for scoring. He played at Penn State and the University of Maryland College Park.

"I only had the privilege to coach Jon for one season," Amatucci said. "I was exceptionally proud to see the development he made in one short year as a player. He went beyond what was expected. He was intense and totally focused on the game in front of him. More importantly, Jonathan is a sensitive and caring young man. He is someone who definitely epitomizes the values of Calvert Hall and always represented the school well. To this day, Jonathan remains close to the program and often stops by school to visit."

DELBERT RANDALL

The lanky forward made varsity as a freshman and was a four-year player. Randall could do everything well. He could score, defend, get out in transition, finish the break, handle the ball, rebound at both ends, and was stout defensively, playing opponents on the perimeter and on the block. "He was just that versatile," Amatucci said.

Randall took over the starting job midway through his freshman year and never relinquished that role. He was a hard worker who never complained and was completely focused on doing his job to the best of his ability. He outworked players in practice, and that carried over to games. Randall routinely finished with double-digit points and rebounds. Delbert was an excellent student and attended St. Michael's College in Vermont. At St. Michael's he scored more than 1,000 points and was the first player in school history to get 100 blocks and 100 assists.

"He reminded me of Robert Parrish of the Celtics," Amatucci said. "Delbert quietly ruled the paint without any fanfare. He was a force inside and was a stopper. He always gave me more than I expected. Delbert deserved the kind of recognition that some of the gunslingers and guys from the 1980s garnered. He deserved more recognition that he got."

• • •

"This was a hard chapter to put together," Amatucci admitted. "The quality of the guys who played for us those last ten years was outstanding. They brought their individual talents and personalities to our teams and were critical to our success. They embodied the spirit of the Calvert Hall basketball family. If space permitted this chapter might never end. The list of contributors would include so many more: Randall Graves, Marcus Thompson, Mike Bryant, Nick Wojnowski, Pat Love, Mike Love, Don Brandenberg, Mike Edwards, Tim Knapp, Braxton Dupree, Chris Knoerlein, Mark Orendorff, Kyle Jarczynski, Mike Kastanakis, Brad Lukens, Derek Potter . . ."

During those ten seasons there was one particular player who would eventually showcase his talents at the highest level: Gary Neal.

18

THE QUIET MAN

Tooch and Gary celebrating his wedding to Leah.

"We have time zones, school zones, end zones,
and then there is The Gary Neal zone.
Gary could shoot it from Mars with his eyes closed
and all you would hear is 'Swish'...
Gary has always played with ice in his veins.
No fear—just get him the ball."

- MARK AMATUCCI

Coming off a disappointing 17-12 season in 2000-01, Amatucci recognized the Cards needed a quality scorer the next season to be competitive in the BCL. Amatucci recalled, "Our season had been up and down. We folded at the end of the year. We lacked the drive that I expect. We need new chemistry, new faces and added fire power." As luck would have it, Amatucci received a phone call about a kid named Gary Neal.

In 2000, Neal led Aberdeen to the Maryland Class 2A state championship as a sophomore, averaging a triple-double per game. Neal also made the game-winning shot in a 50-48 victory over Gwynn Park in the final. Scotty Bowden, a middle school principal and an AAU coach, told Amatucci that Neal's parents wanted him to transfer to Calvert Hall because of the school's stellar academics and athletics. Even though Amatucci had not seen Neal play, he trusted Bowden, who gave the player a glowing review.

Neal had all of the intangibles to succeed at Calvert Hall. He came from a military family, had good grades, and was a big-time playmaker on the court. Amatucci eventually went on a home visit after Neal's mother confirmed she wanted her son to transfer. She liked the structured environment at Calvert Hall. All of the pieces were in place for Neal to transfer as a junior—another boon to Amatucci's history of recruiting.

On Labor Day, Neal's mother informed Amatucci that he was not going to be enrolling at Calvert Hall. There were concerns about transportation from Harford County. "If you're not happy, call me back," Amatucci told her. By the end of the first semester, Neal's mother did indeed admit she made a mistake and now wanted him to enroll at the school. However, the process would have to move quickly because Calvert Hall did not admit any senior transfers.

Neal finished the season at Aberdeen and enrolled at Calvert Hall in the second semester of his junior year. Neal remembers walking into class for the first time and realizing there were no girls. He did not think much about it until later in the day when he had not seen one female. No one had told Neal that Calvert Hall was an all-male school.

"There are no girls. I don't think I can go here," Neal told Amatucci.

"We have conditioning in about 30 minutes. You'll be alright," Amatucci responded. "There's less of a distraction without the girls." Years later, Amatucci reflected, "I didn't know if that was going to work, but he just put his head down and walked quietly out the door. The subject never came up again."

Neal said the structure of his household with a military father and a strict religious mother helped him to quickly adapt to Calvert Hall. He was also used to putting on a tie for church on Sunday. "It wasn't tough because coming to Calvert Hall, I had already qualified academically for college admission," Neal said.

On the court, Amatucci was amazed at Neal's ability to shoot and get up and down the floor. However, he did need to work on his defensive skills and become more adept with using his left hand. Bowden had told Amatucci that Neal could be a point guard, but it was apparent that he was more suited to the two or three position. There was plenty of time for Neal to work on his game before the beginning of his senior season. Neal was already being heavily recruited by several Division I programs and he had his sights on La Salle University in Philadelphia.

"As a player, he got better and stronger over the summer," Amatucci remembered. "He was committed. When he came back for his senior year, he was ready to make a big-time impact. He got used to me. Offensively, he was in the same category as Juan Dixon and John McKay. Once he got in the Gary Neal zone, forget about it."

In summer workouts, Neal managed mostly to escape Amatucci's ire because of his commitment, However, Neal remembers banging his knee during a summer workout and making the mistake of walking off the court.

"Gary, what are you doing? You're not at Aberdeen anymore. You don't walk off the court unless I tell you," Amatucci yelled.

"Okay," said Neal, who learned the lesson and would never walk off the court again.

By the time practice was set to begin for the 2001-2002 season, Neal fit in academically and socially at The Hall. The ease of his transition did not carry over to the court. Amatucci recalled, "Gary's effort was good in practice, but he had difficulty learning the system and adjusting to my personality and demands. His man-to-man defensive skills were suspect."

Neal was willing to take instruction, and over the preseason worked diligently to strengthen his weaknesses and build his confidence. His true potential began to shine.

In his single season with the Cardinals, Neal led the team in scoring averaging 19.5 points per game. Amatucci recalled, "Once Gary got settled in with our style of play, he flourished both in transition and in the half court as our go to offensive threat. He had the green light. If he was open, he was told to shoot it. He was consistent throughout the year with several memorable performances."

In a game against Baltimore Catholic League rival Mount St. Joseph, Neal was held scoreless in the first half. Amatucci ripped him at halftime. Neal responded by scoring 16 consecutive points in the second half. In Amatucci's career number 300 win versus archrival Loyola, Neal had put up 37 points midway through the third quarter. Amatucci remembered, "Early in the third quarter, Gary took an outlet pass, took two dribbles across half court and launched a 30-footer that found all net. The shot left the crowd speechless. His performance that day was amazing. It was definitely one of the best individual offensive outbursts in the history of the program."

The Cards finished the regular season with a 22-8 record, ranked number seven in the area and were the second seed in the Baltimore Catholic League tourney. Amatucci remembered, "Archbishop Spalding was the number one seed, having beaten us twice in the regular season. We were playing well, and I thought we had a chance to take them out in the tournament. Unfortunately, coach Mike Daniel and his Towson Catholic Owls had a different idea." In the quarter finals, the Owls played a box-and-one on Neal who finished with twelve in a frustrating, 50-47 loss. Amatucci lamented, "The season ended with a thud. Gary earned All-Metro and All-BCL honors, but the ending overshadowed Gary's outstanding senior year."

For his college career, Neal committed to La Salle University. La

Salle coach Billy Hahn had sold Neal on the school. "He said, 'I have 30 minutes and 15 shots for you. If you want to come, it's all yours,'" Neal remembered Hahn telling him. La Salle was also the perfect setting for Neal because the campus was just over an hour from his home—close, yet far enough away from Aberdeen. Neal wasted little time making his mark at the Philadelphia school. He averaged 18.6 points and was named the Atlantic Ten Rookie of the Year. During that first season, Neal scored more than 20 points in eight consecutive games. The following year, Neal led the team with 17.9 points per game. He left La Salle as a result of issues related to an off the court incident at the school. Amatucci remembered, "It was a challenging time for him. I spoke to him regularly. We talked about finding the right fit."

Pat Kennedy, longtime Division I coach, who had led schools including Iona College, DePaul University and Florida State University, was then the head coach at Baltimore's Towson University. He actively recruited Neal to join the Towson Tigers. Neal was named to the All-Colonial Athletic Association first team as a senior. He also became only the fourth basketball player in NCAA history to score at least 1,000 points at two programs.

Gary ranked fourth in the nation in scoring with a 25.3 points per game average in his final year. He also averaged 3.5 assists and 4.2 rebounds. Neal did not expect to get drafted to the NBA from a mid-major school, but he was prepared to showcase his skills at a professional summer league. The opportunity never arrived, and Neal was left to ponder an uncertain future. While most players would have been discouraged about their professional aspirations, Neal grew more determined to accomplish his goal and he continued to work out, eventually landing a deal in Turkey to begin his professional career.

Neal said: "At Towson I was one of the top scorers in the country. I graduated and I did not get one summer league invite, not one minicamp invite, and not one inquiry from an NBA team. I didn't get a job offer from a European team until October. A lot of guys would have hit that hurdle and packed it in. They would have stopped working out, got into trouble, or whatever to knock them off course. Not only I was ready to play when I got to Turkey, I was playing at a high level and led the league in scoring. For me, in relation to basketball, that's my biggest accomplishment."

It was a valuable life lesson that he does not take lightly.

"There's always steps to reaching your goal," Neal said. "It was frustrating because I didn't have any money and nowhere to live. I had everybody and their mother asking me about why I wasn't drafted and not going to summer league. It was a lot of pressure. A lot of people would have given up. Everybody that loved me and cared about me told me to stay focused. It will come. So, I stayed ready. When the job called, and I stepped on the court, I was ready. The rest is history."

In his first professional season, Neal played in Turkey for Pınar Karşıyaka. He led the Turkish Basketball Super League in scoring with 23.6 points per game. Neal then spent a season playing for FC Barcelona, which advanced to the Spanish league championship. Neal then signed with Benetton Treviso in Italy before the club ran out of money. Still, Neal excelled and was named to the All-EuroCup Second Team. In 2009, Neal signed with Unicaja Málaga in Spain where he averaged 12.6 points per game.

"My father was in the military, so I lived in Germany and some other places as a kid. It wasn't a tough adjustment," Neal said about playing overseas. "As long as the basketball is going well, everything else is fine."

His performance in the European leagues earned him an invite to the San Antonio Spurs' minicamp. There were 25 players looking to earn a spot with the team. Neal did well enough there to get invited to the team camp. Once again, Neal performed well and the Spurs asked him to play on their summer league team. However, there was a conflict because Neal was planning to marry his long-time girlfriend, Leah, that summer.

"Y'all have not offered me a contract and I am about to get married," Neal told the team. "I can't live in San Antonio for the next two months without knowing if you're going to offer me a deal." Amatucci recalled, "It was a crossroads for him. I have always admired the fact that he was putting his relationship with Leah ahead of his professional career."

The Spurs executives told Neal there was a "99.9 percent" chance that they were going to offer him a contract, but they wanted him on the summer league team. Neal said he would play if the team could accommodate him getting married. The Spurs agreed, and Neal eventually signed a three-year contract a few weeks later.

"The overall athleticism was the biggest adjustment," Neal said about going from Europe to the NBA. "The top teams in Europe might have three or four guys that are athletic. The NBA has eight or nine guys that are athletic. The talent level was about the same. It was the athleticism that separates the leagues."

Neal appeared in 80 games during the 2010–11 season. He averaged 9.8 points and 2.5 rebounds per game. He had one of his best games in the first round of the NBA playoffs against the Memphis Grizzlies when he made a game-tying three-pointer with 1.7 seconds left in regulation. The Spurs won 110-103 in overtime.

"That first year was my best just because it showed that I belonged in the NBA," Neal said.

He averaged almost 10 points per game over the next two seasons. In 2012-13, Neal scored 24 points, making six of ten shots from beyond the arc in a 113-77 victory over the Miami Heat in Game 3 of the NBA Finals. Miami eventually won the series in seven games. Earlier that year, Neal made seven three-pointers and scored a career-high 29 points against the Houston Rockets.

Neal spent the 2013-14 season with both Milwaukee and Charlotte where he averaged 10 points and 11.2 points, respectively. In 2015, Neal was traded to the Minnesota Timberwolves where he appeared in 11 games, averaging 11.8 points.

After that season, Neal signed a one-year, $2.1 million contract with the Washington Wizards but suffered a devastating hip injury that almost derailed his career. Neal was convinced the team did not diagnose the injury early enough before the condition worsened and he needed microfracture surgery. Neal beat the odds again by being able to play after the surgery, which had ended the career of several other NBA players.

"The issue was he was playing with that injury, and it wasn't being properly treated," Amatucci said.

Neal added: "If I had known completely what the nature of my injury was, I would have had the surgery in November or December instead of April. It put me in a bad situation because free agency started in July. I was not able to get a job. It was a mess. It took me 18 months to get back. If I had the surgery earlier it might have taken me 12 months."

Amatucci said, "It was a down period for him. A lot of NBA pundits thought his skills were deteriorating, which wasn't true. The truth was he wasn't healthy. I give him credit. He came to terms with his situation and was thinking about his future after his playing days ended."

In the summer of 2017, Neal enrolled in a graduate program at Towson University to prepare for the next chapter of his life. Amatucci wrote him a letter of recommendation for admission to the school. Neal's wife was also pregnant with their third child. Neal was content with earning his master's degree and pursuing a career in education and coaching.

Two days after his daughter was born, Neal's agent told him that the Spanish club Tecnyconta Zaragoza was interested in him. Neal discussed the situation with Leah, and they decided he should go overseas to play. Neal, not hampered by the hip injury, was named Player of the Month for November when he averaged 22.7 points and four assists. He finished third in the voting as the overall MVP of the Liga ACB.

"I was determined to prove to myself that I could still play," Neal said. "I had been at peace with possible retirement because there was nothing I could do about it. I also knew that given the opportunity I would give 110 percent every time I was on the court. Nobody wants to walk away from the game because of an injury. I believed that opportunity presented itself for a reason."

Neal endured a long journey from Aberdeen High School to Calvert Hall to the professional leagues overseas and the NBA. Amatucci followed his star pupil along the way and called Neal "probably the kindest person I ever met. It's never been about him. He always puts other people's needs first."

Amatucci and Neal remain close. Amatucci was there for the good times, such as Neal's wedding, and the sad times, such as the death of his mother. "People always ask me who is your favorite guy, and I can't do that because we have so many guys, and it's our family," Amatucci said. "But, Gary is certainly one of the best. He's a family guy. His best quality is that he is a great husband and father. He is a humble man who lets actions speak for themselves. Today his NBA jersey along with those of Duane Ferrell and Juan Dixon hang in Calvert Hall's Alumni Memorial Gymnasium. Pretty good company to hang with. That's Gary Neal, the quiet man."

In the spring of 2007, Gary Neal's basketball future was not clear. At the same time, Amatucci's future was a little cloudy. By mid-May there would be new and unexpected changes to the Calvert Hall program.

19

THE HOUSE THAT JACK BUILT

Tooch's court dedication.

"If there was one word to describe Tooch, it would be family.
If there were two words, it would be family and dedication.
And if there were three words, family, dedication and commitment.
I've never seen a guy more dedicated to his program.
He is a great motivator and the kids respected him."

- MIKE EDWARDS

Rising each morning at 6:15, Amatucci starts his day taking a walk with his favorite canine, Charly.

In the guidance office promptly by 7:15 a.m., Amatucci sits at his desk organizing his schedule for the day, which includes appointments with his beloved students, meeting parents and faculty about the academic, social, athletic and other situations that arise in the life of a young adult.

"After forty-plus years in education, I still love coming to work," Amatucci said. "No day is ever the same when dealing with my boys. They challenge me to provide them with the proper guidance necessary for a successful and healthy experience at The Hall."

There are moments throughout the day when Amatucci reflects back on an incredible chapter in his life that ended in mid-May 2007.

"I was a guy who loved to practice 365 days a year; I never took a day off," Amatucci said. "I was always pumped up for practice. It was something I always looked forward to and enjoyed." Joe Baker said, "There is no question that Tooch loved practice. When Jon Capan and I were his assistants, Tooch would occasionally come to practice and say, 'We're going short today'. Cap and I would just laugh because invariably 'short' turned into longer than usual."

"I enjoyed being involved in every aspect of the game," Amatucci said. "I always accompanied my assistants on scouting trips. I was a believer of seeing the game in-person. Those scouting trips often included finding a local establishment to review our notes and have a few adult beverages. In my mind, recruiting and home visits were two of the most important aspects of getting the job done. Recruiting, I believe, was one of my biggest strengths. If you got me alone in a room with mom, dad, and the recruit, I was going to close the deal. It was never a job. I always loved coaching and teaching."

By the end of the 2006 season, Amatucci's basketball frame of mind started to change. He felt his time was coming to an end. "I related it to my baseball days. I had a sense that I was losing velocity on my fastball. It was like going from the nineties to the low eighties. If I couldn't bring the heat, I thought it was time to walk away."

He started giving his assistant, John Bauersfeld, more responsibility. He spent less time scouting in person and used more film to assess players strengths and weaknesses. The motivation to visit recruits in the home began to waver. "It started to become a job, and practice became a grind," Amatucci remembered. "I'm not a good loser. If I knew I could not make the same commitment as I expected from my players, we were not going to be successful. It was time to pack it in."

When the 2006-07 preseason began, Amatucci pulled Bauersfeld aside one day after practice and told him that it was going to be his last year. Amatucci recalled, "JB looked at me with an astonished smile and said, 'Are you kidding?' I told him no, I had made up my mind. I want you to take over and lead the program and carry on the tradition."

Changing priorities and values in the basketball community contributed to Amatucci's decision to leave the game. The rising influence of AAU programs and increasing parental meddling left Amatucci with a bad taste in his mouth.

Amatucci said, "In the AAU world, you had a lot of people talking to kids and not giving them the best advice. Too many people were exerting their influence on the players. It was more difficult to attract players to buy in to the intense, disciplined expectations that we had for our teams. We were successful because we out-worked people and had great team chemistry. It was frustrating having to deal with so many unhealthy distractions that were holding us back from achieving our goals." Amatucci continued, "On the home front, it was getting more difficult to travel during the holidays. I wanted to spend more time with my family."

With little fanfare on May 30, 2007, Amatucci emailed all of the Calvert Hall basketball supporters announcing that he was stepping down. He also forwarded a press release scheduled to be published June 1. On Amatucci's announcement, Calvert Hall Principal Louis Heidrick commented, "Mark has served the student-athletes in the basketball program well. His coaching days will be remembered not only for his success on the court, but more importantly for guiding his players through Calvert Hall into colleges and on to successful lives. His presence in the basketball program will be missed, but we are fortunate that he is continuing his role as a guidance counselor."

For 32 years, Mark Amatucci had been doing what he loved, coaching basketball. During his tenure, Amatucci recorded 389 wins in nineteen years at Calvert Hall, including a 34-0 record and a national championship in the 1981-82 season. Vocal and animated on the sidelines, Coach Amatucci had high expectations for each and every player and guided his teams to three Baltimore Catholic League championships, three BCL tourney championships, and two Maryland Interscholastic Athletic Association championships. Amatucci is Calvert Hall's all-time winningest basketball coach. He was named Basketball Weekly's National Coach of the Year in 1982; BCL Coach of the Year 1980, 1981, 1982, and 1999; the Baltimore Sun and News American's Coach of the Year in 1980, 1981, and 1982.

Amatucci coached more than forty players at Calvert Hall who continued their careers in college, including Duane Ferrell '82 (Georgia Tech); Juan Dixon '97 (University of Maryland), and Gary Neal '02 (Towson University), all of whom played in the National Basketball Association.

Calvert Hall's athletic director, Lou Eckerl, also acknowledged Amatucci's contribution: "When you think of the storied history of Calvert Hall athletics, you think Bill Karpovich (soccer), Joe Binder (baseball), Augie Miceli (football). and, Mark Amatucci (basketball)."

"My success had more to do with the Calvert Hall basketball family than Mark Amatucci." Amatucci reflected.

"Doc" Reif commented, "Jack [Doc's nickname for Amatucci] is genuine, authentic, a builder of community, and is committed to helping others, leaving this spinning rock a better place."

Amatucci offered, "Strong families are built on trust, perseverance, patience, and sacrifice. When you nurture these qualities, relationships thrive with the true meaning of love coming to the forefront. Our success was not in scoring points or winning games, it was in building powerful relationships into a dynamic and caring community. A community that continues today." It was about common experiences - on and off the court from the tragic to the comical. Amatucci continued, "I will never forget the look on the guys faces when Tom Heiderman owner of Ocean

City's famous Hobbit restaurant and a loyal supporter of Tooch's teams told the guys to order anything they wanted off the menu. They went from burgers to Prime Rib in a flash. An unforgettable team experience."

Amatucci realizes that there are those who think his pronouncements on family are just a lot of feel good rhetoric without any substance. To those naysayers Amatucci answered, "I laugh when I hear people take shots at our traditions, values and generations of stars who embraced my philosophy. They haven't been where we were, worked like we did, or lived the experience. It's their loss."

Amatucci's Italian heritage was evident is his insistence from day one that his teams be committed to family. "I firmly believed in family, but I knew my style would at times be pushing people away rather than keeping them together," he said. To build his family, Amatucci needed assistants, who could buffer, re-interpret, temper and who were believers in what they were trying to do.

Coach Baker explained, "Playing for and for that matter coaching with Tooch wasn't easy. He pushed players and coaches to exceed expectations with no limits. Our role as assistants was to help the guys understand Tooch's thinking and give them 'hope'. Some days we were trying to push guys towards Tooch and other days we were trying to keep them away from him. It was a crazy dynamic—but we loved doing it—and it worked."

In choosing his assistants, Amatucci had a clear plan. He wanted coaches who interacted with the players holistically and who brought talents beyond Xs and Os, that could nurture relationships with the players. Amatucci said, "I didn't want yes men. I wanted people who had the confidence to challenge me when it was necessary, whether I agreed or not. I wanted to create an atmosphere where we considered ourselves brothers; brothers who stuck together, fought, made-up, and who never lost a party."

To a man, the coaches who worked with Amatucci, take great pride in being part of something unique in today's world—putting the kids first and their egos second. From Phil Popovec '70 through Vince Williams '95 they are a cohesive and intensely loyal group. If Amatucci were to come out of retirement, a significant issue would be having enough seats on the bench for his former assistants who would readily answer the call to serve. Amatucci's good friend, teammate, and his longest tenured assistant Chris Devlin commented, "I was blessed to be a part of a great team of coaches dedicated to the young men in our program and to each other. The bonds that were formed so many years ago are stronger today. I truly believe that if we were to go back into coaching together again, we would pick up right where we left off."

The players are unmistakably the core of Amatucci's hoop family. They call, they come back to visit, they support the program, and when Tooch calls, they answer (only Dixon is so bold as to send Tooch to voicemail.)

Amatucci commented, "I talk to my guys as much as possible. I still irritate the hell out of them, because if I don't like something going on in their lives, I'm going to stick my nose in it. I probably should not be doing that because they are grown men, but we still have that relationship where I look at them as my children. I am proud of all of them."

The staying power and the attachment to one another is evident by the players enthusiastic participation in the Amatucci scholarship fundraiser, Tooch's annual Christmas party for players and coaches, and the large Calvert Hall contingent attending the BCL Hall of Fame dinners, led by BCL commissioner Jack Degele, to name just a few events. One noteworthy highlight was the 25th anniversary celebration honoring the national championship team in 2007. An outstanding turnout of decades of hoop alumni came out for this memorable event. Amatucci commented, "Nobody has a family like Calvert Hall."

Putting the parts together to build that hoop family structure took countless hours of dedication, commitment, and sacrifice. There were never any shortcuts and no time wasted. The plan for success was a priority, many times at the expense of Amatucci's family at home. Without the support at home, Amatucci would never have been able to have the necessary time for his Calvert Hall basketball family.

"I've been blessed to have my wife Pat, sometimes with a frown, sometimes with a happy face, to have my back through all of the ups and downs over a period of thirty-six years," Amatucci said. "Being a coach's wife takes a lot of patience, a lot of perseverance, and a lot of sacrifice. She was totally unselfish in her support of my career."

Christmas always revolved around a basketball tournament on both the college and high school level. Being on the road the day after Christmas and arriving home often late on New Year's Eve left Pat and the kids alone for much of the holiday break. Many a celebration was missed due to tournament schedules. As the years wore on, it became increasingly tougher for Amatucci to leave just after Christmas. This played a key part with his decision to retire.

The Catholic League Tournament always fell on Pat's birthday in February, another special event that took a backseat to Amatucci's career. "You have to be a very special and devoted wife to endure all of the trials and tribulations that were constant for nearly 12 months each year," Amatucci said. "I am truly grateful, but more importantly, love her for being able to be by my side on this journey."

Tooch's clan – Jacquelyn, Michael and Stephanie

Sometimes lost in the shuffle were Amatucci's three children. Two daughters, Stephanie, 34, and Jackie, 30, were often described as 'gym rats' by Amatucci. Both girls were constantly around the basketball court while growing up. Amatucci remembered changing Stephanie's diaper on the hood of his car outside Northwestern High when he was watching Mike Morrison play. He would often take both girls to Calvert Hall during the week if he could not find a babysitter. "They went everywhere with me," Amatucci said. "They were at the Dome all the time. From all of their experiences around basketball, I am most proud of how they learned to embrace and build relationships regardless of race, color, environment, or social class."

Jackie commented, "Stephanie and I spent long days at practice, rode along to St. Frances or Madison to watch a kid play, and spent many a day at the Cardinal Hoops Camp. We've been here for the winning seasons and the losing one's too. We watched our father weather the storms of his occupational hazard while being present for every track meet and school play. He always gave 150%. My father worked so diligently not just in the gym, but in the community around us, which helped us to become well-rounded adults who value every individual."

Both girls attended local Catholic schools, St. Ursula and Mercy High School. Stephanie was a three-sport athlete, while Jackie thrived being a part of the theater and arts programs.

"They are beautiful young ladies married to two exceptional guys, Jaime and Dennis, but they can be characters," Amatucci said. "They're witty and charming and always willing to share their opinion." Stephanie commented, "Looking back, he did it with such emotion because he cared so much, not to be a mean you-know-what, although hearing the word "BASELINE" come out of his mouth still sends me into a state of sheer panic. He made it so personal because he only wanted the very best for them, like his own kids. Because with your family you fight hard but you love harder; and some of those guys—players and colleagues—are still like my big brothers or an uncle even to this day."

Although now adults, Amatucci's kids can't readily escape their basketball connections. Jackie commented, "Even now as a 30-year-old woman, it's not uncommon to have a grown adult shout out 'Hey Noodle!', my father's childhood nickname for me adopted by most of his players and coaches."

Following in his father's footsteps, Amatucci's son Mike is very interested in a coaching career. "Mike has exceeded all expectations that anyone could ever want from a son," Amatucci said. Mike struggled with ADHD, like his father, and has effectively developed strategies to overcome obstacles typically associated with the disability. Mike worked closely with Fran Vivarito at Immaculate Heart of Mary School in Towson to excel academically. "She was like my Kitty," Amatucci said. "When you have processing issues, you have to work doubly hard. He's a caring kid that loves his family." Mike made the honor roll all four years at Calvert Hall and was a member of the National Honor Society. Mike played baseball from the time he was five and made himself into a good player. He played two years of varsity at Calvert Hall and currently is part of the baseball program at Hood College. He's a marketing and communications major earning Dean's List honors. Multi-talented in the field of communication, Mike has already produced a documentary about Calvert Hall's 1981-82 national championship team.

"I'm extremely proud of his efforts in the classroom and his outstanding work habits—particularly his passion and perseverance in all of his endeavors," Amatucci said. "The biggest thing, though, is how caring he is. It's been a great experience having a son so close to me. He has a bright future."

Mike Amatucci added: "Growing up around my dad and basketball was like a constant montage; something new every day. It gave me the opportunity—as well as taught me—to learn and observe what it meant to be passionate about something you love. Relentless dedication; poetry in motion. Without a doubt it is something that shaped me to be the man I am today."

Amatucci's coaching career came to an end, but his teaching career continues to flourish. Working in his role as a guidance counselor at The Hall, he uses many of his coaching tenets in working with his students: the 4 Ps, time-management, development plans based on individual needs, and no limit expectations to name a few. Amatucci said, "The boys I work with in guidance are a team of their own. I hold them accountable, I am relentless in attempting to resolve their academic and personal issues. I am their advocate with the school leadership, their teachers, their parents, and their peers. When they face tough challenges and adversity, I am in there battling with them to get them to a better place. The situations vary day to day. I have to adjust my approach to the individual student. Just like with the basketball guys, the key to any success I have in guidance is building strong healthy relationships based on trust."

Amatucci is well recognized by the Calvert Hall faculty for his passionate work with his students. His ability to find solutions to situations that appear hopeless is remarkable. Calvert Hall school counseling chair Elizabeth Almeter commented, "On the basketball court, Mark recognized that players must do their best with what they had been given. Some are tall, some are speedy, some just work hard. Mark recognized the gifts of each player and found a place for each. So it is with his efforts in our school counseling department. Mark recognizes the gifts of each student and finds a place for each. He recognizes that students do their best with what they have been given; some are intellectually gifted, some have challenges at home they must overcome, some just work hard. He has a gift of seeing the authentic person in every situation and place."

While he was making a great contribution as a counselor, his contributions on the basketball court were not forgotten. In 2012, Amatucci was inducted into the Baltimore Catholic League Hall of Fame. The school reserved the maximum eight tables with 10 representatives. "It was a true example of the Calvert Hall family coming together for a special event," Amatucci recalled.

At a basketball reception in July, 2014, Frank Bramble, Calvert Hall's Board of Trustees chair, made an announcement naming the basketball court at Calvert Hall's Alumni Memorial Gymnasium in honor of Amatucci. A surprised Amatucci said to those in attendance, "This is an unbelievable honor, and it is truly a tribute to the outstanding student athletes and coaches that have been part of the Calvert Hall basketball family. Only at Calvert Hall would something like this happen to a guy like me."

The dedication ceremony was scheduled to be held before a Calvert

Hall-versus-Loyola game in December, 2014. Leading up to the day of the event, Amatucci was worried if anyone was going to show up. "I wonder how many people are going to show; it might be friends and relatives," Amatucci said to Baker. However, the gym was packed with former and current students adorning fake mustaches to honor Amatucci's signature look.

In the thirty-six hours since the Card's Friday night home game had ended, a team of floor specialists had worked to inscribe Amatucci's signature on the gymnasium floor on each side of the court. By the time, Amatucci's entourage entered through the back door to Aretha Franklin's song, "The House That Jack Built," more than 80 former players and coaches had gathered in the hallway. The group had seats reserved on the gym floor, all of which were taken. "It was truly their day and not all about me," Amatucci said. "Their names should also be included on the floor. The turnout and media coverage was humbling. It was a great day." Included in the crowd were Joe Binder and Kitty Walker, both of whom sat with Amatucci's family.

At the same time as Frank Bramble had announced the floor dedication, he also launched the Mark Amatucci Scholarship. The scholarship would provide tuition assistance to student athletes with financial need. "The scholarship brings me great satisfaction because it takes care of kids in need," Amatucci said. "Through the scholarship we are giving these young students the opportunity to experience Calvert Hall. Without the help of the scholarship, that would never happen. In selecting scholarship winners, we are looking for young men who will represent the school and the basketball program with distinction, young men who will carry on the tradition of Calvert Hall basketball on and off the court."

While Amatucci appreciates the recognition he has received during and even after his coaching career, what is most important to him is the size of the basketball family that has evolved.

One day Teddy Rogers, long-time Calvert Hall staff member, son of the reknowned Charlie Rogers, was sitting in Amatucci's office, looking at the photos of former players that plastered the walls. He remarked how each player had a story about their relationship with Amatucci.

"I was always told by Tooch, it's more than just basketball," Rogers said. "He does more than just coach basketball. My father always told me you will find out who your friends are when things get rough. I had times when things got tough, and Tooch always had my back. Tooch is everything to me"

"Teddy hit the nail right on the head." Amatucci asserted. "What we have done over the years is to build a dynamic group where everyone came together to establish positive relationships. The group had a common vision, what we have accomplished is not about baskets or wins, but rather about people. It's a diverse group—players, coaches, moderators, benefactors, managers, fans … Each person's contribution is different and every contribution is important."

The power of Amatucci's hoop community is clearly evidenced in the growth of the Mark Amatucci Scholarship Fund. After four years, through the contributions of so many, the fund now exceeds $400,000 and is one of largest funds in the Calvert Hall endowment.

Throughout this book, readers have been introduced to and heard from many of the members of Amatucci's hoop family, but there are countless more including:

BENEFACTORS:

Frank Bramble	Todd Binder	Bill Spotts
Dave Marshall	David Gately	Ray Byrne
Bill Karlson	Gary Neal	Mo Bozel, Sr.
Jeff Nattans	Tom Heiderman	Jerry Schiavino
Matt Crow	Tom Murray	Pete Karsos

CHRISTIAN BROTHERS:

Brother D. John	Brother James Nash	Brother Timothy Dean
Brother Andrew	Brother Gregory Cavalier	Brother Rene Sterner
Brother John Herron	Brother John Patzwall	Brother John Kane

Brother Charles Filberg

FIVE STAR FRIENDS:

Lou Eckerl	Pete Hock	Geoff Foltyn
Jack Degele	Rick Palmisano	Eric Rogers
Teddy Rogers	Mary Jo Puglisi	Bill Williams
Steve Connor	Bill Whitty	Jim Dougherty
Doug Heidrick	Tom Blaney	Gary Williams, Jr.
Dennis Morton	Danielle Hladky	
Susan Luchey	Nichole Regulski	

THE COACHES:

Phil Popovec	Darryle Edwards	Dave Iampieri
Chris Devlin	Mark Healy	Ryan Potter
Joe Baker	Mike "Scooter" Warner	Matt Jergensen
Charlie "Doc" Reif	Vince Williams	Rod Norris
Steve Misotti	Todd Binder	John Moeser
Mike Edwards	John McKay	John Bauersfeld
Jon Capan	Jerry Herpel	
Tom Rose	Tom Fan	

And so goes the saga of a coach and his journey. At the end of the day, you have to ask yourself - 'Who is this guy?' Amatucci admitted he was never a one-dimensional basketball coach.

He explained, "My critics, so to speak, would characterize me as volatile, arrogant, rude, crass, selfish, and intimidating. And that's just from my friends. But nothing is further from the truth. I love coaching, and I devoted my entire career trying to be a difference maker in the lives of all the guys I worked with. I also love the theater, arts, fine dining with Pat, red wine and quality cigars. Therapy for me is running a half-marathon, working in my yard, watching a good documentary or a movie on TCM. I love Sunday dinners at home and Ocean City, especially in the fall. I love hanging with my few good friends and intelligent conversation. I love taking walks with Charly and spending time with my children and Pat. I'm a romantic and an atypical jock. I'll always be a crusader for equality, family, tradition and faith."

"This was a journey where I never allowed obstacles to keep me from achieving my goals that were essential not only to athletic success, but a moral blueprint for life. My fellow coaches and players embraced that same philosophy. It's a story of one man's passion to use his energy and leadership skills to make a positive impact on his players and students. I've always seen myself more as teacher than coach. I've told generations of players from campers to NBA pros that the practice floor is my classroom."

"My primary goal was to set a standard of excellence for my basketball family at the high school and collegiate level. It was always about relationships and making the connection off the court to accomplish what was necessary to win. I took no prisoners and sometimes went beyond the limits of what was acceptable in a traditional basketball world. I broke social barriers and changed the cultural traditions wherever I went for the benefit of my students and players. In the end, I was better than most and worse than some. So, here ends the journey or maybe not … Karp and Joe are already thinking about Volume II."

"This is the House That Jack Built, ya'll.
This was the room that was filled with love
This was a love that I was proud of
This was a life of a love I planned
Of a love and a life we loved
In the house that Jack built.
Remember this house!"

- ARETHA FRANKLIN

CATHEDRAL FOUNDATION PRESS *a division of:*

PARENT COMPANY OF:
The Catholic Review • Park Chase Press
Cathedral Foundation Press • Catholic Print Solutions

320 CATHEDRAL STREET • BALTIMORE, MD 21201 • 443-524-3150
PO BOX 777 • BALTIMORE, MD 21203 • CatholicReview.ORG
PUBLISHED IN AMERICA'S PREMIER SEE – THE ARCHDIOCESE OF BALTIMORE